Life, death & Hurling

Michael Duignan
with Pat Nolan

IRISH SPORTS PUBLISHING

Jon 8-2-12

Published by Irish Sports Publishing (ISP)
Unit 11, Tandy's Lane
Lucan, Co Dublin
Ireland

First published, 2011

A CIP record for this book is available from the British Library

ISBN 978-0-9563598-6-5

Printed in Ireland with Print Procedure Ltd
Typesetting, Cover Design by Jessica Maile
Photographs: Sportsfile, and Michael Duignan's own collection.

DEDICATION

To my late wife, Edel, and two wonderful sons, Seán and Brian.

To Mam and Dad.

To the memory of my two great friends,
Noel Farrelly and Sean Conway.

ACKNOWLEDGMENTS

In some ways I have had a difficult life but, in general, I have been very lucky to have led the life I have. I have met many wonderful people, mainly through sport, and, through adversity in recent years, I have seen at first-hand the love and goodness in those people closest to me.

To Mam and Dad, you have always put family first and, without you, I don't know how Seán, Brian and I would have got through the last few years. Thanks for all the sacrifices and hard work over the years – I hope it was worth it!

To my brother, Pe, and sisters Brenda, Maura, Róisín and Sinéad, thanks for your love and support, especially to the lads.

To Edel's mam, Chris, and dad, Jerry, thank you for your kindness and friendship down the years. This book will bring back painful memories but I know you will always cherish the happy times Edel brought to us all.

Edel's sisters Jacinta, Anne and Linda and brothers Ronan, Niall and Diarmuid, were a constant source of support throughout her illness – thank you. We all had many great times with Edel and our annual trip to Kilkee, where all the cousins meet, is very much a legacy of that.

Linda, I know what you did for Edel and will never forget it. You were always there, day or night, and you, more than anyone, helped us through the really tough times.

Thanks also to Dr John Kennedy and all the oncology nurses at St James's Hospital, Dublin. Also, to AIB, with whom Edel spent her entire career, for the caring and understanding showed during her illness.

I have been blessed in life with many great friends. I'm loathe to name people but I must single out a certain few. Joe and Marie Dooley, and Martin and Evelyn McKeogh – thanks for your great friendship over many years and for being there through the tough times as well as the many happy times we shared. Olly and Siobhán Ryan, for your kindness since we moved to Tullamore, thank you. Ciarán 'Sod' Daly, we go back a long way. You've always been at the end of the phone no matter what the problem and thanks, especially, for listening and for your straight talking.

Edel and I spent eight great years in Naas and have many wonderful friends there. To you all I say thanks for then and thanks for now, eight years on. I miss ye all, but look forward to Punchestown and the Monday Xmas Lunch every year to catch up with my great friends.

When we moved to Durrow, just outside Tullamore, little did we think that we would meet so many remarkable neighbours who have now become some of our closest friends. Margaret and Donal Fox, thanks for looking after the lads over the years and making them part of your family. Michelle and Ian Crilly, and Maura and Pat Murray – you may no longer be neighbours but are not forgotten nonetheless. Joe and Lily Regan, thanks for your kindness and willingness to help. A special thanks to Dolores and Stephen Ravenhill, and Breeda and Willie Fogarty for your patience, understanding and kindness towards us all, but particularly to Seán and Brian – we genuinely could not get by without your friendship.

To Bríd and Michael O'Brien, who minded the lads from when they were three months old in Naas, thanks for the great start in life you gave them and your continued presence in their lives. We do not consider you friends – you are family.

I have played with many great men throughout my career in different sports, and with many different clubs, and I would like to thank you all for your camaraderie and friendship. I was lucky to play with so many great players who were also my closest friends in the St Rynagh's and Offaly jerseys in particular, which meant so much to me. Lads, thanks for all the great days, on and off the field.

To all the managers, trainers, selectors, members of the back room teams and County Board officers that I worked with over the years, I'd like to say thank you for your contribution, much of it voluntarily. I have the utmost respect for all of you and even if I had the odd falling out here and there, it was never personal and always in the interests of the jersey!

Offaly is known as the Faithful County and we have had many great days on the field over the last fifty years. First and foremost, I am an Offaly supporter and I would like to thank all the people who travelled all over Ireland to follow us and support us during my playing career.

Thanks to John and all in the Flanagan Group for the trust you placed in me over the past few years.

I would like to thank Irish Sports Publishing, and Liam Hayes and Kevin MacDermot in particular, for making this project possible.

However, the one who deserves most credit is a Tullamore man, journalist Pat Nolan who has written this book with me. Pat, you have put a huge amount of time and commitment into this book and spent many a late night working while we all slept. Over the past twelve months, I have told you everything about my life and it has been an emotional roller-coaster which I found very tough at times. You bore the brunt of that when I went to ground or got lazy, but you never lost focus. You have moved back to Tullamore since we started the book and I want to wish you well in your future career where I think your honesty and integrity will carry you a long way.

Finally, can I say that writing this book has been hard at times but, I hope, worthwhile. There are many people going through difficulties in life and maybe this book will help some of them. Unfortunately, cancer is something that affects every family at some stage and perhaps my story might help some people to deal with living with the disease. There are many people out there struggling at the moment, as I did at times. Please talk to someone and don't try to carry the can by yourself because it's not possible.

This is my story. I hope you enjoy it.

Michael Duignan
October, 2011

ACKNOWLEDGMENTS

Writing a book is something that I've aspired to for a number of years, though it is an onerous task and not one that I took on lightly. Therefore, the help and advice of several people was something that I leaned on throughout the project. To Micheál Clifford, Jim Lalor, Jackie Cahill, Christy O'Connor and Martin Breheny – thank you. However, three individuals in particular gave of their time relentlessly to read my work and offer feedback. To Paul Keane, Damian Lawlor and Dr Paul Rouse, my sincerest thanks. All three have put their names to truly outstanding books and I know I couldn't have sought guidance from better sources.

Thanks to my sports editor and editor at the *Irish Daily Mirror*, Neil Fullerton and John Kierans respectively, for giving this project their blessing. Also to my colleagues in the paper, Michael Scully and Orla Bannon, for at times allowing me breathing space to concentrate on writing this book.

Thanks to Liam Hayes, Kevin MacDermot and all at Irish Sports Publishing for bringing this book to fruition.

The Offaly hurling team, on which Michael Duignan played, illuminated my childhood and gave me heroes that I could identify with. Although this book is about much more than sport, the opportunity to write about their exploits is something that I found deeply gratifying. For that, I'd like to thank Michael for trusting me to do his story justice. The decision to write a book was one that he mulled over for quite some time and I believe it has been, and will be, a rewarding experience for him. Some of the material tugged at my emotions; I can only imagine what it was like for him.

I'm fortunate to have a good circle of friends, primarily in Tullamore and Dublin, and their interest and encouragement throughout the year is greatly appreciated. If my moods fluctuated somewhat over this period, I'm sure you'd all acknowledge that it's rarely any different!

Finally, to my family, which is large and varied. Thanks for believing in me and encouraging me in the career path which I have followed.

Pat Nolan
October, 2011

CONTENTS

PROLOGUE

Pat Cleary's name flashed up on my phone. A former Offaly team-mate, he was calling me purely as a friend, though not without first coldly analysing my misdemeanours like the good detective that he is. My most recent indiscretion, which had occurred a couple of days previously, was referenced early in the conversation. There'd been a serious dust-up in a pub in Tullamore on the night a much-loved local character, who had died suddenly, had been laid to rest and I was in the middle of it. While drawing back to throw a punch at one stage, my elbow accidentally caught a barmaid and sent her sprawling on the floor. Though no-one was seriously injured, an ambulance was called and the guards arrived and cleared the pub.

It wasn't the first flashpoint I had been involved in, however. I'd become somewhat susceptible to incidents like these throughout my wife Edel's illness, which had culminated in her death just five months earlier in September, 2009. A couple of years previous to that I put a man out through the front door of a pub. I'd been recounting a horrific episode a close friend of mine had endured when this man made a flippant remark to which I took grave exception.

On another occasion, a few months before Edel died, I swiped a mobile phone from a chap in a bar who thought it would be useful to have footage of some Offaly footballers taking their tops off during a session after they were knocked out of the Championship. I eventually gave the phone back but, when he and his brother accosted me over the row as I waited for a taxi outside afterwards, they both got a slap for their troubles.

These incidents, which were happening before and after Edel's death, were not affecting me the way they should have. I can't say that I was greatly perturbed by any of them at first. I often wouldn't give them a second thought the next day and, if I did, it extended no more than, "What about it? They deserved it."

As a player I often lacked confidence and, ahead of a big game, it could sometimes take me a week to convince myself that I could compete against my direct opponent. But, in a fight situation, I've always been fearless. My father was a serious boxer and won numerous titles during his days in the Air Corps. He would have given us tips on how to defend ourselves when growing up. I had fast hands and could protect myself. In any scuffle I was in over the years, nobody ever scored a direct hit on me.

However, this latest incident in the pub – the one Pat was calling me about – was the most chaotic yet, though I was largely oblivious to the error of my ways.

"Michael," Pat said, "me and the lads have been chatting about you and we're worried about the direction you're taking. Take the last couple of years – this is going on the whole time."

"What are you on about, Pat?" I asked intolerantly.

"Sure, how many incidents is that?"

"I don't know how many... "

"Well, where do you want me to start?"

He began to reel them all off. Not just the skirmishes, but other scenes when I would have heated arguments with fellas. Ok, sometimes whoever I was exchanging verbals with could be bang out of order themselves, but I'd have to meet fire with fire every time. I couldn't just make my point back at them: I had to ram it down their throats.

But, meanwhile, I was still on the offensive with Pat.

"Sure, that only happened because your man was being an idiot, and that other fella had it coming to him, too. It was only a one-off," I reasoned.

"But they're not all one-offs. Who's the common denominator in all these incidents?" he asked.

"Look," he added, "I'm not giving out to you, I'm just a friend of yours at the end of the day."

Pat wasn't the only friend who had tried to get through to me. About six weeks after Edel's death, Joe Dooley, who I hurled with throughout my Offaly career, called to the house and put it to me that I had been out drinking too much following Edel's passing. The slightest opportunity for a night out, no matter how tame the occasion, and I was out the door. The neighbours were only too happy to take our sons, Seán and Brian, off my hands and I had been taking advantage of that facility.

"Why don't you give up the drink for a while and I'll give it up with you?" Joe suggested. "Jaysus, Joe, I'm only going out at the weekend, here and there," came the reply, as I dismissed his offer out of hand.

Of all the players I hurled with, I'm closer to Joe than anyone so his words did bring about something of an improvement but still didn't have the impact they should have.

The conversation with Pat, however, had a snowball effect on my thinking, though the penny didn't quite drop straightaway. A couple of days later I was driving to Birr for the funeral of Johnny Pilkington's father, John, when everything crystallised in my mind. If you like, the N52 between Tullamore and Birr became my Road to Damascus. While I had made some calls the previous day in a bid to patch things up following the latest incident, I still wasn't seeing the bigger picture in terms of the other scenes that I had been involved in. As Pat's words continued to sift through my mind I thought, "You know, he's right." It was like somebody had opened my head and moved things around, putting a completely different perspective on my thought process.

But was it just simply 'somebody'? I firmly believe that this was Edel's influence at play here. It wasn't so dramatic as her spirit gushing through me in a ghostly manner, or anything like that, but I'd say she opened my eyes and allowed me to see the type of person I was becoming. Or had become.

I started thinking about all these incidents with much greater clarity.

I was wrong.

It was the first time it had dawned on me: I was wrong!

Now, quite often the other parties were far from blameless themselves, but that was for them to deal with. I could only account for myself. I wasn't getting involved in dust-ups or sharp exchanges every night I went out, but it was happening often enough to put my closest friends on edge. One of them, Ciarán Daly, known to us all as 'Sod', later told me that it had reached a stage where he didn't enjoy going out with me any more. He never knew when it might kick off. Coming from him, that revelation rocked me to the core. While it's not in my nature to reach for excuses, there was a correlation between the worsening of Edel's illness and the rate at which these incidents were happening. I'd think I was handling her condition just fine; that it wasn't affecting me in a major way – the typical Irish male's way of dealing with matters. But, looking back now, it had to have been a major factor. I hadn't slept properly for years, often lying awake in bed at night for hours on end. It was obvious to my friends that I was under pressure, but not to me. And it was manifesting itself in a most awful, ugly and unbecoming manner, which isn't me at all.

Over the years I've enjoyed an active social life and craic, humour and good friends would be my mainstay. I'd be seen as good company. Still, my priority was always home, particularly in the three years after Edel was diagnosed with secondary breast cancer. Within the household I'd like to think that I ticked all the boxes as a husband and father to my sons, Seán and Brian. I've been a conscientious businessman and was always disciplined both on and off the field during my playing career. But the stress I was under had to come to the surface somehow and, just occasionally, it happened in these social settings.

With the path I was on, something serious was going to come to pass sooner or later, and what then? Seán and Brian, having just lost their mother, could have been left completely isolated, and that was the scariest aspect, coupled with the fact that I was so oblivious to what was happening to me. And yet these implications didn't dawn on me until it was almost too late. It was, and is, deeply unsettling to think that I had become the sort of person who simply wasn't treating people with the basic respect they deserved. But, mercifully, driving to Birr that day to pay my final respects to John Pilkington, Edel's outlook helped steer my thoughts in the right direction at long last. I immediately lifted the phone and began the process of apologising in earnest.

It was the turning point of my life.

PART ONE

Chapter 1

Healthy children will not fear life if their elders have
integrity enough not to fear death.
Erik Erikson (1963)

Edel was initially diagnosed with breast cancer in 2002 but came through her treatment successfully and was given the all-clear the following year. However as anyone who has had cancer, or is close to someone who has, will know any all-clear comes with provisos and, following a check-up in June 2006, we received the dreaded news that Edel had contracted secondary cancer from which she could not recover.

We went through the motions of dealing with that shocking revelation in the coming months and years. It was a very slow process and at times, in the early stages, Edel's fate was the elephant in the room. We didn't talk about it. We weren't ready to. It took a while for us to get our heads around the fact that she was eventually going to succumb to this illness. Gradually, as time went by, we started ticking the boxes. Making wills. Whether to get hospice care or not. Funeral arrangements. The music. Who would sing. Who the celebrant would be. Choosing prayers. Where the plot would be located in the cemetery.

But there was one glaring duty that had yet to be fulfilled: telling our sons Seán and Brian that their mother wasn't going to get better.

Edel had never been a Bible basher, or anything like it, but she became much more devoted to religion in her latter years – not in a forlorn attempt for salvation, but because it helped her and it was good for her. She became more spiritual and it gave her a sense of perspective about where she was going, and this framed the context in which we explained things to the lads.

We hadn't necessarily been putting the issue on the long finger, but it took us so long to absorb what was happening that telling the boys simply wasn't a runner, not least for the fact that they were very young lads that had childhoods to enjoy. We weren't going to weigh them down with news like this for any longer than we had to. Naturally, Seán and Brian knew that Edel had cancer and had been receiving serious treatment over the previous few years, but, by June 2009, we couldn't put off telling them any longer.

Edel had a scan around this time and the results weren't encouraging. She had been fighting secondary cancer in her spine and liver over the previous three years. Spinal cancer is more containable, but the liver is so central to your bodily functions that it can't hold out indefinitely. She had already got three years – the optimistic outlook at the time of diagnosis was twelve months. The chemotherapy goes in cycles from drug to drug as, eventually, a drug becomes ineffective in fighting the cancer and you move on to another one. Eventually, you run out of drugs. Edel knew that her time was coming. She had already been through, at times, a horrendous three years given the intensity of the treatment she was undergoing. The results of that scan weren't reassuring and, with the cancer spreading and forms of treatment almost exhausted, it was time to sit the lads down for the chat.

At the time Seán was eleven and Brian was eight. They're two very different characters in lots of ways yet very close, though they'd never openly admit it. Seán is certainly the more guarded of the two. He doesn't talk about his feelings much – he's too private for that. He's an exceptionally well-balanced young fella, though, and an expert mimic. One of his teachers in primary school once commented to me that she had never come across a lad that was so fluid in his dealings with the various factions that develop in a class, while at the same time maintaining his own independence. He was able to mix with everybody and treat them all more or less the same. If he were any more laid back he'd be horizontal and I often find myself trying to cajole him if I want him to do something.

Brian is the polar opposite of Seán in so many ways. For a start, he's incredibly driven and determined. He always seems to be in good form.

Perhaps it's an age thing to a certain extent, but he never stops talking. He'll articulate whatever is on his mind, sometimes with hilarious consequences. He's honest, genuine and sincere. There's no hedging of bets with him: what you see is what you get.

On the Saturday afternoon that we resolved to tell them about the true nature of Edel's illness, we cooked them both their favourite lunch. Seán had his rashers and fried potatoes, and Brian his margherita pizza. Being the incredibly organised person that she always was, Edel had already researched information from the HSE on how to tell your children about such matters, whereas I'd tend to be more off the cuff. But when the boys had finished eating, she began.

"Lads," she said, "you know that I have the cancer. It's getting a little bit worse all the time. I'm still getting treatment for it but they're not going to be able to cure it and I'm not going to be able to get better."

Being that bit older, the penny dropped with Seán straightaway, but Brian didn't fully grasp the gravity of her words. Not that many eight-year-olds would.

"What do you mean you're not going to get better?" he asked.

Seán threw a look at him and then came another question.

"Are you going to die?"

"Well, we're all going to die some time but, hopefully, not for a while yet," we reasoned with him.

With a startled look on his face, Brian replied: "But I don't want you to die!"

We chatted about it for another few minutes and, given Edel's unshakeable faith, assured them that she would be going to a better place when the time came. Obviously, we didn't know how long she had left but, having already gone three years since the second diagnosis, it was more likely to be months than years. Not that we put any such timelines in the lads' heads. They finished up at the table and were outside pucking around shortly afterwards. There may have been a few tears shed by Brian but, overall, they didn't make a big deal of it. It wasn't, isn't their way. The manner in which they have dealt with everything from that day on has been nothing short of inspirational to me.

Looking back now, it's clear to me Edel had thought rigorously about the repercussions her death would bring and did as much to offset them as she could. More often than not I was oblivious to how she was engineering things to this end but, with hindsight, I can see what she was doing. She was trying to prepare us all as best she could for what was coming down the tracks.

Around the time we told the lads, Edel insisted I get counselling from a lady she had seen in St James's Hospital in Dublin, where she'd been undergoing treatment since first being diagnosed back in 2002. Ranging in periods from one to three weeks, she would get the early train to Dublin while I got the lads ready and out to school. I'd drive up to the hospital then and bring her home that evening. The days were long but much of the monotony was removed once the counsellor became part of her schedule a few months before we explained things to Seán and Brian. While I wouldn't have any great hang-ups about seeing counsellors in the way a lot of men do, I didn't think it was necessary for me to see this woman.

"There's no problem, I'm grand. I'll be strong," I told Edel, but she had her doubts and, as usual, she was right. Despite my reservations, I bought into the idea and in due course found the counsellor was really very helpful. It was a sort of pre-bereavement counselling, if you like, with the counsellor putting across the practicalities of how my life would change when it was just the two lads and myself. She teased out my relationship with the lads and how my role with them would have to evolve pretty dramatically, all vital stuff that I needed to have laid bare before me. In terms of things I would have to forsake to look after the lads, I had no qualms with any of that and, to be fair, Seán and Brian weren't neglected after Edel's death. I've always got on brilliantly with them and was never found wanting within the household but it was still difficult to get the overall balance right.

I only got three of those counselling sessions in before Edel passed away. They certainly helped, but I didn't get near enough of them.

· · · · ·

Over the nineteen years or so that Edel and I spent together, we had some great holidays. During my playing career, most of those holidays would have been courtesy of the Offaly hurlers as there was a team holiday every January after each of the four All-Ireland finals we played in from 1994 to 2000. There were trips to Florida, Lanzarote, Cape Town and Thailand – brilliant memories. Apart from that, I think I only had one holiday with Edel during my playing career which was a trip to Corfu. Between Offaly and St Rynagh's, it was all hurling, with a bit of rugby and football thrown in, right up until late autumn year after year. Even when we got married it was in October, though I still cut the honeymoon short to play in the county final replay against Seir Kieran. That changed once I retired from inter-county hurling in March, 2001, and we often frequented our good friend Tom Mangan's villa in Spain, bringing the lads with us. We also went skiing in France for my fortieth birthday in February 2008, but, having looked forward to a trip like this for so long, Edel wasn't able to take part though she still knocked great fun out of my clumsy efforts to master the slopes. The following October we brought the lads to Disneyworld Florida.

In later years, however, Edel had a hankering for holidaying in Ireland and keeping things simple rather than heading for more exotic climes as we had often done before. She wanted to get back to basics, to nature, the fresh air and the sea breeze. And, in the end, it was just as well, given how our last holiday together worked out.

When she was a child Edel's family used to go on holidays to Kilkee, in Co Clare, and she longed to rekindle those memories before she died by uniting the O'Connells down there again years later, something she achieved initially in 2008. She also had a grá for West Cork, and that summer we also spent a week there with our friends, Ian and Deirdre Brophy.

In August 2009, we decided we'd do something similar. Although we wouldn't have said it out loud, there was a feeling of finality about this trip as the following summer was a long way away. That feeling didn't impact negatively on the holiday in any way and, in fact, it enhanced things because we appreciated what we had so much more and were determined to make the most of the time we had left together as a family.

I covered the All-Ireland semi-final between Kilkenny and Waterford for The Sunday Game and, a couple of days after that, we loaded up the car and pointed it for Leitrim, of all places. I'd hardly ever been there in my life and I'm not sure why we chose it as the starting leg to our break, but it eased us into the holiday nicely. Edel exuded positivity as we set off, despite the staggering amount of medication she was on and the pain she was enduring. She'd never wallow in self-pity and drag the mood down, particularly on family excursions such as this, which were, quite literally, what she lived for. She was all about engendering the right atmosphere among the four of us, and she did it so well. With Drumshanbo as our base, we tried a bit of horse-riding and Seán and Brian got a great laugh out of seeing me perched in the saddle. The horse didn't seem too amused, though. Edel was so happy there, spending quality time with the lads. We went to the Arigna Mines, in Roscommon, and the Lough Key Forest Park, in Boyle, things the lads still talk about now. After three nights there we linked up with Edel's brother Niall, in Sligo, for a couple of days and took a spin to Bundoran as well. Edel and Dympna, Niall's wife, went off for a seaweed bath while I took the lads to play crazy golf.

Through my friendship with former Galway hurler, Joe Connolly, we then moved on to Ballyconneely, where he has a mobile home. Part of me was thinking, "Edel is sick and I'm taking her to a mobile home", but I needn't have worried, it was really comfortable and the area was alluring, looking out on the Atlantic Ocean. In the context of this holiday, it was perfect. The first night we arrived down Joe and his wife, Cathy, had the place set up for us with dinner cooked and everything ready. We were fortunate to be surrounded by a lovely bunch of people for the week we spent there. Brian Feeney, another ex-Galway player, was there with his wife, Orla, and family. So, too, was Proinsías Kitt, a well-known accountant in Galway whom I hadn't properly met before. We also ran into some former work colleagues of ours from AIB and then there was Pat "The Scrapper" King, who owns the caravan park down there. A woeful character, he only drinks sporadically and our luck was in because this was one such occasion when he did. We had some craic with him. Brian and Mary Cowen, who we've been friendly with for years, were also there. I had a round of golf with Brian at the nearby course. Another day we met him and Mary coming back from a Gaelic football tournament in Clifden. Mary was very helpful throughout our time down there, dropping in to our caravan with various bits and pieces. We had a great evening with them and Brian's driver, Mick Cleary. Obviously Edel wasn't going to town on the drink, but a few glasses of wine here and there were no problem. In fact it was good for her.

One of the best nights we had there was with Brian and Orla, when they invited us over to their place for dinner. I like to cook so we returned the compliment to them on another night. Orla cooked a fabulous meal and Edel was particularly taken by her pasta starter. She went to the trouble of writing to Edel after we got home with the recipe and sent up a parcel with all the various ingredients – such kindness from people we had never even met before.

It was all so relaxed and off-the-cuff in Ballyconneely; we didn't know what was going to happen next, we just took it in our stride. People would be popping in and out of each other's places for breakfast, lunch, a drink, a chat or whatever. We'd go for walks on the beach and into the water for a swim, though Edel couldn't go all out given the risk of infection. She was so happy there, spending quality time with the lads. It was idyllic from her point of view. We all have our own idea of what the perfect holiday is and this was most certainly hers. The sun holidays we had taken before were hugely enjoyable in their own way, but that type of break wasn't really where we were at by this stage. The simplicity of this holiday was permeating through me. I could see why it appealed to Edel so much to do something like this. It was all so pleasant and uncomplicated. It was all we wanted.

There was no real standout moment as such, just a sustained period of relaxation for all of us in the most ambient of atmospheres. There was also a real sense of, "Why didn't we think of this ten years earlier?" There are so many beautiful parts of the country to explore, but I always felt that we should go where we were guaranteed the sun. However, there's more to a holiday than just greasing up on a beach to maximise your tan. The other aspect to it, of course, is whether I would have been in the right headspace to, ten years earlier, take a holiday like this and appreciate it fully. If I'm honest, I most probably wouldn't.

In the end, the only complaint we could have was that the week passed too quickly and we had to move on to Kilkee to link up with Edel's family, as we had done the year before. Not that it was a chore, or anything like that, but that week in Ballyconneely was as perfect as could be and we didn't want it to end. It's a time that will always stay with me and is a special memory to have.

In Kilkee we stayed in an apartment looking out on the sea, linking up with Edel's parents, Jerry and Chris, her sisters, Jacinta, Anne and Linda and brothers, Niall and Diarmuid. Her other brother, Ronan, couldn't make it down. All the respective husbands and wives were there, too, and Seán and Brian could mix with their cousins, something Edel was very keen on. It would be very easy now for me to just drift over to my side of the family and not maintain the same contact with the O'Connells but, again, Edel was meticulous in her planning in ensuring that this wouldn't come to pass, and it hasn't. In most families there is someone who binds people together and maintains a level of contact between everyone who might otherwise drift apart. While I get on well with all my brothers and sisters, I don't pick up the phone as often as I should so I wouldn't quite fit that role within our family, but Edel appeared to be the conduit among the O'Connells. She's a huge loss in that respect, as well as everything else.

I had always enjoyed a good relationship with Edel's family, though I did get off to an inauspicious start. Edel and I had been going out for a few months around the summer of 1991 when I went down to Portlaoise for the afters of Brian and Claire Rigney's wedding, Brian being of that well-known rugby and hurling family from the town. Edel's sister, Linda, is married to Brian's brother, Mick. Linda and Mick's son, Mark, Edel's godson, is now a strapping young man, well over six foot, but, back then, he was just a baby and Jerry and Chris were looking after him for the night while we were at the wedding.

I exchanged pleasantries with the family when I landed and off we went to the wedding. Back then, however, I had a habit of sleepwalking and, typically, I was in wandering mode that night soon after I hit the pillow back in the O'Connells' house. I arrived into Jerry and Chris's room and tried to climb into the cot with Mark. Jerry ushered me out, but I floated into their room again shortly afterwards, only this time I was trying to get into bed with them!

"Mick, Mick, Mick," said Jerry in his Kerry brogue, "come on, come out!"

Fortunately, for them, their sleep wasn't disturbed again, but I was mortified when the flashbacks hit me at breakfast the next morning. Luckily, they're an easy-going family so they saw the funny side and never held it against me. I haven't gone sleepwalking since.

Jerry, a retired Garda inspector, is a very well-liked man. I've met loads of people over the years who would have known him through his work, particularly his time at the prison in Portlaoise, and I've yet to hear anyone say a bad word about him. He's a very outgoing and interesting man and a great chat. He is a keen follower of sport and always took a big interest in my playing career. Chris, who hails from Mount Bolus in Offaly, is much quieter, though she has a good sense of humour in her own way. The sleepwalking incident aside, I got on well with them from the start and that was reassuring for me as I always felt they had a bit of a soft spot for Edel given the role she fulfilled in the family. As time went by I got to know the rest of the O'Connells well and it was never a case of being forced to spend a dreaded week with the in-laws in Kilkee.

Around this time, Edel had mentioned to me that her short-term memory had been affected by the treatment and she would find herself having to write things down. She was fanatical in terms of researching various things, such as diets, in order to keep herself at the optimum. To help keep her mind sharp, she started doing *The Irish Times* crossword and, after breakfast each morning, we'd have a go at that together and then head out for a walk. Again, the simple things.

Seán and Brian mixed well with their cousins and they all went swimming daily in the popular Pollock Holes down there. At night we'd all head out for a meal and a few drinks. Sleeping wouldn't have come easy to Edel at times, so a glass of wine or two was helpful to that end. One of the days she went off with Linda's daughter, Emer, and got her nose pierced. It was quirky and looked nice. She may have been a little old to be getting something like that done but she didn't care. She wanted to squeeze as much life as possible out of what time she had left.

Our time in Kilkee was broken up by a session of chemo so the two of us got the train to Dublin from Ennis, had a nice meal afterwards and spent a lovely evening together before linking up with the O'Connell clan again the next day. It's a measure of Edel's toughness that, after a long day of chemo, followed by a few hours on a train, she just had a shower when we got back and then straight out for the family meal. That the family was together for that week was a credit to Edel, and perhaps it was hard for some of them not to underestimate the seriousness of her illness. A year had become a year and a half, then two years and now three years had passed and she was still around.

Maybe people relaxed a bit and perhaps started to expect a miracle. Now, given that a few of Edel's family are nurses they would have been more pragmatic about these things than most people, but I suspected that Jerry and Chris were hoping against hope for a miracle, and it was hard to blame them. The fact that she looked well, and was still in good form, would have given oxygen to that hope, I'd imagine.

Much of Edel's family are scattered around the country, so we all went our separate ways on that Saturday, August 29, 2009. We stopped for a bit of lunch in Ennis and got home later that evening after two-and-a-half weeks of pure bliss. Of course, Seán and Brian would say that the skiing trip was the best holiday they were ever on, as any two young lads would, but, for Edel and myself, as well as the O'Connells, it was a hugely gratifying time together and its importance was accentuated by what was coming next.

· · · · ·

The week after we returned from Kilkee passed like any other. Having been away from work I had a number of things I needed to catch up on. I wasn't run off my feet though, given that the auctioneering trade had slumped significantly by then. The lads started back at school and, Edel being Edel, had all the books and copies covered and labelled, pens, pencils and everything in two new schoolbags – all of which had been prepared and ready to go before we had left for Leitrim weeks earlier. I was heedless to it. It was a side of things that I had never got involved in. All the lads had to do was slip into their uniforms that first morning, pick up their bags and out the door to school.

The week ran into All-Ireland hurling final weekend, and I would be working alongside Ger Canning on the RTÉ live commentary for the game between Tipperary and Kilkenny, who were aiming to become the first side since 1944 to complete the four-in-a-row. The day before the game there were a number of underage county finals down for decision, which Joe Dooley, Sod and I attended at O'Connor Park. I went home that evening and was getting myself organised for heading to Dublin with Sod the next morning. I always stay overnight in Dublin the weekend of the All-Ireland and we were booked into the Croke Park Hotel.

I don't go into any sort of preparation for my match commentaries, not even for games as big as this, which was the most anticipated All-Ireland final in years given what was at stake. I don't bring notes with me, what I say on air is all off-the-cuff, though I may jot down the scorers as the match progresses. Working on the highlights programme in the evening is different, but I'd have virtually nothing planned for a live commentary. It surprises some people in there but it's my hobby and I'm taking mental notes on players from when I first see them as minors, or earlier. Other pundits may get a bit stressed about it, but I just take it in my stride.

Having packed my essentials for the following morning, I kicked back and watched a bit of television with the lads while Edel was on the laptop, researching to find any angle she could that would help her along. As I said, sleep didn't come easy for her, given the amount of steroids and other medication she was on, and she was as happy to engross herself in the internet to hasten the drowsiness.

I would often go to bed first and, as I rose from the couch, she said, "I'm not feeling 100 per cent." It's not something she would have said too often, despite the travails she had endured over a number of years. It wasn't that she was in pain any more than she usually would have been, but felt more like she had a touch of the 'flu. Immediately after chemotherapy there is a higher risk of infection but, curiously, over the three years she had never been struck down by 'flu. We knew that if and when that came to pass she'd have to go into hospital and go on an intravenous drip; there was no other way of fighting it. She checked her temperature and it was high.

"What's the next step?" I queried.

"We'll leave it until the morning and see what it's like then," she replied.

Her temperature hadn't dropped the following morning so she called her sister Linda, a nurse, who advised her to ring the hospital. The staff in St James' told her to come in so they could monitor her. I probably wasn't as tuned in as I normally would be, between cooking breakfast and other distractions, and I had to get to Croke Park for midday to do an introductory piece at the top of the programme. But there really was no need for panic anyway. Although

Edel hadn't been so hastily whisked to hospital like this over the previous three years, there was no great cause for alarm at this point.

I set off for Dublin with Sod while Linda came over from Portlaoise and brought Edel up to St James's. My father collected the two lads and brought them to Banagher. I immersed myself in the day at Croke Park for what turned out to be the greatest All-Ireland final of the modern era. It was a pleasure to be there to witness it. I made a quick stop to say hello to some friends at the Hill 16 pub on Gardiner Street after the game before moving on to St James's to check in with Edel. I thought I'd never get out of the pub having run into John and Renée McGrath, two staunch Tipp supporters who own a pub in Cabra. Renée was like a bull, given the result of the game, and was seething over Benny Dunne's sending off. She wasn't happy with my commentary that he could have no complaints at referee Diarmuid Kirwan's decision either. It was hilarious.

"But Renée, he pulled across his head," I reasoned.

"He didn't!" she stormed back, "he pulled straight across his chest."

As if that was okay in any event.

"You believe whatever you want to believe," I chuckled back at her, trying to get out the door.

By then the doctors had seen Edel informed her that she had an infection and was going to be admitted, but she was still waiting for a bed. There were no doctors there to see her, given that it was a Sunday night, though she had been told she would be going on intravenous antibiotics. I arrived to allow Linda to go home and Edel and I waited for a number of hours, though there was still no sign of a bed. Now, she wasn't deteriorating, or anything like that, she was still much the same as she had been that morning, apart from being a little annoyed at hanging around a waiting room all day. They eventually brought her into a room where she could rest, and she looked at me.

"Go off and get a few pints."

"Ah, I'll hang around for another while," I said.

She nearly ran me out of the place in the end!

Paul Flynn, Ollie Canning and John Mullane had been on The Sunday Game that night and I met them in Chaplin's in town, along with Sod, Vinny Claffey and David Reynolds. I had been critical of Mullane on the show before for showboating.

"I don't know if you want to fight now or have a pint!" I said jokingly.

Of course there was no problem with him, but that's not always the case. I remember John Gardiner haranguing me on the night that Cork won the 2005 All-Ireland title after I had said on air that he was able to dish it out, but not so well able to take it. Ben O'Connor and Joe Deane were trying to move him on as I defended my position but, just to get rid of him, I eventually had to say to him wryly, "Listen, John, would you ever just do me a favour and feck off!" He was inadvertently proving my point. With the Cork lads, they sometimes seem to think they have to challenge absolutely everything for fear of otherwise showing a weakness.

The following morning Sod and I went over to St James's, where Edel had finally been given a bed. She wasn't on a drip full-time so she was up and walking around in grand form. It was a lovely sunny morning and I was still on a high from the game the day before. As I tend to, I became rather impassioned when discussing an aspect of the game and Sod later told me how Edel rolled her eyes as I became more animated. We stayed a few hours and then I had to get off home to the lads, who had been looked after by our neighbours, Liam and Breeda Fogarty, the previous night. The two of us were always keen on the lads maintaining a routine as much as possible in order to minimise the impact Edel's condition had on them. With that in mind, I didn't even go to Dublin on the Tuesday. We were in regular contact on the phone all day and other people were in to see her, so we agreed that I should stay put with the lads.

Unfortunately, Edel's regular oncologist, Dr John Kennedy, was on holidays at this time. She had built up a tremendous relationship with him over the years. He has his own unique personality and the two of them just bounced off each other. Often when we were away she'd bring him back his favourite type of dark chocolate, or something exotic like that. They really clicked. It would have been reassuring to have him there at this time, having liaised with him for so long, but that's no reflection on Dr Dearbhaile O'Donnell, who stepped into the breach and was excellent. The news she imparted to Anne, Edel's sister, and me on the Thursday was far from excellent, however.

She explained to us that Edel had pneumonia and an infection in the lung, which they were finding very difficult to get a handle on. So, all of a sudden, from just being a routine few days in hospital, it all became very serious. They didn't say that in so many words but Anne, being a nurse, didn't need it spelled out for her. Perhaps I did, initially, but then it dawned on me. They had tried five different antibiotics but none had anything like the desired effect, though they hadn't given up hope just yet. By then Edel had developed breathing difficulties and tubes were inserted in her nostrils to help her. She was weakening to the extent that I had to bring her to the church in a wheelchair on the Friday morning to say a few prayers. She also had an oxygen mask, which she didn't need all the time, but her breathing was getting shorter. I noticed that she had become relatively quiet and wasn't inviting too much conversation with anyone. We had already had our chats together about her fate, so there was no need for us to get into any morbid stuff like that at this point. Any words we exchanged were bits of banter and small talk.

Later that day I was told that the only way they could accurately reflect the nature of her pneumonia was if they performed a biopsy. An x-ray had shown a lump forming in her lung and, while it was unlikely to have been cancerous at that early stage, the idea of the biopsy was to define its characteristics. The most critical aspect though was the fact that the biopsy would be very invasive. Even after all that, they mightn't have been able to treat the lump successfully. Though the staff didn't say it in so many words, the likelihood is that the treatment wouldn't have been a success, given the number of antibiotics they had already tried.

"I don't think that's going to happen," I told Dr O'Donnell on the possibility of doing the biopsy, knowing how Edel would feel about it.

And that's when it hit home: this was effectively the endgame. I went in to Edel to explain the situation to her and immediately she said, "No way". Again, this was something we would have discussed together. We had covered as many aspects as we could over the years, whether to get home help in the latter stages or possibly avail of a hospice. It never came to that in the end but she wanted to die with as much dignity as possible, something that would most likely have been taken away from her if we had opted for the biopsy, which was the last option. It was effectively me having the conversation with my forty-one-year-old wife that it was all over for her.

Later that evening I drove home to pick up a few bits and pieces for Edel. Joe Dooley called me and I ended up meeting him and Sod in town to explain the situation in the snug of Digan's bar on William Street. I went to the toilet at one stage and bumped into Johnny Pilkington, who was managing Kilcormac-Killoughey at the time and they had played a game up in O'Connor Park that evening. After chatting with Johnny it occurred to me that I should tell him what was going on. Word hadn't really got out at all that Edel was particularly sick, as there had been no real cause for alarm up until the day before. But Johnny and Edel had always enjoyed a good relationship and I thought he might be disappointed when it eventually came out if I hadn't taken this opportunity to tell him. After all, I had soldiered with him for Offaly over so many years.

"Look, Johnny, Edel is fierce sick," I said to him.

He looked at me with a perplexed expression as if to say, "Sure I know she's sick".

"But, Johnny, she's really sick now. She's up in James's and it doesn't look like she has much time left."

He struggled to deal with it. He was shocked and left quickly.

While I've mentioned how keeping Seán and Brian in a routine was a big thing for us, it probably went a bit over the top the following day. Brian went off on a football blitz to Cavan that Saturday morning, while I drove Seán up to the hospital. My intention was for the three of us to go in together the following day. The blitz was a huge thing for Brian and he had been looking forward to it so much. I felt I couldn't deprive him of it and I'm sure that would have been Edel's thinking as well. But, when we got to the hospital, Anne asked, "Where's Brian?" They probably thought we were mad, but that's the way we were. She pulled me to one side.

"I think you should get Brian up here as well," she said.

"Do you think it's that bad?" I asked.

"It could be."

Edel's breathing had deteriorated and she was on the oxygen mask virtually all the time, though she did take it off to talk to Seán. I called Dolores Ravenhill, another neighbour, and asked her what time they were expected home as her son Ross, Brian's best friend, was on the blitz as well. Like most people, she had been insulated from how serious Edel's condition had become over the previous forty-eight hours or so and was taken aback by the news. She drove Brian to the hospital as soon as they got back from Cavan.

Seán, being older, was more aware of what was happening. I had chatted with him about it going up in the car anyway, more or less telling him that Edel wouldn't be coming out of hospital this time. It probably came as a bigger shock to Brian.

Anne and Linda were in tears at the sight of them going in to see Edel. I was, too, standing at the end of the bed as they cuddled up to her one last time. Seeing adults show this type of emotion brought home the gravity of the situation to the lads, if they had any lingering doubts. I've never been afraid to shed a tear, but anyone would have been incredibly moved by that. You never forget things like that particular moment. Two little lads going in to their mother in such circumstances and they're never going to see her again afterwards.

We were all a bit upset, but there were no hysterics. There was a peaceful air to it all. Edel said her few words to them, but there wasn't a whole lot of talking done; she had already imparted the most important things to them in the previous few years. How she handled that whole exchange was incredible, given how she was so immersed in the lads in everything she did. In a calm and serene manner she was able to have her few words with them and then let them off without any fanfare. After a few minutes they exchanged hugs and kisses and Seán and Brian left the hospital. I knew she'd be in a casket the next time they saw her.

It's just as well I heeded Anne's advice because, by the following day, Edel had deteriorated significantly. She was in critical care and was capable only of minimal communication. Out of nowhere, the former curate in my native Banagher, Fr Simon Cadam, arrived at the hospital that day. Shortly after we moved from Naas to Tullamore in 2003, Edel travelled to Lourdes with a group from Banagher, of which Fr Simon was the leader. They got to know each other and would often meet when we'd go down to Banagher to my parents. They kept in touch, even after he was transferred to Longford. Whatever talking Edel did over that Sunday and the following day was mostly done with Fr Simon, who also had a man called Stephen Leary, who had just joined the priesthood, with him. I was out in the corridor while they were inside with her. I spoke to them as they were leaving. They were in tears. Fr Simon had never come across someone who was so ready to die.

"The time I've just spent with her has done more for me than all my years as a priest combined," he told me. "She really wants you to know that she's ready. She's not afraid. She told me that she'll look after you and the lads from heaven."

Curiously, he didn't administer the Last Rites that night. It was as if he knew that she'd still be there the following evening when he came again.

That night, Linda, Anne and Jacinta, another of Edel's sisters, booked a couple of rooms in the nearby Radisson Hotel in Kilmainham. Their brother, Ronan, was preparing to bring their parents, Jerry and Chris, up from Portlaoise. Diarmuid was also a constant presence over the few days. The nurses told us there was no great point in us hanging around, that we were as well off to try and get a few hours' sleep and they'd call us if necessary.

I was on autopilot at this stage. We were only gone a couple of hours when we were called back in, but Edel hung on throughout the day. I believe that this was fuelled by a determination to see one of her brothers, Niall, who had been out of the country working at the time and had yet to make it to the hospital. We would all still talk to her, and she would squeeze your hand to let you know she was listening, but she didn't say much throughout that Monday other than "Where's Niall?" Thankfully, he arrived and was able to say goodbye.

Word slowly filtered out about what was coming and a stream of visitors arrived at the hospital throughout the day, close friends like Nicky and Anne English, Tom and Paul Mangan and Ollie and Siobhán Ryan. I dropped over to the oncology ward in the hospital to inform the nurses that had been treating her for years. They were shell-shocked. Edel had only been in with them a couple of weeks earlier in flying form. Despite the number of patients that pass through their hands on a daily basis, they were heartbroken given the phenomenal relationship they had enjoyed with Edel.

I had a number of missed calls on my phone and, when I got around to returning some of them, three of the neighbours, Dolores, Ciara Leonard and

Breeda Fogarty were already outside the hospital having just decided to make their way up anyway when I hadn't been answering their calls. It was nice to have them there. Although Edel had a wide circle of friends, Dolores and Breeda had been particularly supportive over the previous few years, given that they have sons the same age as Seán and Brian and were often the first port of call when help and assistance was needed. It was wholly appropriate that they would be present in Edel's final hours. Others would rightly feel that they deserved to be there, too, but, if I had called everyone that was close to Edel, the ward would have been thronged. Also present were Joe and Marie Dooley, Martin and Evelyn McKeogh, Ian and Deirdre Brophy and Sod, all of whom were our best friends; Edel's family obviously and then Fr Simon and Stephen.

Father Simon administered the Last Rites this time. He led the decades of the rosary and I felt the strangest sensation as he said the Hail Mary. Like most Irish Catholics, I generally just rhymed off the prayer without putting any thought into it throughout my life. But this time it was different, and the words rang true like never before.

Now and at the hour of our death. Amen.

It was so powerful. It was also uncanny, because Our Lady was a huge influence on Edel throughout her illness. She had been to Lourdes and then Medjugorje several times, which was a place of real serenity for her. She also took great solace from Our Lady of Clonfert, near where I come from in Banagher, and we went there frequently. I still feel that same tingle to this day when I say my few prayers.

By now Edel had a bowl-like breathing apparatus around her head and, eventually, with the end drawing near, I asked the nurse to take it off. She was on a lot of morphine so didn't suffer for a minute. She was just drifting away. The nurses on duty were so caring and gentle.

"It's very close now," one of them said.

I whispered into her ear. "I'll look after the lads."

At two o'clock that Tuesday morning, September 15, 2009, she stopped breathing.

It was such a peaceful death. There was something so spiritual about it. Of course it's still terribly sad because the person I had been with for so long had just died in front of me, but she was surrounded by her family and friends, which is exactly how she would have wanted it.

We knew this day was going to come, and that she passed away in such a placid atmosphere, free of pain and with her dignity intact, was gratifying. On the other hand, you would have liked some more time because it had all happened so quickly. She was only admitted to hospital a little over a week earlier and now she was gone.

But, in both life and death, you can't dictate all the terms. I didn't get to have a final conversation with her, which is something of a regret, but not an overriding one. While we had spoken in depth about her dying in the months and years beforehand, it was more in a general sense rather than focusing on the moment itself. By the Saturday the chances of holding a proper conversation with her had more or less diminished, so it had just crept up on me. From then on we got only got to talk together for a brief couple of minutes here and there. But then Edel drew the parameters with these kinds of things. She was ready to go and if she wanted to talk she would have. Of course I told her I loved her, but we were never going to start spouting the sort of bullshit you see on American television dramas. It wasn't our way and Edel wouldn't have appreciated it if I went through some sort of emotional metamorphosis at this stage. We knew how we felt about each other without going into it. In the spiritual setting that was Medjugorje we had some great old chats, while we had only just arrived back from the family holiday out west, which was also very special. In the overall scheme of things, it would have been satisfying to have signed off with a proper chat between ourselves, though not having a final conversation isn't a massive regret, given that everything else about her death was pretty much as she would have wanted it to be.

She was surrounded by people who loved her and, in the coming days, Seán, Brian and myself were, too.

· · · · ·

Joe and Marie drove me back down home from the hospital. My parents, Peadar and Jo, had decamped to my house from Banagher at this stage and were looking after Seán and Brian. I've always looked on my father as something of an iron man, but I saw him cry for the first time when I arrived home. My mother was desperately upset, but that wouldn't have come as a surprise to me – she's always been an emotional person anyway and was very close to Edel. On the drive down I had been steeling myself for what was ahead of me. It was one thing telling the lads a few months earlier that Edel wasn't going to get better but another thing entirely informing them that she had actually passed on. I had spoken to them on the phone over the weekend and I instructed my mother the night before to inform them that Edel's condition was worsening. I didn't think this was something they should hear over the phone. As it was still the middle of the night, I wasn't going to wake them so I just went up to bed to lie down for a couple of hours. Sleep was never going to come to me at a time like this.

I called them at eight o'clock and brought them into the sitting room for the hardest conversation of our lives.

"Mam died a few hours ago," I told them. "It was all nice and peaceful and she wasn't in any pain. She was talking about ye and she loves ye very much. She's gone to a better place now."

They were upset, of course, and tears were shed. After a few minutes we emerged and my parents embraced them. They were contained though; it wasn't a case of them bawling their eyes out.

A neighbour, Donal Fox, called soon afterwards. Donal is one of these go-to guys in Durrow, the rural community just outside Tullamore, where we live. His wife, Margaret, looks after Seán and Brian three days a week after school. Even when Edel stopped working the lads still went to Margaret's to maintain that link. We didn't want to break it because we knew they'd have to go back there at some stage. They've always been a wonderful support. They tragically lost a son, Peter, in a car crash before we moved to Durrow and it was thought that taking on the lads might have been good for them.

Being no stranger to tragedy, Donal was upset when he arrived at the house. The two of us went up to the graveyard to pick out the plot. Brendan Ward, the former Offaly County Board Chairman, looks after these affairs in Durrow. Settling on the exact location was one of the few things that Edel and I hadn't got around to but, once I was happy with where the plot was situated, I returned to the house where 'Team Durrow' was already clicking into gear. I barely had to lift a finger over the next couple of days such was the level of community support. It was incredible.

Edel had already laid out many of the arrangements surrounding her funeral and one of them was that she would be waked in the house. When I got back from the graveyard a friend of Donal's was already cutting the grass. Hedges were being clipped. Another neighbour, Joe Regan, who is also originally from Banagher, was there as well and he had the paint brush and tin out, touching up the window ledges around the house. It was like watching an army mobilising, with Joe the commander-in-chief.

I saw Seán tipping around with a hurley in his hand out on the lawn. I went over to check that he was okay. Having done that, I was walking away when he called me back and said something I'll never forget.

"Dad, I'll wear a suit if you want me to wear a suit."

Getting Seán to wear anything but a tracksuit and runners has always been a struggle, regardless of the occasion, First Communion, Confirmation, whatever. I thought it was an amazing thing for a young lad to say at a time like that. It showed such integrity and understanding of the situation.

"I think Mam would like that alright, Seán," I replied to him proudly.

Brian was different, of course, and dressing up is something that naturally appealed to him. My sisters, Róisín and Sinéad, took the two of them off to Athlone later that day for a break and to get fitted with suits.

I had been in touch with Phil O'Reilly, a local undertaker, in the preceding days to put him on standby. I played with Phil for the couple of years when I was on the Offaly senior football panel and I've always had good time for him. He's a good character and an awful sneer; we'd often be ribbing each other about the North Offaly-South Offaly divide. "Fucking hurlers," he refers to us as. I'd quickly remind him that he was only a sub on the Offaly football team while the "fucking hurler" was starting! He was a model of professionalism from start to finish regarding the funeral arrangements. In my innocence, I had planned to go up to Dublin with him and bring Edel back down home.

"You need to be around, you have plenty of things to do," Phil told me.

Edel even had her clothes laid out, exactly what she had worn to Brian's First Communion a couple of months earlier.

"Give them to me and I'll bring her down for you safely, don't worry about that," he assured me.

He told me he'd meet me at the entrance to the hospital in Tullamore after they had readied her to be waked.

In the meantime I went into town with Joe Dooley to get some clothes for the funeral and we grabbed a bite to eat as well. Back at the house people were beginning to file through, with John Flanagan, Tadhg Sheedy, Brian Digan, Donal Rigney and former Offaly teammates, Daithí Regan and Pat Delaney, among the first to call. We went to the hospital to meet Phil at around five o'clock. Four or five cars went in with Phil leading us back out to the house. He later told me that, when he arrived to collect Edel at St James's, all the nurses from the oncology ward had come over to see her off. He'd never seen anything like that before. It underlined just how special and unique she really was.

She was waked in the sitting room and looked great. Before I left St James's I had asked a nurse to restore the piercing to her nose. The house was heaving that night with visitors. Literally thousands of people converged on Durrow to pay their respects over the few days, the majority of them to the house and, while I greeted them all, I made sure to stay in the room with Edel virtually all the time. She was my wife, it was my house and there wasn't anywhere else I should be only by her side. That Tuesday was more of an informal wake and there was something of a party atmosphere, which is how Edel wanted it. She wished for her funeral to be a celebration of her life rather than have people moping around with long faces, and the spirit with which she lived was certainly evident in the vibe among the people who were there. The wake proper was the following day and the same mood was maintained.

All the while, the community effort had gone into overdrive. Joe Regan had tables and chairs organised outside the house, given that the weather was beautiful. Three or four sets of furniture were dropped off. Sandwiches were being prepared and people I hardly knew were leaving in all sorts of food and drink in vast volumes. Roast beef, ham, bottles of whiskey, wine. I only found out not too long ago that, with the number of people that were streaming through the house, the septic tank out the back was full to capacity and somebody brought a tractor in around the back and emptied it. I still don't know who did it.

Naturally, there was a strong GAA presence in the house over those couple of days and at the funeral. You always hear about how GAA people rally around so well at times like this, and this was reinforced for me by what I was seeing. The likes of Henry Shefflin and Eoin Kelly were pucking around with the lads out the back. There was a broad cross-section of GAA players from all around and even Niall Quinn, who comes from the GAA gene pool, was there. Seán and Brian were particularly glad to make his acquaintance as he handed them €50 each. Joachim Kelly emerged as a hero in Seán's eyes, given his warrior-like playing style after he viewed old footage of him in action on TG4, and he was smitten when he arrived at the house. He later took Joachim as his Confirmation name.

I didn't know a lot of the people that came but it was pointed out to me afterwards that they were county board chairmen and secretaries from all around. One county that perhaps made a bigger impression on me than any was Clare. Brian Lohan, Anthony Daly, Liam Doyle, Seánie McMahon, Jamesie O'Connor and Ollie Baker were all there. We had hurled our hearts out against each other a decade before. Another one that stuck in my mind was Pat Hartigan, a Limerick hurler from a different generation to me that I had met only a couple of times before, but he felt he had to be there. Brian and Dessie Donnelly came down from Ballycastle in the Glens of Antrim. Football men like Joe Kernan and Nudie Hughes travelled too. That's the GAA community for you.

As the crowd dispersed on the Tuesday night and into the early hours of Wednesday morning it was down to the likes of Joe Regan, Willie Fogarty and a few other neighbours, including Jim Troy, my former Offaly teammate, who lives just up the road from me. Jim and I have always been good buddies from our days hurling together and, being from Lusmagh, Banagher would have been his nearest town. But, despite the fact that we are living even closer to each other now, we don't mix as often as we should. Jim's two eldest children are girls so they wouldn't have moved in the same circles as Seán and Brian, and he doesn't tend to drink in the same pubs around town that I do. But it wouldn't diminish our friendship in any way and we'd always pick up where we left off any time we'd meet. The Troys are a truly remarkable family.

"I'll stay with you for the night now," Jim announced.

"You don't have to Jim, I'm going to stay up myself anyway," I said.

"No, someone has to stay with you. I'll stay with you."

And that would be Jim. I wasn't too well versed on funeral traditions but Jim was. He stayed in the room with me from around two o'clock to half-past seven later that morning. The night before I had taken a call from Páidí Ó Sé, who offered his condolences and said he would do his level best to make it up. I don't know Páidí that well and said to him, "Páidí, there's no great need for you to come up at all, to be honest." Not long after Jim left though I saw Páidí striding up the driveway, resplendent in a fine suit only hours after I had been talking to him when he was below in Ventry. He stepped in, paid his respects, wouldn't even have a cup of tea, and straight back out the door again without any drama.

The house was private for the hour before we went to the church in Durrow for seven o'clock that Wednesday evening. As we prepared to put the lid on the coffin, I gave a screw each to Seán, Brian and Jerry, Edel's father, for them to apply, while I added a fourth.

"Will that keep her safe?" Brian asked me.

"She'll be as safe as a house on fire," I remarked back to him.

"But how would she be safe then!" he shrieked.

We all laughed. A child's innocence had lightened the mood.

Nonetheless, there's a huge finality about that moment, even more so when she was going out the door of the house, crossing that threshold for the last time. That was the part that I found the most difficult, leaving the house that she had put such an indelible imprint on. It had always been a huge ambition of Edel's for us to make a home in a rural area and live that type of life. Now she was leaving that home behind her for good.

I asked Joe Dooley to carry the coffin with me from the house to the front gate, with Edel's brothers following in behind. It was the only time I carried the coffin over the course of the two days, as I was conscious of being close to Seán and Brian all the time. Sod was among the pallbearers from the churchyard to the grave the following day. He and Joe were the only two non-family members to fulfil this role. The Offaly lads that I played with, as well as representatives from St Rynagh's and Ballinamere-Durrow GAA Clubs, formed a guard of honour around the hearse, a lovely touch that I greatly appreciated.

Edel had wanted Fr Simon to celebrate her Funeral Mass the following day but it wasn't straightforward given that it wasn't his parish. Fr Seán Heaney was understanding in that regard and stood aside as chief celebrant. He still joined Fr Simon on the altar on the day, as did Fr Pierre Pepper, from Banagher, Fr John Naughton, from Clonfert and Fr Shay Casey, the chaplain from Athlone IT. The turnout was massive. There were stewards kitted out in fluorescent vests directing traffic, while makeshift car parks were set up around the church. They were so shrewd in their judgement of what the numbers would be. One of the few things that I did make a call on surrounding the funeral was for loudspeakers, to Cyril Mongey of Mongey Communications in Naas. Edel had been in school with his wife, Sinéad, and they were good friends. Cyril looked after that, had them erected outside the church and refused payment afterwards. Tyrrell's Deli and Scally's Centra sent food out to the house, too. A lighting tower had also been installed for the removal.

It was a beautiful morning once again, and a really lovely Mass. Edel wanted Carmel Horan from Banagher to sing. She and Edel spent a lot of time together in Clonfert, where Edel used to go quite often to pray. Carmel is married to former Rynagh's player, Aodh Horan. They have an apartment in Medjugorje and we stayed there a couple of times. Fr Simon suggested a few readings, and Edel had more picked out herself. It was just a matter of delegating them among her family and friends to read. A number of symbols were carried up at the start of the Mass: the family picture of the four of us from Brian's First Communion the previous June, one of Edel's paintings, a Bible and a camera, given how she was so into taking photographs. Edel had set aside a prayer she wanted to be read for Seán, Brian and myself.

As you journey on the path of life don't feel alone and cry for me. Raise your eyes up to the sky. My pain is over, my spirit free. Though you can't see me, never fear, I walk beside you always near – to face each dawn a brand new start and I'll live forever in your heart.

Fr Simon delivered a touching homily on Edel that struck all the right notes and, at the end of the Mass I got up to say a few words. It actually wasn't something that Edel and I had discussed, but I felt it was expected of me. I didn't mind anyway. I was careful in choosing my words though. The last thing Edel would want would be for me to deliver some dramatic eulogy praising her from all sorts of heights. But she'd want the people who were good to her to be acknowledged, so I mentioned the likes of Dr John Kennedy and all the staff in St James's Hospital, as well as the Dóchas support group in Tullamore and, obviously, Edel's close friends. I held myself together pretty well. I'm not afraid to cry, but it never came to the fore over the course of the formalities of those few days, though the lads still say to me now that my eyes were red on the day.

She was laid to rest in the adjoining cemetery and we must have been an hour accepting condolences at the graveside. The number of people that came was truly bewildering, but virtually everything was taken out of my hands, given the community spirit that wafted in around me. In Durrow Hall, which splits the church and the cemetery, tea and sandwiches and all sorts were laid on immediately, as is the tradition there. That amazed people who weren't from the area and so many of them commented on it to me afterwards. It gave me a chance to chat to people that wouldn't have been coming along for the meal in the Tullamore Court Hotel afterwards.

For the two days that she was waked in the house there were tears and laughter, there was craic and a few drinks, the type of setting that would have found Edel in her element. It was a celebration of her life. The funeral itself represented the spiritual element of her, in a pleasant, rural setting. All in all, it was a lovely send-off. The perfect funeral for Edel in that it honoured everything that she was about.

Chapter 2

I sat down on the couch after seeing the lads off to bed. The neighbours had been around earlier for a few drinks, as was the custom in our house. The respective children from the various families rhymed off songs to keep us entertained. When everyone left and it was just me, Edel's absence hit me then more so than at any other time up to then. The atmosphere in the house was so markedly different. It was Christmas Eve.

For any young family, there's great excitement at times like this and, with the children gone to bed, you're almost as giddy at the thought of Santa Claus as they are. Not this year, though. At least not for me anyway, whatever about Seán and Brian. I found that Christmas Eve and into Christmas morning to be terribly difficult. Edel was hugely into Christmas, with the trees and decorations and, as well as the presents, there were all sorts of nice little touches and stocking fillers to supplement the whole occasion every year. I wasn't quite able to tap into that in the same way. The absence of a wife and mother from the household left a gaping hole. Of course we put the decorations up and my parents came over to help, but it wasn't the same. It couldn't be. Time seemed to move so much quicker that first Christmas without her. Last Christmas wasn't exactly a ball of fun either, though the lads assure me that they enjoyed themselves greatly over the past two years, which was comforting to hear, and I believe them.

Edel was all about the family home at Christmas. The first two years after we got married we alternated between Portlaoise and Banagher but, after that, we stayed put in our own home in Naas and then Durrow. That first Christmas after she passed away I was grateful to be able to go to Banagher and I couldn't get out of our house quickly enough that morning. We paid a visit to the grave first before heading for Banagher.

There was a card and a little crib there, which my mother had erected on behalf of the lads. A placard in front of it read, "Mam, Time goes by without you, And days turn into years, Each moment holds a memory, And many silent tears". We said our couple of prayers and the lads told Edel what Santa had brought. They don't talk openly every time we visit the grave but I encouraged them to this time, given the day that was in it. It was a chilling contrast to previous Christmases we had spent as a family.

In Banagher, Edel was offered up in the prayers at Mass that day, something that I really appreciated. It was nice to have her acknowledged in Banagher because she was held in high esteem down there, too. The place means a lot to me and virtually the whole town turned up at her funeral. I felt a genuine sense of mourning from the people of Banagher when she died. Emotions were high back in the house as well. My two youngest sisters, Róisín and Sinéad, were there, too, and there was a real feeling of loss among everyone over Edel, particularly with my mother. Of course it was sad, but, in another way, it was touching to see the extent of the love and respect that my own family held for Edel.

Generally speaking, I had been on a wayward path in the three months since Edel had been laid to rest. Only a few days after the funeral I was pacing around with a cheque book in my hand, trying to settle bills.

"Michael, relax," Joe Regan told me. "There's no rush on that kind of thing for a month or two."

With my Rynagh's days long behind me, I was still lining out for the local Ballinamere-Durrow team, who operate at intermediate level in Offaly. I was also managing the team with Pat Cleary and the county semi-final against Brosna Gaels was two days after the funeral. I hadn't been playing much that year but the game was going away from us in the second half and I said I'd enter the fray, hoping I might make a difference. I barely remember anything about it, though I think I scored a point. We lost the game in any event.

I probably got too caught up in the moment with all the support that I had received from the community that week, thinking I could come in and save the day but, looking back, even the writers of Roy of the Rovers would stop short of producing a script like that. I wouldn't be too hard on myself over it, but, out of respect for Edel, I shouldn't have put myself in that position. If it was a big game at my peak with Rynagh's or Offaly that would be a different story. But this was an intermediate county semi-final, I was forty-one years of age and had enough to be contending myself with anyway seeing as I was managing the team.

It was different with Seán and Brian, though. Seán had an Under-12 'B' football county semi-final with the club the following morning and there was never any doubt that he would play. They beat Ballycumber-Tubber and went on to win the final against Gracefield a couple of weeks later, after which there was a lovely barbecue at the clubhouse. It would have been wrong to detach him from his friends in that situation, unless he didn't want to go, and it never even came up as an issue. I wasn't in the right frame of mind to play, though, and was doing it for the wrong reasons. For Seán and Brian it felt natural, and it felt right. They went back to school the Monday after the funeral, which also might seem a bit abrupt, but I still think it was the right thing to do. They had endured a long week with everything surrounding the funeral and I thought it was best to get them back into a routine. The advice from the school would have been along those lines as well.

At the time Seán was in sixth class and Brian was in third in Durrow National School and the school staff were incredibly supportive. From time to time the teachers would bring their classes down to the grave, which is just across the road, and lay flowers. That's something that meant a lot to me, and certainly helped in terms of the grieving process for everyone involved. The worst thing would have been to ignore what had happened. It's not very often that primary schools encounter the death of a student's parent, but yet everyone in Durrow NS knew exactly how this situation should be dealt with among all the pupils. Brian really enjoyed that, the whole class going down to the grave, whereas Seán would be more reserved, but it was good for them both. Their friends really rallied around them, and the way the school dealt with it neatly reflected how we go about our business at home, where we involve Edel in virtually everything we do.

In the weeks and months after her death things were generally fine within the household. Well, as fine as they could be, given the circumstances. The home has always been my focus, but the lines became a bit blurred all the same, particularly at weekends. From Monday to Friday, by and large I fulfilled my duties consummately at home but I found myself seizing on any social occasion I could, however small, on successive weekends and the odd night during the week as well. That whole period is very much a blur, and I sometimes need my friends to fill in the gaps for me. Not that I was out getting inebriated the whole time but, with everything that had happened, my head was all over the place, though I never realised it at the time. People would ask me how I was coping and I'd tell them that I was fine, that we were well prepared for it and that she had a peaceful death. It was true up to a point, but not as much as I wanted it to be.

The former Kilkenny goalkeeper, James McGarry, whose wife, Vanessa, died in a car accident in 2007, wrote me the most astonishingly heartfelt letter shortly after Edel died. Among other things, he cast doubt on whether time is a healer at all; that it didn't seem to be of much solace to him. I called him for a chat and outlined how, in effect, I had already started the grieving process long before Edel died, which was a completely different scenario to where he found himself as Vanessa was taken from him and their son so suddenly without any prior notice.

At the same time though, it simply isn't possible to fully prepare yourself for something as traumatic as your wife's death. In some respects, it's like knowing that you're going to be on the receiving end of a ferocious shoulder in a match: You can brace yourself for the contact better than if you were caught unawares, but it doesn't mean you're not going to get lifted out of it to some extent. Although I knew it was coming, Edel's passing happened so quickly in the end. We had just been away on holiday, she came home and fell ill and, just over a week later, she was gone. I always thought it would have been more protracted than that. In the aftermath of her death I was in shock without being aware of it.

As I said, my recollections of this period are hazy at best, but I was putting myself in social situations that I shouldn't have been. When Tullamore unexpectedly won the county hurling title in October 2009, there was a great buzz around the town following the final. I went on a couple of benders and didn't cover myself in glory, only weeks after my wife had died. Again, the support from the neighbours was huge, and I took advantage of it in some respects. Dolores Ravenhill, Breeda Fogarty or Teresa O'Reilly would take the lads off me for a couple of nights over the weekend, assuring me that I needed the break, and I was happy to take their word for it. In a way you'd be feeling that you deserved the time to yourself after everything that had happened. I went through a lengthy phase of being like that after I retired from playing with Offaly. It's a selfish mind-set. Back in 2001 it was a case of, "I've been training hard for fifteen years, now it's time for me to enjoy myself", when my priority should have been to use the new-found time I now had on my hands to support Edel more in raising the kids.

A similar mind-set prevailed after she died. Now, it wasn't like I was sending the lads to a prison camp; they were very well looked after in these households and were good friends with the Ravenhills' and Fogartys' sons, so it wasn't as if they were suffering in any obvious way. But, still, I should have been more conscientious. Regardless of where I was sending them, they ought to have been at home with me more often, and it must have been unsettling for them to be landing in a different house almost every weekend. It should have been me that was looking after them. It was only natural that, as the sole parent, I was now going to have to rely on the support of others, given that other commitments of mine, such as the punditry work for example, would still have to be fulfilled. However, in the few months after Edel died, I was showing up at every cockfight and embracing the slightest opportunity to go on a session.

I'd be performing master-of-ceremonies duties at some fundraiser or other, presenting medals and attending other such engagements and overindulging in the process. All of these events would have gone ahead without me anyway, while there was no need to go out drinking after games. I should have just gone to the game and then gone home. I don't think there's any problem with having a couple of pints in these settings but, with the lads being looked after at that time, I had to milk these 'occasions' for all they were worth. I wouldn't say it was a thirst for the drink per se as I've often been able to abstain for lengthy periods and wouldn't brand myself an alcoholic by any stretch, but, when you go on sessions for spells like this, you tend to lose perspective about everything, both good and bad.

And, as some of the incidents which happened during that period of time showed, the out-of-character flashpoints weren't all drink-related. It was effectively the stress of the previous number of years manifesting itself. Before and after Edel died I was letting off steam in public, clashing with people and thinking nothing of it. I didn't think I was stepping out of line at all, which makes my transgressions even worse. Thankfully, I never portrayed that side of myself while I was at home. The lads can read me like a book at this stage. If I say there's no television, they know it'll be on in five minutes anyway!

In fairness, while I would feel now that I was taking advantage of the neighbours at that time, they wouldn't have seen it that way and were only too happy to take Seán and Brian off my hands. It never occurred to me that I was leaning too heavily on them until my mother suggested to me that I should drop the lads to Banagher rather than sending them around the houses in Durrow. That got me thinking a bit and I began to avail of my mother more, but it wasn't where I was sending the lads, it was that I was sending them anywhere in the first place. My social habits needed to change and, after Joe Dooley called out to me some six weeks after the funeral, I did straighten myself out to a certain degree.

Not too many people would have noticed the extent to which I was overdoing it, as I was dipping into various circles of friends in different locations like Tullamore, Banagher, Naas or Dublin on successive weekends, and it might spill over into a Monday session, too. Being closer to Joe than most, he was more tuned in to my movements and suggested I come on a long weekend to Spain with him and a few other friends. I went, but wasn't up for it at all. I became physically and mentally anguished by everything and didn't really mix, and my back went into spasm. I played golf the first day but, after that, I just left the lads at it and barely touched a drop out there so, without knowing it, I had begun to address my lifestyle to some extent. I also took the opportunity to spend more time with the lads by spending a couple of days with them over the Hallowe'en break at the Connemara Coast Hotel.

Once Christmas passed, like most people do in the New Year, I got myself back into more of a settled routine and had definitely improved from where I had been in the previous three months or so, but I was still prone to lapses and hadn't fully worked my way out of the fog. It took the mayhem of the dust-up that night, and tarnishing the funeral of a well-known character and friend, and the picture that Pat Cleary then painted for me in terms of my antics at times over the previous couple of years, for me to finally see the wood from the trees while driving to Birr that day.

I remember waiting to offer my condolences to Johnny Pilkington in the churchyard and feeling as though every pair of eyes were fixed on me, given how quickly word of the row had spread. As a sports writer once put it brilliantly, Johnny never saw a bush he wanted to beat about and, true to form, he strolled over.

"Heard there was a mighty row, what the fuck were you at?"

Meanwhile his father was being placed in the hearse. Only Johnny.

The process of apologising to the people I hurt and offended wasn't easy, but it was a very cleansing exercise. I made a call to one of the main protagonists in the row in the pub and asked that he convey my apologies to the others involved. I didn't know the family of the deceased and thought it would be antagonistic of me to approach them, so I met three of his closest friends to outline how sorry I was for all that happened so that they could impart it to his wife and family. I also tracked down people from the other incidents going back over the previous couple of years and expressed my regret.

I was fortunate that charges weren't pressed by anyone, and the fact that it was well-known that Edel was either sick, or had passed away, in the midst off all these incidents certainly played a part in that. People were cutting me some slack because of what I was going through, but that goodwill wasn't going to last indefinitely. The way I was headed I was going to use up all my credit eventually, though, thankfully, that row was the last tranche I drew down.

These days, if I go to a match in O'Connor Park, I might have a couple of pints afterwards and then come home, or I just might not bother at all. I can take it or leave it. I have retained my sociable ways but have ditched the tantrums. There have been one or two instances since, where I've been the peacekeeper, whereas, previously, I was more likely to have thrown petrol on the flames.

While I can't possibly be at home all the time with Seán and Brian, I carefully pick and choose what I attend and don't attend and, by and large, week nights are sacrosanct. There's a balance to my life now that I didn't have before. From the point where I was only too happy to offload the lads to the neighbours, now there's a reluctance to lift the phone at all. I wonder if I had continued the counselling with that lady in St James's would I have been able to slip more smoothly into the routine I'm in now, rather than coming to the point where I was on the verge of pressing the nuclear button? The counsellor had been very concise in terms of how I would need to live my life, striking that right balance between responsibilities at home, at work and then having a life away from that, which is something we all need. It's very easy to put it that simply, but not so straightforward to put it into practise and get it spot on. Three sessions wasn't enough for her to instil that idea of lifestyle equilibrium in me. Conversely, I can't help thinking that, given my personality, that final flashpoint is something I probably had to go through in order to come out clean the other side. In some ways I could say that it was the best thing that ever happened to me, but it came at the expense of a lot of heartache for people, and I'll always carry guilt and shame for that.

While I wouldn't have branded myself as a hellraiser beforehand, I'm much more comfortable with who I am now, which is great but regretful in ways, too, because I'm only reaching this plane now and Edel is gone. Overall I think I was a good husband, but could I have been better and more supportive at times? Undoubtedly, yes. It took until I was into my early forties before I reached a level of maturity that many people achieve much earlier in life. Now, rather than being out on the town, I genuinely prefer to be at home with my lads. It's a shame that Edel can't be there, too.

The more time that passes, the more I miss her.

PART TWO

Chapter 3

Walking out the front door of my family home on Cuba Avenue in Banagher, you couldn't move for iconic hurling figures. Straight across the road was the home of Roy Mannion, whose hurling career dovetailed with mine until he found himself too much at odds with our manager Eamonn Cregan and left the Offaly senior panel in 1994. Months later we were All-Ireland champions.

Next door to Roy then was Tony Reddin, the legendary former Galway and Tipperary goalkeeper, who was selected on both the Team of the Century in 1984 and the Team of the Millennium sixteen years later. Tony relocated to Banagher to work in Bord na Móna many years ago and made a huge contribution to the St Rynagh's club. Chatting to him as a young lad, he'd tell you some amazing stories that would have me captivated. He showed me all his medals and artefacts, including a hurley that Christy Ring fired at him one day. It hit Tony on the knee and he just threw it into the back of the net and kept it afterwards. He's still fit and well at ninety-two years of age.

Two houses further down then came the Fogartys, of which Aidan and Declan were the most famous, winning All-Irelands with Offaly in the '80s. Frank, Andrew and Ger also hurled for Rynagh's and their father, Tommy, was a serious hurling man himself who played for Offaly during the lean times. He had a huge influence on us as young lads and was a master at maintaining hurleys. He had a big lock on the press out the back of his house where he stored them, and even Ocean's Eleven would refuse to plan a heist on it on the grounds that it would be impenetrable without Tommy's co-operation.

Moving closer towards the hurling field on the far side of the road from

Fogartys were the Whites. Seánie, Stephen and Thomas, known as 'Tiddler', hurled for Rynagh's for years while Seánie was on Offaly's All-Ireland winning panel in 1981. Further on up the road was Shane McGuckin's house. Shane was corner-back on the Offaly team that won the 1994 All-Ireland and later went on to captain the county. Micheál Conneely, also a member of the 1994 panel who spent his best years abroad, later lived on the same road after he got married. The journalist, Tom O'Riordan, once carried an interview with me under the headline, "Duignan from the street of champions," in the *Irish Independent*.

• • • • •

I was the second child born to my parents, Peadar and Jo, in a family of six on February 21, 1968. Brenda is two years older than me and we both were born and lived in Birr until the family moved to Banagher when I was a few months old the following October. Next came my brother, Peadar, known simply as 'Pe', who was quickly followed by Maura. There's a gap then of ten and five years respectively to my youngest sisters, Róisín and Sinéad.

Brenda went to England for the summer when she was eighteen and we're still waiting for her to come back! She liked it over there and has stayed ever since. She's married to an Englishman called Graham Day and has four children, who are all nearly grown up at this stage. She was good at camogie but packed it in at an early age, while Sinéad was a good footballer, though wasn't particularly interested in keeping it up either. Maura and Róisín never played at all.

Pe played at underage level with Rynagh's, but could only be described as a hatchet man. There's no other way of putting it. There may have been a bit of pressure on him coming up through the ranks just after me but I'd be a shrinking violet compared to him in many ways. I remember once he was playing a minor game in Birr when a high ball dropped in around the opposition goal. The goalkeeper caught the ball and was preparing to clear it but, for Pe, getting the ball or the man was sometimes a fifty-fifty choice at best. He pulled wildly and straight into the goalkeeper's face.

"He was spitting out teeth and everything, but it was fierce peculiar because there wasn't that much blood or anything," said Pe to us afterwards, more in disappointment than anything else. Not a jot of shame or embarrassment.

It turned out that he had merely shattered the plate in the poor lad's mouth to which he already had false teeth fitted, and it didn't bother Pe in the slightest. He was probably a better footballer than a hurler, though he was still good enough to win a county minor hurling title in 1986 despite the fact that he was still U-16. He moved to Paris when he was nineteen and stayed there for about ten years. He's been in Toronto ever since, though his Offaly accent remains as strong as ever despite the fact that he speaks three other languages and rubs shoulders with Canadians and Americans every day. He's a very bright guy who has done really well for himself. He has a daughter, Sinéad, who is the same age as Seán.

Maura lived locally for a while after finishing school before relocating to Dublin. She's married to a chap called David Doyle and lives in Sallins, in Kildare, with two children, Ciara and Eoin, who I stood for as Godfather. She's very much the adhesive in our family in the way that Edel was for the O'Connells.

Róisín, then, is the academic in the house and has a PhD in electronic engineering and currently lectures in UCD. She got married a couple of years ago to Barry O'Donnell and lives in Dublin. Sinéad was a beauty therapist and managed the spa down in Dromoland Castle before returning to college in Dublin to study business and management. It's interesting in that Róisín and Sinéad were both born after I had left home to go to boarding school in Garbally College, and it's only over the last couple of years with spending Christmas at home that I'm really getting to know them as adults, which is nice.

Banagher isn't a big town now, but it was particularly small fifty years ago before there was an influx of people, such as my own family, mainly due to the employment brought about by the ESB, Bord na Móna, Banagher Concrete and Green Isle, where my father was working. My mother was employed in Dooly's Hotel in Birr, and they lived in a flat on Connaught Street until shortly after I was born when the house on Cuba Avenue became available and they snapped it up.

My father is from Connemara and his brother, Frank, hurled a little bit for Galway. Dad was more into athletics and boxing, though he did dabble in hurling and football, too. He's a very cool character and a man of few words so I'd look for signals from him after games to gauge my performance. If I played well, and we won, he might sit and have a cigarette and chat with me when we got home, but then he might not if the game hadn't gone my way. He'd be very shrewd and would often give me tips, particularly in athletics, which was his natural field. He was tactical in his thinking and would tell me to take a certain line coming around a bend in cross-country running, for example, but he would never have put any pressure on us growing up. Although he's quiet by nature, he can mix with anyone. Seán and Brian absolutely adore him and enjoy a brilliant relationship with him. They hang on his every word when they go to Banagher.

My mother was a bigger influence in a sporting sense, given that she has a much more outgoing personality and would encourage us to be the very best we could be in anything we did. She's originally from Lorrha, just the wrong side of the border between Offaly and Tipperary. She'd lavish me with praise if I played well but it would be a case of, "What happened you today?" if I didn't. My father would be wittier, interjecting with comments such as, "Ah, no, he wasn't too bad now, it was one of those days when you did most of your good running off the ball" – his way of telling me so that I never felt the weight of it. It was the perfect mix with my parents in that regard because, no matter what modern-day players say, you need your ego stroked from time to time, but too much of it can be detrimental also. My mother was the one driving me on, instilling that passion in me to succeed, whereas my father was the cool head to temper all of that.

Mam's mother died suddenly at the age of 51 years old so, at one stage when I was growing up, my aunts, Kay and Marie, and uncle Jim O'Meara, came to live with us before moving on to England when they came of age. My grandfather, William, also lived with us before passing away when I was twelve after years of ill-health. He had a great interest in horse racing and used to send me around to the bookies to place bets for him, having been down on my hands and knees reading out the form to him. Looking back, it must have been hard on my mother because she was only a young woman in her early twenties when she got married and had four children in quick succession. She then had to take in three of her siblings and look after her father full-time in his latter years. But, when you're a young lad, you never think of your mother in terms of being young or old.

My father worked as a fitter and worked very hard. He squeezed in overtime and shift work on top of that when required in order to maximise what he could provide for us and, against that backdrop, my mother was the bigger influence within the home. Everything was channelled towards the family to ensure we got the very best that they could provide for us. Good food, decent clothes and the best possible education. Apart from a few trips down to my father's home in Connemara, there weren't too many holidays, and certainly no frills, but I had a very happy childhood with sport, particularly hurling, at the centre of virtually everything I did.

· · · · ·

Shannon Rovers and Cloghan merged to form St Rynagh's GAA Club in 1961 and, with the increasing population in the area, the club really hit the ground running, particularly in hurling, for which Banagher is the power base with Cloghan very much the football stronghold. The club won its first county hurling title in 1965 and then added nine more by 1976, when I first got involved, as well as competing in the first All-Ireland club final in 1971, which was lost to Roscrea. Tommy Fogarty and Jackie Ryland ran the underage hurling scene in Rynagh's and kept us interested. Jackie was a Protestant, though an absolute fanatic about hurling. Never mind soccer and rugby, Gaelic football was a foreign sport to him. He never married and hurling was his life. From the time we first appeared in the field he treated us as if we were adults. He'd fall out with you, and then back in just as quick. He called me "that man" and Roy Mannion was "the other man". Often he'd be worried about some altercation he might have had with us and would report to my mother for reassurance.

"I had a bit of a row with that man the other night there now, the other man got into it as well and the two of them got thick, but I didn't mean anything by it," he'd say.

"Ah, sure I know that Jackie," Mam would reply.

He brought us everywhere and looked after us. He had a bigger influence on me than anyone in the club, such was his passion. He'd be shouting and roaring on the sideline, clashing hurleys, but even as a young lad you'd know that it was just a bit of harmless aggression. He had a shop in town I'd pop into every day and he'd be enquiring as to whether he could bring me anywhere or do anything for me. Even when I started playing with Offaly seniors he was involved as team secretary and would bring Jim Troy and myself to training. Sadly, he fell into ill-health and died a few years ago.

St Rynagh's used to run the school teams in Banagher as well, which was highly unusual at the time given that, in most other schools, there were teachers only too willing to fulfil that role. I started school in Banagher NS the same day as Roy. He was always a superior hurler than me in a technical sense, but I had a fierce determination to match him stride for stride in terms of achievement. I remember he was picked for a Community Games team one year and I wasn't. They went on to win the Leinster title and I swore that he wouldn't be on any team ahead of me again, and it more or less worked out like that. Now, I had no qualms with Roy's selection, he was the better player, but we were such close friends that it was very difficult for me to swallow at the time. It wasn't a rivalry, or anything like it, but it acted as a motivation for me and spurred me on to have that iron-willed resolution to make any team I was involved with. The following year we were both on the Community Games team together, though we only came third in Mosney this time. I was also competing in athletics there that year.

When I won my first under-fourteen county medal in 1979, I was just eleven and playing corner-back, while Roy was a sub. We won four in a row, and I was full-back the second year, then centre-forward and full-forward. I knew by then that, while I didn't have the skill of the likes of Roy, I could more than hold my own. Such was my mind-set, I wanted to be the first from that batch of players to make the club senior team and then the Offaly team. Roy and I were more or less on an even keel by then, and I made the senior team before him in 1986. That had been my goal from a very young age.

Playing senior for Rynagh's was, for me, box office back then, given the string of famous hurlers the club had produced and they were routinely winning county titles. The likes of Barney Moylan, Pádraig Horan and Damien Martin were hurling for Leinster when Offaly was seen as nothing only a hurling backwater. Pat Joe Whelahan was another Rynagh's and Offaly stalwart, and then the Fogartys joined Horan and Martin in winning All-

Irelands with Offaly in the '80s. Martin Hanamy would have been a couple of years older than me then as well.

Roy and I would spend hours as young lads watching the Rynagh's. They were our idols. Damien Martin, the first-ever All Star, was one of the all-time great goalkeepers. I remember he used to have us take shots on him in goal to sharpen his already keen-edged reflexes after the rest of the team had finished training. Damien would sometimes arrive late and, despite having put in a hard day's work on the bog, wouldn't be spared in training often putting in extra effort which was no sacrifice to him and helped make him great. He'd stand in goal with his back to us and we'd take shots from the twenty-metre line. When he turned, the ball would have travelled most of the way towards the goal but he'd still be blocking the shots. He was something else.

The same year that I broke into the Rynagh's team, Roy and I were both on the first Offaly minor side to win Leinster and All-Ireland titles. By then our lives had diverged somewhat in that I went to boarding school in Garbally College, in Ballinasloe, while Roy stayed and went to Banagher Vocational School. My father was on reasonably good money but it still would have been a strain to send me there. It was typical of my parents' outlook in resolving to provide the very best they could for us. Generally, my father would never go outside the door. He used to socialise quite amiably as a younger man but more or less just gave up all that, preferring to invest his money in his family rather than the publicans. Later, Green Isle closed after he had been working there for twenty-seven years and he went on to work in Banagher Concrete before setting up a security business. Around this time my mother returned to work in Dooly's, where she ended up as manager without having had any formal training as such. She's just a brilliant operator and hardest-working person I have ever come across.

My father left school at fifteen to become an apprentice fitter with the air corps in Baldonnell, though his father, also Michael Duignan, had taught in Garbally for a period while his brothers, Frank and Danny, attended the school. With the family connection to the place, its reputation and the fact that I was a sports fanatic, sending me there was seen as giving me the best opportunity to maximise my potential in various fields. Pe followed me there a couple of years later but couldn't settle and returned to Banagher to study for his Leaving Cert.

The convent in Banagher, La Sainte Union, had a huge reputation, so there was never any question of my sisters being sent anywhere bar there.

• • • • •

Going to boarding school was exciting but daunting at the same time. I was fortunate in that it was only a half-hour drive from home so my parents would visit every Friday evening with sandwiches and fresh clothes. We got home roughly every six weeks. A neighbour of mine, John Tim Dalton, started at the same time. There were a number of Offaly lads in the school, such as Aidan Ryan, Cathal Ryan, Mike Devine, Kieran Egan and Daithí Lynch. There was a massive dormitory for the first-year students, with partitions between every eight beds. Going from your family home to living with strangers was testing but you get over it after a while. The night after I arrived we were out at the gates to see the Galway team bus pass by as they headed for the home-coming celebrations after winning the All-Ireland hurling title for the first time in fifty-seven years the day before.

Rugby was, traditionally, the main sport in Garbally but hurling rose to prominence in the '70s when the likes of Ollie Kilkenny, Seán Silke and Iggy Clarke attended the school. Ciarán Fitzgerald, the former Ireland and Lions' rugby captain, was also a past pupil. My time there was really dictated by sport and I did little else bar train with the various teams I was involved with, be it hurling, rugby or Gaelic football. One year we won the Connacht title in juvenile hurling and football, as well as the junior cup in rugby and I was on all three teams. It would be unheard of for Garbally to win even one of those now. Football wasn't taken too seriously and was shelved after juvenile level, even though we beat St Jarlath's of Tuam to win that title.

When I look at Seán attending secondary school now, he maybe has one PE class a week and the odd training session but, in Garbally, we trained every day from four o'clock to half-past five in various sports and I would have been involved in cross-country running as well. It paved the way for my playing career because, while I wouldn't have been one of the most skilful players, I certainly wasn't lacking in most of the other areas. I was very strong and fit from a young age as a result of what was almost professional training. I rarely tired in matches throughout my career. I won a lot while I was in

Garbally and it gave me confidence to a certain extent.

Away from sport, it instilled in me an ability to mix with people from various walks of life, which stands to me to this day. I was comfortable dealing with a wide range of people regardless of their background and, without a doubt, that was the single biggest reason why I have been able to succeed as a television pundit. Although I was a boarder at Garbally, I got on well with the day boys and had an affinity with the lads who were from rural farming backgrounds and then the townies from Ballinasloe. If I hadn't had that experience in Garbally I don't think I would have been as likely to move away from Banagher and do other things in my life, such as spending the summer of 1987 in Boston, going to college in Waterford, moving to Dublin and then going out on my own in business in later years. Doing transition year and going to work in a psychiatric hospital and with St Vincent de Paul was brilliant for my personal development as a teenager too.

There were two deans in Garbally at the time, Fr Colm Allman and Fr Dan O'Donavan. Fr Allman is now president of the school. A typical day would see you rise at about ten past seven for breakfast at half-past. Then you'd come up and wash and go for morning prayers and school hours were from nine to four, after which we'd usually go training. It was tea at half-past five followed by study at quarter-past six for two hours. That could be shortened by half an hour if you took up the option of going to Mass at quarter to eight and we usually developed a rather angelic streak around that time of the day. A second study session ensued from quarter to nine until quarter past ten and we'd round off the day with a glass of milk and a bun followed by night prayers. The meals weren't great but you'd get by. On weekends there'd be study sessions in the morning and evening but you'd have a bit of free time to yourself. Once you got older you'd be allowed down the town in Ballinasloe on a Saturday night. Other than that you weren't allowed outside the school grounds. But then you could venture as far as you wanted as long as you weren't caught. There were various forms of punishment for indiscretions, which could include cleaning duty or, worse, being kept back until Saturday morning on a weekend you were due to go home. I was a victim of that a number of times.

There was very little corporal punishment and, certainly, none of the horrific stories of abuse that have come to light in recent years were comparable to my time in Garbally. There might have been the odd clip here and there but they were different times. If you went home and told of it, you would have got another couple. The threat of the wooden spoon, or of being sent up to Michael Hyland, the principal who was hard but fair, was deterrent enough.

There was a common-room where we could watch television and quite often we'd sneak down after hours. I remember in 1985 a group of us went down to watch the epic snooker World Championship final between Dennis Taylor and Steve Davis. I was standing beside the door when Fr Allman burst in and ordered everyone out. However, he didn't notice me and, as soon as the coast was clear, I switched the TV back on and watched as Taylor sank the black for a famous win. A group of us got away with taking a teacher's car out for a spin one night, but, on another occasion when I wasn't involved, a few of the lads took Bishop Cassidy's car as far as Shannonbridge and were caught.

I was suspended at one stage, however, when I busted a lad's nose. He got thick over a game of pool and hit me with the cue across the back. I hit him a shot back, harder than I meant to, and broke his nose. He didn't squeal on me but Fr Allman inevitably noticed his bloodied face. It wasn't a huge incident but I would always have been encouraged by my father to stand up for myself and I wasn't going to take being hit by a pool cue from behind. Garbally was a tough place and there were fights of some sort most days. I wasn't involved in many flashpoints but I never had a problem with defending myself when I had to, a trait I retained into adulthood.

I had played at U-14 level for St Rynagh's from the age of eleven so, a couple of weeks after I started in Garbally, I saw a notice for junior cup rugby training and reported for the first session as bold as brass despite being twelve and never having played rugby before. The coach, Johnny Farrell, asked me where I was going. "Sure I'm under-fifteen, what's the problem?" I had to be content with playing for the first year and under-fourteen teams, though I played two years junior cup and three years senior cup, as well as four years on the senior hurling team.

I also played for Connacht Schools in rugby for two years. I won two junior and two senior cups with Garbally and I always felt that rugby was the game I was most naturally talented at. I played at outside centre and enjoyed the physical contact and was very attack-minded in my play. The standard at schools level in Connacht wouldn't have been exceptionally high compared to Leinster and Munster, but we played friendly games against the likes of Roscrea, Rockwell, Blackrock and Gonzaga and competed well with them. At interprovincial level Connacht only played the 'A' teams from the other three provinces.

In the summer of 1985 there was a week-long training camp in Clongowes for those who would be in the shake-up to play for the Ireland schoolboys' team the following year and I was one of the few Connacht players invited along. Nicky Barry was among the big names in schoolboys' rugby at the time and he went on to play for Garryowen and Ireland. I made the final thirty and played at full-back in a 'probables' versus 'possibles' game in which I broke my collarbone. I didn't receive any further contact the following year when the squad was being finalised.

In hurling we won two Connacht senior titles under the tutelage of John Molloy, a very good coach who did a lot for my game. We were beaten fairly comfortably in both All-Ireland semi-finals that we played in, by North Mon of Cork in 1985 and Birr Community School the following year as they went on to win the All-Ireland. When I first went to Garbally I had been playing mostly in defence with Rynagh's but John reckoned I was a corner-forward and that's where he played me most of the time. I found myself moving up the field back at the club too.

I dabbled in a bit of athletics in Garbally and became the first boarder to win the first-year cross-country race down there. I never did a formal athletics training session but I won Offaly cross-country titles at various age groups as well, including one at Under-14 straight after hurling in a county final. I won the Offaly Community Games at 600 metres when Under-12, 800 metres when Under-14 and 1,500 metres at Under-16. The last time I didn't even bother going to Mosney as I had no long-term interest in athletics and thought it better to allow someone else take my place. Hurling was always my priority and if I could fit a bit of rugby and football in around that then fine.

Academically, I probably let myself down a bit in Garbally. My Leaving Cert results weren't great, though I had broken my hand in an intermediate hurling match for St Rynagh's a few weeks earlier and only cut the cast off a couple of days beforehand. It was a handy excuse to fall back on because I hadn't much work done. Admittedly, I had paid my own fees for a few of the years I was down there. I worked on the bog in Derrinlough with Roy Mannion one summer while during another summer I worked for Anthony O'Reilly in the Stroll Inn pub in Salthill. I had ability and I could have done a lot better at school but I suppose I found it hard to motivate myself because, whereas my sporting ambitions were clearly mapped out in my mind, I hadn't a clue what I wanted to do professionally. I repeated my Leaving Cert in LSU in Banagher in 1987 and it was interesting to observe how I had matured rather differently to the other students, given that I had spent six years in boarding school. I was nineteen by the time I sat the exams and was on the Offaly senior panel.

Edel also attended boarding school at Cross and Passion in Kilcullen, Co Kildare. As her father was a guard and her mother a nurse, they worked awkward hours so it was practical on a number of levels to send their children to boarding school. She liked the routine that came with it and was quite sporty. In fact, she was the school's sports captain and, unlike me, dovetailed her sporting interests with her studies rather well. She loved the whole experience and would have been very much in favour of Seán and Brian going to boarding school as well and, if she was still with us, that's probably what would have happened. We had Seán's name down for the Cistercian College in Roscrea but, after losing his mother, I wasn't going to send him away and it'll be the same with Brian when he finishes primary school. I'd miss them too much anyway and couldn't imagine them being away from home for weeks on end.

Chapter 4

Croke Park, September, 1986

Given the importance that pulling on the tricoloured hoops of Offaly held for me, I must say my early experiences of wearing that famous jersey weren't the most cheerful. I have sketchy recollections of going to Dublin with what I think was an Offaly under-sixteen team and, while still under-sixteen, I got a call once to play in a minor challenge game against Galway. I thought I had done reasonably well but never heard anything back from the management. The following year, 1985, I made the team but the set-up was appalling. I just got a phone call informing me that we were playing Wexford in the first round of the Championship in Carlow and that I should make my way back from Garbally to Banagher to catch a bus to the game. We didn't have one training session. Sean Rigney, from Rynagh's, was selected at full-back and Mick Hogan, from Birr, at centre-back but, for whatever reason, neither of them turned up. Apart from the few Rynagh's lads, I was in a dressing room with strangers. All I could think was, "I'm playing on Garbally teams that are far better organised than this". I didn't know the names of the lads playing beside me. It was a complete joke. It was particularly hard to believe that this was the level of preparation, if you could call it that, for the county minors in a year when Offaly won the senior All-Ireland. We patched up a team and only lost by a few points. Wexford went on to reach the All-Ireland final, where they lost to Cork by seven points.

Later that year Birr and Rynagh's contested the county minor final in what was an exceptional game of hurling, so the talent was certainly there for Offaly to have had a much more successful minor team. Birr scored six goals to beat us narrowly, though we unquestionably played the better hurling. Pat

Joe Whelahan, a former Rynagh's great, was in charge of the Birr team. He had moved to the town years earlier and finished out his playing days with them at junior level. When Rynagh's emerged as the dominant force in Offaly hurling in the '60s, '70s and into the '80s, Birr weren't really a factor. We grew up thinking that Birr just couldn't beat Rynagh's. Their county title win in 1971 was their only one in a forty-three year period. But, at underage level, they were getting their act together and a serious rivalry had been simmering between the two clubs as we moved through the ranks. The sparks first flew in a tournament game we played at Under-14 level in 1982. We both won through to the final and an almighty row broke out and we felt hugely aggrieved following an incident involving Alan Kelly and Birr's Mick Hogan. There were skirmishes after the game with even parents getting involved. There was a lot of bad blood over that and familiarity with each other bred further contempt between both sets of players as the years progressed. Still, after they had beaten us in that minor final, I made it my business to shake hands with each of them, much as it pained me. It's something I always preach to young lads now.

Pat Joe was given the Offaly minor job and it was hugely significant. To us he was a Rynagh's man to the core but he had that Birr background too. He was instantly agreeable to both sides. If Offaly were going to go anywhere at minor level at that time the Birr and Rynagh's lads had to be singing off the one hymn sheet and Pat Joe was the perfect conductor. He got us together early in the year for a challenge game against Laois – a marked difference to the shambles of 1985.

As we sat in the dressing room the Rynagh's and Birr lads were all grouped together according to their factions. Pat Joe came in and grabbed me by the arm, brought me to the other side of the dressing room and put me sitting between Daithí Regan and Gary Cahill. He might as well have been tossing me into the fires of hell as far as I was concerned. "The Birr lads won't take a bite out of you," he said. He then moved one of their lads over the other side as well. I didn't appreciate it at the time but it was a brilliant piece of management on his part and something that had to be done, particularly when you consider that Mick Hogan was centre-back and captain while Alan Kelly was midfield.

In terms of team selection, Pat Joe couldn't really see past Birr and Rynagh's. By the end of the year we had twelve players on the starting team between us. He had a massive influence on me from a confidence point of view. "We won't win an All-Ireland without you playing well," he'd tell me. I was used to good training sessions in Garbally but Pat Joe's were at a different level altogether. They were hugely enjoyable, with brilliantly innovative drills. The ball work was excellent and he wasn't shy in terms of working us hard either. He had a real affinity with young lads and how to train them. He's someone I have immense regard for and he later came back to train Rynagh's to a senior county title in 1990 against Birr.

Things were coming together nicely as Birr Community School won the All-Ireland Colleges title, while Banagher did likewise in the Vocational Schools' competition. John Kilmartin, from Kilcormac/Killoughey, and myself were the only two players on the Offaly minor team that weren't involved in either of those successes. For all that, we very nearly came unstuck in our first Championship game against Kilkenny, needing a late score from Declan Pilkington to secure a replay, which we won. I was full-forward and scored a goal shortly after half-time, which gave us breathing space playing against the wind and we held out. Generally, in the last fifteen minutes, Pat Joe used to bring me out to the middle of the field to help us see out the game. We went on to beat Dublin and then Wexford in the Leinster final to claim Offaly's first ever provincial title at minor level.

The team was well-balanced. Roy Mannion was full-back with Hogan in front of him. Daithí was centre-forward and I was on the edge of the square. Then we had the likes of Ronnie Byrne, Declan Pilkington and Gary Cahill down the flanks. Joe Errity was an absolutely outstanding prospect as a centre-back but played in goal that year as it was felt that a certain John Troy was just a little too young. Troy had only just turned fifteen but he was on the panel all the same. Of course he didn't end up as a goalkeeper, but he had all the skills to make it to the very top and would have been more than comfortable in the company of all the great netminders that have graced the game in the last twenty years. Without doubt he is the greatest stickman I ever came across and he had the hurling brain to complement it, too. Although he wasn't yet playing, he was very much a part of the set-up that year and it was the first chance I had to observe him at close quarters. Some of the tricks he had were breathtaking. He could trap a ball instantly, regardless of what speed or angle it was coming to him at. He could be running flat out to the ball and suddenly decide to pull on it rather than lift it without having to adjust his stride in the slightest, whereas most lads would fall over themselves trying to do it. He had such balance. There was no drama; he just made everything look so easy.

I ended up getting on very well with the Birr lads and a team spirit developed very quickly, thanks to Pat Joe's handling of the affair. They were massive craic and, as we began to socialise together, I realised they weren't the unbearable ogres we believed them to be. They had won an All-Ireland colleges' title together and didn't care about whatever opposition we came up against. There was great swagger about that team but no over-confidence. Our support base swelled as the year progressed and the families of the players became close. It was a tightly-knit group.

We overcame a good Galway team in the All-Ireland semi-final after Ray Duane, who was the big name in their side at the time, nearly beat us on his own. I scored 1-5 and had been handed the free-taking duties by that stage. Ronnie Byrne and Deccie Pilkington had been on them up to the Leinster final and were more natural free-takers than me but Pat Joe must have felt I could handle the responsibility better. I really immersed myself in ensuring that this minor team maximised its potential, to the extent that I didn't take up the option of playing with the county Under-21 team that year even though several of the other lads did. They lost a Leinster final to Wexford after a replay.

Our All-Ireland final was against Cork, the defending champions who retained Ger Manley, among others, from the previous year's final when he was one of the star players. However, the prospect of taking on the famous blood and bandage didn't faze us in the slightest. Daithí had a bit of previous with Rory O'Connor, when Birr CS beat North Mon earlier that year in the colleges' final, and O'Connor got sent off shortly before half-time after the two of them had another altercation. I was marked by Damien Irwin but very little ball came down between us so the game passed me by to a certain extent, though I did convert a couple of testing frees. It was a feature of the campaign that different players stepped forward in each game to make critical scoring contributions. Ronnie had a great day in the Leinster final, I did most of the damage for us in the semi-final and then Deccie hit 2-2 in the final. Daithí scored a hand-passed goal late on to clinch a 3-12 to 3-9 victory for us and we all cheered as one as Mick Hogan, of all people, became the first Offaly man to lift the *Irish Press Cup*.

There was a great reception for us in Power's Hotel and then, the following afternoon, came the function in the Burlington for the two senior and two minor teams, as was the tradition at the time. We arrived early and when one of the lads ordered a drink he was pleasantly surprised to learn that it was complimentary. We furiously began ordering vodkas and all sorts and, by the time the other three teams arrived, the tab had been exhausted. We were back down to Birr that night and a great week of celebration followed. Ronnie Byrne missed much of the festivities after he had broken his jaw towards the end of the final. Pat Moylan, one of our selectors, and later Cathaoirleach of the Seanad, rushed into him.

"What's wrong with you?"

"Ah, me jaw, me jaw," roared Ronnie.

"Get up," Pat said to him, "for feck's sake haven't you got another one!"

Ronnie finally got home to Lusmagh from the Mater Hospital on the Wednesday evening and the cup was coming to nearby Banagher that night. He was one of three Lusmagh lads on the panel, along with Brendan Kelly and John Troy, and he and Brendan called in for John on the way to Banagher. What Ronnie didn't know, however, was that John had been in a bit of trouble at home that evening having got caught up in the celebrations and gone AWOL for a couple of days. He was only fifteen while most of us were eighteen, quite a difference at that age. Ronnie stepped into the Troys' sitting room and John was in the corner with his head down. After chatting with Jimmy, John's father, for a while about the game Ronnie eventually said, "Well we may head on anyway, the cup is coming to Banagher at eight o'clock... Are you coming in John?" John looked over at Jimmy.

"By Jaysus," says Jimmy, "Go in there for a few hours tonight and behave yourself. If I hear anything about you drinking..."

They were just going out the door then when Jimmy chased John down and said, "Here's a tenner in case you have to buy a round!" He wouldn't let him out the door with nothing. He didn't want him drinking but he wouldn't have anyone else buying it for him either. He'd stand his round; that was the Troys for you.

You'd have to wonder what direction Offaly hurling might have taken in the next fifteen years or so had that minor team not emerged. On the back of our success, Offaly won a further two All-Ireland minor titles in 1987 and '89 and Troy stands alongside Jimmy Doyle as the only men to hold three medals in that grade. I think our team paved the way for the other two to follow. Of those three teams I felt we had the best balance and spread of hurlers, even though the more virtuoso performers like Brian Whelahan, Johnny Dooley, Johnny Pilkington and Adrian Cahill emerged on the '87 and '89 sides. To win a colleges', vocational school and minor All-Ireland in 1986 with the same hard core of players was a fair achievement. But, if Pat Joe hadn't broken down the barriers that were there between the Rynagh's and Birr players, what direction would our careers have taken? We might well have just knocked lumps out of each other at club level for years afterwards without realising our potential together with Offaly.

· · · · ·

Before the year was out there was the matter of the county minor title, which was contested between you know who. Birr had seven starters on the Offaly minor team in the All-Ireland final and we had five. Both clubs had two players each on the subs. Make no mistake about it, we were the two best minor club teams in the country. It ended in a draw, fourteen points apiece, on a day when I shipped two fierce belts on the head and refused to come off. I later required twenty-four staples to the wounds. I wouldn't have got the second blow but for the first as, when I looked up for a high ball coming in my direction, the blood flowed down into my eyes and, before I knew it, I was pole-axed again. Pat Joe was managing Birr again and came out to me. I could see how concerned he was. He treated us like his own but, at that moment in time, he was Birr and I was Rynagh's and I told him where to go because I was playing on. Believe it or not, Daithí and I were selected to play for Offaly seniors that day in a National League game against Clare but my debut would have to wait as I was rushed to hospital in Tullamore having collapsed after the game. The minor final was the curtain-raiser to the League game in Birr. Could you imagine that happening now!

When I arrived home that evening it was almost like a wake with the flood of visitors that had called wondering how I was. The following weekend I played a Connacht Under-20 final for Ballinasloe against Galwegians and my debs was that night. I couldn't wash my hair because of the staples. The state of me.

We won the replay against Birr by 3-7 to 0-14 and they were probably the better team on the day but, then, we would have said the same the previous year when they got the better of us. We just got the goals at the right time. I finished the game at centre-back after Mannion struggled uncharacteristically on Daithí, whom he nearly always had the measure of. I caught Daithí square with a shoulder shortly after I went back on him and buried him, legitimately of course. It was probably the sweetest shoulder I ever hit someone with and Daithí admitted himself that he felt it all the way from head to toe. He was a spent force for the rest of the game and we held out. My brother Peadar came on as a sub that day and had a couple of pints afterwards with us. He was only sixteen so it didn't take long for him to get jarred and I sent him off home. When he got in the door it was obvious he was in a bit of a state. He thought he was able to cover it up, though of course he wasn't. My parents are easygoing and got a great laugh out of it and then sent him in to school the next day just to rile him while I was allowed to lie on and bask in the glory. He's still slagged about it to this day at home.

It was a huge win for us and a game we couldn't afford to lose. We had won four Under-14 titles in succession together but then just one Under-16 title and failing to win a minor would have been a big let-down. While that Offaly minor side of 1986 helped sustain the senior team for years to come, the same was true of Rynagh's success in the grade that year. We won four Under-21 titles around that time and also four senior titles up to 1993. Similarly, Offaly and Rynagh's experienced barren times after the underage success ran out. The club went another nineteen years without winning a minor title and we haven't won the senior since '93. Having won four minor titles since 2005, hopefully that statistic will be amended sooner rather than later.

Chapter 5

Boston, June, 1987

Losing to Kilkenny in the 1986 Leinster senior final was a watershed moment for the Offaly team of the '80s. Diarmuid Healy stood down after seven glorious seasons in charge in which he had won four Leinster titles and two All-Irelands with a county that had achieved virtually nothing in hurling before 1980. Many of that team had given everything to come back and win the 1985 All-Ireland having been well beaten by Cork in the Centenary final in Thurles the year before. Sadly, Pat Carroll passed away in March, 1986, and, as well as Healy's exit, stalwarts like Pat Fleury, Pádraig Horan and Damien Martin retired.

The team was ageing and Offaly weren't going to re-emerge without the infusion of new blood so our minor success couldn't have come at a better time. Daithí, Brendan Kelly and I were added to the panel straightaway. Georgie Leahy, another Kilkenny man, was appointed as Healy's replacement. He was a great hurling man but preparations and training were completely different back then.

We were coming into a dressing room that was full of legends. Eugene Coughlan, Ger Coughlan, Pat Delaney, Joachim Kelly and Aidan Fogarty were gods to us and we were very much overawed to be in their company. Paudge Mulhare was a selector and also chairman of the county board. I remember one team meeting where Delaney blew a gasket over expenses and fired a pair of boots at Paudge. Then that'd be it and they'd just move on to the next item as if it never happened while us young lads went pale. They were seriously tough men but very straight and honourable. Joachim stood out to me as being particularly welcoming to the younger players. He was delighted that a new generation was breaking through and he fed off it. It was like the players from those minor teams gave him a fresh impetus and he ended up playing on until he was thirty-seven.

Around May, 1987, there was a panel picked for the Championship and both Daithí and I were selected. However, contact had been made with us by a chap called Jamesie Donoghue in Boston in connection with us playing out there for the summer with the Fr Tom Burke's club, which was mostly made up of Galway players. Between the jigs and the reels we decided that we'd go as we might never have a better opportunity. Unlike a lot of the trans-Atlantic jaunts at that time, this was all above board as Boston was properly affiliated to the GAA. We had to fill out transfer forms and stay there for a minimum of thirty days. Once you landed back in Ireland then you were immediately eligible to play for your club again. We told Georgie and there wasn't any fuss.

I remember the day we left so clearly. I had never been on a plane before. I borrowed money from the bank in Banagher to pay for the flights and the club would refund us when we arrived. They would also fix us up with accommodation and try to get us a job. There was no question of being paid to play. Daithí's parents, Alf and Bridie, brought us down to Shannon to get the flight. Alf was a great character who, sadly, has died since. We wouldn't have been drinking much at the time but we had a going away do the night before and were feeling a bit tender, though Alf bought us a few more pints anyway. The flight was delayed and when we finally got on board the captain announced that there would be free beverages on the way over as a result!

When we landed in New York our connecting flight to Boston had already left so here we were, we had never been anywhere before and we were standing in JFK airport with hurleys in our hands. We were spotted by Norbert Hennessy, a prominent figure in New York GAA circles, who was on the same flight as us. We explained our predicament and he said he'd put us up and we could sort another flight for the next day. He was very good to us and brought us down to Gaelic Park the next day, where Tipperary and Galway were playing in the New York Championship. Some of the main protagonists that defined the fierce rivalry between the counties around this time back home were in action. Norbert asked us would we hurl for Tipp. It went against our better instincts but he had been good to us so we agreed.

As we togged out though I had second thoughts. There was a photographer present and if word got out that we had played illegally God knows what the repercussions would have been. I faked a hamstring injury but Daithí played. The hurling was animal, particularly in the first fifteen minutes or so with the dust flying off the ground on a tight pitch. Daithí came off after about twenty minutes with a "tweak". We actually spent another couple of nights in New York and quite liked it there but eventually fulfilled our obligation and moved on to Boston.

We initially stayed with Gerry Martin and Pat Costello, who more recently was chairman of Oranmore GAA Club. We later moved in with Pat and Laura Magee, a couple from Loughrea. We did a few odds and ends for the first couple of weeks before I got fixed up with work. It was labouring with a fella called Eamon Meehan, from Newry. The day started with breakfast at five o'clock in the morning on Dorchester Avenue and though the work was tough it did me the world of good. The whole experience over there was great for my social development. I'd mix the plaster a couple of times in the morning, drag it up a few flights of stairs maybe and then we'd get lunch at around ten o'clock in the morning seeing as we started so early. I was perplexed to find that you could walk into a shop and get various forms of coffee and a roll prepared. There was none of that back home. There were numerous instances where I was like a rabbit caught in the headlights, but then you learn quickly.

To say that Daithí didn't work quite as hard as I did would be a polite way of phrasing it. He did a few bits and pieces, roofing and painting, but certainly didn't work as fanatically as I did. We had a system whereby we placed whatever money we earned in a drawer between our beds and our spending money came from that. Daithí tended to get rather homesick and would talk about "Ma and Da" quite a lot. They'd send a copy of the *Midland Tribune* out to him every week. During one period when I was working flat out and Daithí was at a loose end, the money was running scarce in the drawer and I dropped down to the pub to find him half-jarred. I called him outside for a word and gave him a severe dressing down. He was taking the piss. "If I hear one more word about Ma or Da I'll kick the living shit out of you!" I fumed.

The hurling out there was a pantomime. We had plenty of good players like Tom Hennessy, who was Limerick's sub goalkeeper for the 1994 All-Ireland final. John Considine, from Cork, was corner-back and went on to win an All-Ireland in 1990. Aidan Staunton was on the Galway panel in 1987 and '88 when they won the All-Ireland and he later won a club title with Kiltormer. Pat Nolan, from Castlegar, was centre-back. I thought he was a phenomenal hurler and could never understand how he wasn't a regular with Galway. Then again, he was vying with Tony Keady for the centre-back spot. Dick O'Hara, corner-back on Kilkenny's All-Ireland winning teams of 1982 and '83, was a few years older than most of us. The standard was high among all the teams and we trained hard. Needless to say, the hurling was tough. We played Cork a few days after we arrived and they hammered us by about fifteen points. Pat Kenneally played centre-back for them, just as he did for the Cork minors the previous year in the All-Ireland final. There was a certain spillover between Daithí and him from that game and a few strokes were pulled early on. Daithí eventually landed a haymaker and Kenneally was stretchered off.

There were five teams in the Championship and we all played each other twice, with the top two progressing to the final. We recovered from the early setback to reach the final when Cork were our opponents again. We were six points down after about fifteen minutes and our corner-back John O'Connor was sent off, even though he didn't have a streak in him like a lot of the defenders out there. Once again Daithí and Kenneally were taking lumps out of each other but Dick swapped with Daithí, who went in corner-forward and immediately scored two goals. All the while, Dicko pulled a couple of strokes under dropping balls before turning to Daithí: "Go back out there and hurl away." We won after extra time and moved on to Pittsburgh for the North American Championship, which we also won.

It was a phenomenal experience over there, on and off the field. The freedom of living in your own place and going for a few jars. I loved the lifestyle over there. One night I was in the pub, unusually before Daithí, when he arrived in telling me that my mother had called with my Leaving Cert results. I got a few honours and did well overall, much better than the previous year, and I suppose it was some justification for my parents sending me to Garbally. Daithí was nearly more excited about the results than I was. All my family knew him quite well and he even went out with my sister, Maura, for a period. He was always in and out of our house. He's a great character and he brought quite a lot to the party as I would have been rather shy then, but Daithí was outgoing and witty and passionate about certain things and would sing his few songs as well. The possibility of staying on in Boston was mooted and Eamon offered me the opportunity to serve out my time with him. It was mildly tempting as the economy was hardly booming back home at the time but an offer of an accountancy course in Waterford RTC cropped up. I had no great ambition of becoming an accountant but it was a start, somewhere to go. More importantly, going back and establishing myself with Offaly and winning as much as I could over the next ten years was the primary objective.

While we were in Boston another Offaly minor team had come along and retained the title we won the year before. That '87 minor team included three very special talents, Adrian Cahill, Johnny Dooley and Brian Whelahan, all of who were still Under-16 and who had won another minor title two years earlier. Unfortunately, Adrian never fulfilled his vast potential due to injury. Johnny Pilkington was also on that team but was a year older than the lads. Everyone around Birr and Banagher knew that Brian Whelahan had been marked out as a great hurler from an early age. Given his family connections Brian had always knocked around Banagher as a young lad with a hurley in his hand. There was a movement in Offaly hurling again and I wanted to be part of it.

Chapter 6

I only spent a year in college in Waterford and it was mayhem. Let's go through the number of teams I was involved with that year. In Waterford alone I was playing for the freshers in rugby, hurling and football, as well as the senior hurling and football teams. In Rynagh's I was involved with the Under-21 and senior teams in hurling and football. I was playing with the Ballinasloe Under-20 rugby team, as well as their seniors and the Connacht Under-20s, with and against players like Noel Mannion and Eric Elwood. Then there was the small matter of playing Under-21 and senior hurling for Offaly. In case you've lost count, that's fourteen teams. One of the few teams I wasn't involved with, the Offaly Under-21 footballers, had a brilliant campaign and won the All-Ireland in 1988. I was invited onto the panel midway through their run but declined as I felt it wouldn't be fair on the lads who had brought them that far. I still regret that I wasn't involved though. If I had been, I would be the only Offaly man to hold All-Ireland medals at minor, Under-21 and senior level.

Anyway, I had more than enough to keep me occupied. I definitely played too much at adult level too soon. If I was advising young lads now, I'd tell them that they're time enough waiting until they're at least nineteen before getting into all that. At sixteen or seventeen I was playing intermediate football and hurling with Rynagh's, as well as senior rugby with Ballinasloe. I now have back trouble, which comes at me now and again, and various different strains that I believe are as a result of taking heavy knocks at a young age. I was able to absorb them at the time but it catches up on you. By the time I was in my mid-twenties I was having scans on my back. I had an ankle problem before that, which limited my involvement with Offaly from 1992-94. The schedule

I had in my late teens and early twenties knocked a couple of years off my elite career. Given how naturally athletic and strong I was, I should have been able to play on for another couple of years but, at that stage, I was on and off the treatment table with various ailments, mostly hamstring problems. Burn-out has been a hot topic in the GAA for the past few years but, when you're young, you don't see it coming. In hindsight, I needed someone to tap me on the shoulder and tell me that I couldn't do all these twice-a-day training sessions and three matches at weekends, often going from one field to another without getting out of my gear. It was unsustainable and had to have affected my performances on some level.

Getting to and from Waterford and Banagher that year was a nightmare at times. I'd get a train from Waterford to Portarlington and then Portarlington to Tullamore where my father would pick me up. Fortunately, Cathal Ryan, from Banagher, who was in Garbally with me, started work with Ulster Bank down in Waterford and often gave me a spin. Some Monday mornings my father would drop me back to Waterford at five o'clock and get back in time for work at eight. Aidan Fogarty was living in Kilkenny and put me up the odd night after coming from Offaly training. I went to a few lectures here and there but most of my time was spent socialising, training and playing matches.

I played in the Fitzgibbon Cup weekend up in Belfast but Queen's University, who had the likes of Séamus and Henry Downey and Ciarán Barr, beat us. At one stage our wing-back, Paul Phelan, from Glenmore, was soloing up the sideline and someone stepped out and planted him with a box. A row broke out and I was caught unawares by Barr, who thumped me in the mouth. I ended up over the sideline and had to fight my way back on to the safe haven of the pitch.

Colm Bonnar was training us and we took it very seriously. I'd have to say that much of the training done for third-level competitions is completely over the top and unnecessary, even back then. Playing at that level was a good experience, though, and we actually won the Shield competition that weekend. I played well and was chosen on the Team of the Fitzgibbon. I also played at centre-back on the Freshers' football team in one game against UCC and scored a couple of points while holding Maurice Fitzgerald scoreless.

With Offaly I got a good run of games in the National League as we reached the final. I played mostly at midfield, alongside Sean Donoghue from Kinnitty, but we were dropped for the final against Tipperary as Joe Dooley and Joachim started, having only rejoined the panel late enough that year. I was very sour over that, having played particularly well in the quarter-final and semi-final against Galway and Wexford respectively. I was trying to establish myself and we had a couple of great wins to get to the final. Tipp beat us reasonably comfortably, and the way that game turned out summed up where we were at that stage in our development. The older lads were just gone off the boil that little bit while the younger players hadn't quite come of age yet. We were good enough to beat most teams but weren't ready to move on to the next level just yet. Eugene Coughlan and Pat Delaney moved up to the forwards that year in a bid to bridge the gap but it was still a great learning curve playing alongside those players. We won the Leinster title, beating Dublin and then Wexford in the final. By then I had reclaimed my place at midfield and the advice from the stalwarts when playing Wexford was simply to move the ball quickly and you'll beat them. If you put it in the air they'd destroy you. Move the ball fast and low, hook them and block them and, when you put them under pressure, they'll drive the ball wide. That's pretty much how it worked out between us and them up to 1996.

We played Galway in the All-Ireland semi-final and I was very nervous on the morning of the game. I used to go to the first Mass with my father the morning of matches and my mother would have breakfast ready for me when I got home. I was only shifting it around the plate when my father said, "Eat up that, there's no point being out in Croke Park making a fool of yourself and being hungry as well!" Being from Galway, there was always a bit of craic with my father when we played them. Although he wouldn't have been an avid follower by any stretch, he'd let on to be shouting for Galway. Even now he'd say, "When I die I don't mind where you bury me, but bring me over the Shannon. Just dig a small square and drop me into it rather than wasting the ground." Later that day in Croke Park, Joachim and I were at midfield against the Galway pairing of Pat Malone and Brendan Lynskey. I was due to pick up Malone but, when it came to matching up at the throw-in, Joachim was nowhere to be seen so I ended up with Lynskey. Before the referee threw in the ball Lynskey looked me in the eye.

"A mhaicín, what are you doing here? The minor match is over."

I resolved that I was going to pull wildly for the throw-in, which I did, but Lynskey just dropped his left hand and took the ball, elbowed me into the nose, walked over me and took off down the field. He could hardly be described as one of the game's great stylists and the solo run wasn't the most elegant and he pucked the ball wide. However, he had completely knocked the wind out of my sails. I felt I settled in quite well after that and scored a great point but I was moved into corner-forward and then taken off at half-time. I felt I was scapegoated somewhat by the management as a number of the more experienced players were getting roasted. We lost by seven points but it was quite an experience coming up against that Galway outfit, who could be a rather fearsome bunch. They just had too much power and pace for us with their running game. It wasn't a bad start to my inter-county senior career though, winning a Leinster medal and nailing down a starting spot.

· · · · ·

I didn't go back to college in Waterford as a job came up in AIB. My mother saw it advertised, filled out the application for me and, the next thing I knew, I was going for an interview in Ryan's Hotel in Galway in a horrendous grey suit, which, once I started the job, had to do me for a good while. There were a couple of hundred vacancies for which thousands had applied. At twenty years of age, picking up a permanent, pensionable job at a time of rampant emigration in the '80s wasn't to be scoffed at. I did a week's training in Dublin and was then dispatched to Celbridge where I started as a junior bank official in September, 1988. The general rule of thumb was that, after five years, you progressed to be a senior bank official and then an officer rank after a further five years. I liked it from the start, though you have your ups and downs as you learn the ropes. I interacted well with the customers and that was my strong point.

Having missed out on playing for the Under-21s that year, I was called into the Offaly senior football panel by the manager, Michael McBrearty. I looked on it as another challenge and said I'd give it a go. The hurling training didn't get serious until well into the New Year so there was no major problem in terms of the crossover initially. In fact, it was handier to get to football training from Celbridge as it would be held somewhere in north Offaly and I'd get a lift down most of the time.

Although I trained very little with St Rynagh's footballers, I always had a grá for the game and it came more naturally to me than hurling. There were real football stalwarts in the club like Sod's father, James Daly, Donal Kilcummins and James Whelan, and we won the senior 'B' title in Offaly in 1988, two years after coming up from intermediate. Offaly had slipped rather alarmingly since winning the 1982 All-Ireland but there was still the nucleus of a good team, with players like Vinny Claffey, Peter Brady, Richie Connor, Padraig Dunne and Brendan Lowry with Tom Coffey and Jimmy Stewart coming through from the successful Under-21 team. They ought to have been much more competitive at senior level around that time but then Dublin and Meath were very strong and confidence was low.

I made my Championship debut for the footballers at wing-back against Westmeath in 1989 in a very poor game at O'Connor Park, which we won by a couple of points. That sent us through to the Leinster semi-final against Meath, who were the reigning All-Ireland champions. I was detailed to play corner-back on Colm O'Rourke and I had a stormer. He barely touched the ball for the first hour and we were well in the game. Then Colm Coyle kicked for a point on the Hogan Stand side of the field in Croke Park and I stood rooted to the twenty-metre line when I saw O'Rourke rocket past me. "Oh, shit," I thought. As I turned around the ball hit the post and dropped into his arms. Goal. He got another one a couple of minutes later following an overlap and we ended up being well-beaten. It was a great lesson, though, and, for the rest of my career, I always followed the ball just in case it deflected off the post.

I spoke to O'Rourke about that game years later and he told me it was one of the few times in his Meath career when he was taken completely out of the game and feared he was going to be substituted. But he showed his class by coming up trumps in the end. It was nice to have pitted myself against that great Meath team, and their full-forward line of O'Rourke, Brian Stafford and Bernard Flynn were a handful. Bernard and I didn't know each other at all back then but he's one of my very best friends now.

Georgie Leahy stepped down as hurling manager after the 1988 campaign and was replaced by Pat Joe, who was also in charge of the Under-21s. He was the de facto manager of the minor team as well and won the Leinster title in all three grades. I was delighted when he took over but, in hindsight, maybe he would have been better off getting it a few years later. We played Laois in the Leinster semi-final and beat them easily. I was marking John Taylor, one of the very best players I ever came up against. Two years earlier, when Rynagh's played Portlaoise in the Leinster Club Championship, he hit me a dunt into the stomach and I was shook for twenty minutes afterwards, but, in '89, I was ready. I scored two goals, my first in the Championship. For one of them, after I had struck the ball Laois defender John Bohane followed through and knocked me over but it wasn't caught on camera. I didn't wear a helmet too often but I did that day and it flew off my head as I hit the ground. Marty Morrissey was a fledgling commentator at the time and, when the highlights were broadcast on The Sunday Game that night, he said, "Michael Duignan takes off his helmet so everyone in the crowd knows who he is!" as the camera panned back on me.

The Leinster final against Kilkenny was an amazing game, which we won by 3-15 to 4-9. Mark Corrigan went on the rampage for us and scored 3-7. Two of his second-half goals came after I had been moved in to full-forward and made a couple of big catches and laid it off to him. His third goal put us well out of sight and I remarked to John Henderson, "We have ye now!" It wasn't something I normally did on the field but he glared back at me. "It's not over yet." Next thing I knew they scored a couple of goals and cut the deficit back to two points before Corrigan nailed another point to see us home.

It was my first Championship game against Kilkenny and, although it wasn't one of their vintage teams, it was always great to beat them. I had another Leinster medal, had made quite a contribution to our victory and was now fairly well established on the team. Having won an All-Ireland minor title, played in a National League final and now won a couple of Leinsters, the natural progression at that point was to contest an All-Ireland senior final. All we had to do was beat Antrim in the semi-final.

Our heads were all wrong going into that game. Séamus Coughlan, a brother of Ger's who was on the panel the year before, was in New York for the summer and tragically died in a drowning accident. He was a good hurler and a lovely fella who was liked by everyone. The funeral was just a few days before the game. It was definitely a factor and I think it affected the older lads on the team, and the Kinnitty contingent particularly. Ger played the game and had a difficult afternoon on Brian Donnelly. But then the mind-set was very much, "Ah, sure, it's only Antrim", with one eye on the final. We definitely took them for granted despite the fact that they had beaten us twice in the National League that year. The second game was a relegation play-off and, while we weren't too bothered to lose, the Antrim players later said that they took great belief from those games.

They had some excellent hurlers, like Sambo McNaughton, the Donnellys, Ciarán Barr, Dominic McKinley and Olcan McFetridge, and had spooked Cork, Tipperary and Kilkenny in the previous few years so there was no excuse for taking them lightly. Yet we went out with the wrong attitude and although we were four points up at half-time, when they hit us with a couple of goals after the break we weren't able to respond because we just weren't ready for it. We were terrible, myself included, running over balls and missing them and dropping them, all indicative of a team that wasn't tuned in. In fairness, they got some great scores. Olcan McFetridge buried one as he was falling over and, as soon as they got ahead, I knew we weren't going to come back. It was all over. Other games ebb and flow and, if you're prepared for that before you take the field, once a team gets a run on you, you should be able to respond but that day we couldn't. If your attitude is wrong beforehand you can't just suddenly change tack and say, "Right, we'll up it now for ten minutes". It just doesn't work like that. Instead there was an awful sense of panic as they grew in stature and pulled away from us.

As we trooped off the pitch afterwards in a daze, someone suggested that we form a guard of honour for the Antrim players. I was used to it from rugby but this was unheard of in GAA. The gesture was very well received by the Antrim players, but why we did it, I don't know. I couldn't imagine any other team doing it. I remember Ciarán Barr once saying that, although we were the team of the '80s, they would have feared Kilkenny much more than us if they had been their opponents that day. That rankles with me a bit. Why couldn't they just apply themselves the same way against the traditional powers? They went out in the final against Tipperary and didn't raise a whimper.

I often wonder how a final between ourselves and Tipperary would have turned out. They would have been favourites and the pressure was on them to win their first All-Ireland in eighteen years. I think whatever was left in the old stagers from the '81 and '85 teams would have come out and, supplemented by the young players, I'd like to think we would have produced a serious performance. Whether that would have been good enough at that stage in our development we'll never know, but even competing in a final at that point might have hastened our ascent to the top rather than waiting until 1994. Our problem was that we were thinking of the final and forgetting that we still had to beat a good Antrim team. As it was, I didn't have to wait too long to tackle Tipperary in an All-Ireland final.

• • • • •

With our minor team of '86 supplemented by the best of the minors in the intervening three years, the Under-21 All-Ireland was there to be won in 1989, and Pat Joe made me captain. We played Laois early on in the Leinster campaign and they had a serious team. In fact, they were the best outfit we came up against all year. The day of the game I got a phone call in work explaining how my sister Róisín, who was eight at the time, had been taken to hospital after my parents couldn't wake her that morning. However, the last call I got before I left work that evening informed me that Róisín had pulled through and was fine. Alf Regan picked me up in Celbridge and brought me down for the game, which we won after a ding-dong battle. It was one of the best games I ever played in an Offaly jersey. I scored one of my favourite goals direct from a free from about 25 yards. I was fouled for the free and quickly got to my feet and belted the ball into the top corner.

I went home to Banagher afterwards only to find that, in fact, Róisín wasn't out of danger and my parents had only told me otherwise so that it wouldn't bother me when going to play. She had status epilepticus, which can cause you to drop into a coma and, in twenty percent of cases, die. Thankfully, she snapped out of it and was placed on medication to prevent it happening again. She was always very academic, however, and the medication caused tiredness that would curtail her ability to study so she eventually stopped taking it of her own accord in her teens and has never looked back. She gave us quite a scare that time, though.

We beat Kilkenny in the Leinster final, and Antrim in the All-Ireland semi-final, to set up a final meeting with Tipperary. The game was played in Portlaoise a week after we had won the minor and they had won the senior All-Ireland. Interest in the game was huge and a crowd in excess of 30,000 turned up. They had a decent team, with players like Declan Ryan, John Leahy, Conal Bonnar, Conor Stakelum, Mick Ryan, Liam Sheedy and George Frend. We had four players from the minor team starting, which, generally speaking, may have been too many, but then we're talking about stickmen of the quality of John Troy, Brian Whelahan, Adrian Cahill and Johnny Dooley. We had such an exceptional team and played some brilliant hurling all year, including the final, but yet we didn't win it. We were far superior to Tipp on the day but kept handing the initiative back to them. Anything that could go wrong, did go wrong. I went into the game with a very bad groin injury and probably shouldn't have played. I didn't feel right the moment I hit the field but I was doing well at corner-forward on Frend early on. I won a couple of frees and any ball that came in I won. Ronnie Byrne was on Sheedy in the other corner and didn't start so well and Pat Joe decided to switch the two of us. It was a bad move because I was doing fine on Frend and it was easier to play on him given my injury, as he was light, whereas Sheedy was much stronger physically.

We went a few points up after a bad start but Troy, who was playing in goal, shipped a heavy knock from Declan Ryan and so, too, did Cahill at the hands of Leahy. I'm not saying there was anything wrong with the challenges but it took the wind out of our sails. Tipperary got four goals and three of them were the softest you'd ever see. Troy didn't have his best day between the posts after the Ryan collision. Damien Geoghegan was sent off for us. It seemed that with each setback we suffered we'd then hurl our way back into the game and completely dominate them only to shoot ourselves in the foot once again by conceding a bad goal at the other end. Even at the death, when we were two points down, Roy Mannion came up to hit a twenty-metre free with the last puck of the game and it flew off Mick Ryan's shoulder and past the post. Mick told me years later that he didn't see a bit of the ball from that shot.

It broke my heart to lose and it remains the single biggest disappointment of my career. Worse than the two senior finals I lost. It was partly because I was captain but also because we had such an outstanding team and were much superior to Tipperary that day. They weren't even the best team we had played that year. Declan Ryan was their captain and, as he collected the trophy, he showcased that brand of arrogance that Tipp have been famed, and disdained, for at times. In a sneer at the fact that we had lost to Antrim in the senior semi-final, he said, "I'd like to thank Antrim for the game ... oh, sorry, I mean Offaly". Having beaten Cork in the minor final it would have been nice to have accounted for them in this one, as the minors had done in 1987. Despite what Tipp people may like to think, there was no fear factor with playing them, or anybody else for that matter. We just dug our own grave that day. I believe that defeat had a big impact on us and played no small part in the fact that it took a few more years to really get it together at senior level. While our minor title in 1986 paved the way for two further successes in that grade, this defeat was the first of three final losses at Under-21 level in four years.

· · · · ·

I doubt if my parents look back on 1989 with any great fondness as, not only did Róisín have a health scare, but I also had a brush with death. After most of the serious hurling had finished up that year I was playing a friendly game for Ballinasloe Rugby Club against Young Munster in Limerick one weekend and felt that the soles of my feet were rather itchy and sore. It accelerated to the point where my hands were being affected and I didn't feel well at all. I didn't go to work that Monday and went to the doctor in Banagher. She put me on antibiotics for a few days and said that if there was no improvement to come back but, after another day or so, the rash was spreading to my mouth and lips. It was just a savage itch that was extremely painful and agitating. It was like I had blisters under my skin.

I was referred to Dr Humphrey O'Connor, in Tullamore General Hospital, and he immediately diagnosed it as Stevens-Johnson syndrome. He explained how there were different extremes to it and that sometimes it can come under control very quickly. There's no specific cause and neither is there a cure as such, but he told me to stay on the antibiotics while he ran some blood tests. He was trying to find something that might have sparked it but the only thing that showed up was a slight chest infection. My own theory is that the gruelling schedule I had subjected myself to through my various sporting pursuits in the previous few years had to have been a factor, though there was nothing medically to support that. Dr O'Connor told me to come straight back to the hospital if I deteriorated further.

The following Sunday Jim Troy and Jackie Ryland called to bring me to a Walsh Cup game that Offaly were playing but I wasn't fit to move. I went to bed for the rest of the day. Mam was working in Dooly's Hotel in Birr and Dad thought it best to leave me resting. That period while I was in bed was the most distressing experience of my life as my body just broke down completely and blisters came out everywhere. It was frightening that I could deteriorate so quickly. My mother checked on me the next morning and I was rushed to hospital. I was out of it, but I remember being placed on a trolley and being wheeled up to intensive care. I overheard the doctor talking to my father.

"We really need to get him to St James's but we can't move him. He's too weak. It'll be touch-and-go whether he pulls through this."

They pumped me full of steroids and I was critical for a couple of days, drifting in and out of consciousness. Gradually I started to recover and the considered view from the medics was that it was purely because I was so fit and strong. I was just about able to fight it off but I had shed four and a half stone in a very short period and looked desperate with the number of blisters that had invaded my body, particularly my feet, hands and mouth. Even after I snapped out of it I was still very low for about another week and wasn't quite with it. People told me later that they called to see me but I had no recollection. Some of them didn't even recognise me and a few of the lads thought it was hilarious. Mam couldn't bear to see me in that state. She was so upset that she just stayed away altogether but Dad came and sat by my bedside every night.

There was a man across from me in intensive care from Birr who was dying of cancer and I remember the roars of him one night. He was in agony, calling for his wife and family. It was horrendous. He died the next day. It was my first real experience of seeing somebody dying and it was terrible.

A couple more people died as well before I was shifted out of intensive care after about a week. Initially I was feeding on milkshakes because my mouth was too sore to eat but, once that subsided, I wolfed down the hospital food. I remember thinking, "I'm definitely ok if I think this stuff is tasty!"

I spent another few days in hospital and then began to recover pretty quickly. I was on a reducing dose of steroids for about eight weeks having started on a very large dose initially. Naturally I was told not to play sport again for a number of months but I wouldn't be one for taking that on board. While I was in hospital the Under-21 county final of 1988, which was delayed for the best part of a year, was played and, a couple of weeks after I was discharged, the 1989 Championship was winding to a close. We played Drumcullen in the semi-final and I went along to the game. We were struggling at half-time and Dad turned to me.

"Did you bring the gear?"

"Yeah, it's in the boot," I said.

"You may get it."

I was still grossly underweight but went on for the second half. We won the game, then beat Birr in the final having lost to them in the '88 final only a few weeks previously. It meant that I never lost an Under-21 match that I played in at club level and won four county medals.

The Friday before I fell ill I was told I was being transferred from Celbridge to Dublin but that obviously didn't happen until a lot later than planned. Nonetheless, I started in AIB Rathfarnham in January, 1990, when Edel O'Connell entered my life.

Chapter 7

New York, Chicago, Toronto, San Francisco, October, 1994

When I first moved to Dublin I settled in an apartment in Norbrook Avenue, Ranelagh, living with Mike Devine, the Offaly footballer I had been with in Garbally. I got the bus to Rathfarnham that first Monday morning and jumped off at the Yellow House near the Grange Road not knowing exactly where the village was. The first person I met was the parish priest, Fr O'Hanlon. A Longford man, he knew me from the hurling and sent me back up to the village where I would spend close on the next five years. I was nearly twenty-two and excited at the prospect of living in Dublin. There was a young crowd working in the Rathfarnham branch and there was a great social side to it. Dan Ryan was the manager and Gerry McGrath was his assistant. Dan ran a tight ship and I learned a lot from him.

Edel had been transferred to Rathfarnham a couple of months before. I wouldn't quite say it was love at first sight because both of us were in relationships at the time. In fact, Edel later told me that she found me cocky and arrogant when I started in Rathfarnham. She was probably right. You could see straightaway that she was very diligent in her work, and was assigned extra responsibilities very quickly. After my illness, I didn't play with Offaly footballers in 1990 and the hurling training hadn't really cranked up until a few months into my time in Rathfarnham so I slipped into the social scene within the branch quite quickly.

Edel was living in Rathmines, which is quite close to Ranelagh, so we'd often get the same bus home together. The relationship I was in was pretty serious at the time and I had even met Edel's boyfriend a couple of times so there was no question of anything developing, but I still felt there was something there between us. I could see straightaway that she was genuine.

No bullshit about her. While she was conscientious in her work, she was great craic away from it. That summer, however, the girl that I was with suggested that we go on a break, a concept I was at odds with. When she made contact with me again the following year I was already with Edel, who had also finished with her boyfriend by that stage. It was a slow burner in terms of us getting together even after we became single. After we'd have our few pints with the work crowd in Rathfarnham, we might have one or two more on our own in Rathmines on the way home, though it wouldn't have been an official date.

We finally got together when Gerry McGrath suggested we go to the AIB GAA dinner dance together. Gerry proved to be quite the Cupid as he also persuaded Ray Lynch and Mary O'Donnell to go together. They ended up getting married, too. This was towards the latter end of the year and I had been nominated for an All Star, won the AIB Sports Personality of the Year and the ACC/*Sunday Independent* Man of the Match for the Leinster final. There were various black-tie functions attached to each of those, which Edel attended with me. The All Stars was a brilliant night. I was nominated for full-forward, along with Kevin Hennessy, of Cork, and Dublin's Brian McMahon, who won the award.

It could be awkward at times in terms of going out with Edel and working with her, but, overall, I settled in well in the job. She was very structured in how she went about her work whereas I'd be chatting and having the craic, yet I had an ability to fly through my work in a short space of time, something that would drive her around the twist. I had a bit of a reputation for cashing almost anything for customers. If they had an account with us, or in another AIB branch, there'd usually be no problem. I rarely got caught for a bounced cheque.

One day a hard-core Dub lost the rag with me when I wouldn't cash a Bank of Ireland cheque for him. In a bid to calm him down I asked him if he had any identification to prove he was the person the cheque was made out to. He pondered for a moment and then pulled up his sleeve to show me how his Christian name was tattooed on his arm. Only a Dub would think of it.

The funniest episode from my time in Rathfarnham came when an individual entered the bank with an AIB deposit book from a branch down the country. It was a partnership account with a substantial amount of money and he wanted to check the balance. However, while a number of his family members were on the mandate, he wasn't, so I wasn't permitted to impart any information on the account to him. When I told him this he became absolutely hysterical. He claimed to be a substantial shareholder in the bank and read me the riot act, saying how the chief executive was a personal friend of his and insisting that he was entitled to the information. It was lunchtime on a summer's afternoon and we only had skeleton staff. There was a lengthy queue building up behind him taking in this spectacle. He insisted that I write a letter for him outlining how I wasn't giving him the information he wanted. I told him I wasn't in a position to do something like that so I went up to Dan, who wrote a letter. When I handed it to him he insisted that I sign it as well. I refused.

"If you don't sign that letter I will have you transferred to Achill Island," he screamed.

"Will you?" I said.

"I will," he snapped. "I'm personal friends with the chief executive. I will have you transferred to Achill Island."

"Well, if you're going to," I replied, "could you try and do it straightaway. I heard it's lovely down there at this time of year."

I remained stony-faced while everyone present, who, by then, included quite a large number of customers and staff, erupted in laughter. He snarled and whipped up his letter and walked out. Enquiries were made about the incident afterwards but I hadn't done anything wrong, regardless of this man's standing.

Apart from that it was plain sailing in Rathfarnham and, after a couple of years, Edel and I moved in together. While it was a natural progression it carried its own difficulties as we were then living and working together. In 1994 she was transferred to Terenure and, a few months later, I was sent to Tallaght. Although we weren't staying together professionally, we knew we would be in every other way.

• • • • •

Paudge Mulhare took charge of the Offaly hurlers after Pat Joe lasted just one year despite having won Leinster minor, Under-21 and senior titles in 1989.

Sensing that Offaly were entering a transitional period, Pat Joe wanted more than just a one-year term to allow him to rebuild with some comfort. The county board wouldn't budge on their year-by-year policy and they went their separate ways. Losing to Antrim, as well as the Under-21 reverse, would have weakened Pat Joe's position while, I think, some of the older players may not have been overly enamoured at the likelihood that he was going to focus on the younger players.

Paudge was a long-serving selector and was involved in the management teams for each of the four All-Irelands that Offaly won. That didn't happen by accident. He was a very shrewd hurling man, though the feeling was that he was only put in place as a stop-gap appointment. I think Paudge was more comfortable in the selector's role anyway. It was some craic training under him though. A clubmate of mine, some of the tales spun about Paudge are legendary. He might tell us to do forty press-ups and, before we'd have ten done, he'd roar, "Get up, ye fucking eejits, and do a few laps of the field!"

However unconventional he may have been by today's standards, he oversaw Offaly's biggest-ever victory over Kilkenny in Championship hurling in 1990. Brian Whelahan and DJ Carey made their first Championship starts that day marking each other and DJ was taken off before half-time. These two players had been heralded as they moved up through the ranks, so it gave us a lift when our lad was more than holding his own while DJ was substituted. We cruised to a 4-15 to 1-8 victory in what was a poorly attended game, largely due to the fact that Ireland played Egypt on the same day in the World Cup. Giving Kilkenny a beating like that was a massive fillip but, at the same time, we were trying to move on having failed to build on the Leinster titles we had won in the previous two years. We played Dublin in the Leinster final, a team we had no real gripe with so Paudge was trying to find an edge in the build-up with hilarious consequences.

"Are Dublin going to bate ye? Are they, are they, are they?" he asked us in a team meeting.

He had this habit of saying things three times. We just shrugged. Next thing he picked on Daithí.

"Are they going to bate ye, Daithí?"

"I don't know, Paudge," answered Daithí, somewhat taken aback.

"Well, you know everything fucking else!"

We all burst out laughing, but Paudge wasn't finished yet.

"If they bate ye, if they bate ye, if they bate ye, are ye going to give them a guard of honour? Are ye, are ye, are ye? Are ye, Daithí?"

"I don't know, Paudge," he said, totally perplexed.

"Well, if they bate ye, and if ye give them a guard of honour, I'll fucking puke on top of every one of ye!"

It was absolutely hilarious but helped to focus minds all the time. I was playing full-forward on Vinny Holden, who was an outstanding player, but who was getting on by then. I scored a few points and we had a number of clashes in which he broke a couple of hurleys off me. I was well on top and didn't give a damn.

"Vinny, I hope you have plenty more of them in there," I told to him after he received his third camán of the day.

That bravado would only carry us so far, however, and, once again, we came up short in an All-Ireland semi-final, well beaten by Galway. In terms of hurling ability we were as good as anyone but there were very few players who were in their prime years. Those who had won All-Irelands in the '80s were just past their best, whereas most of the rest of us were still learning the ropes. We were too young and yet we were too old. A lot of our young players had played exceptionally well against Kilkenny but maintaining consistency from game to game was the conundrum. I think if Pat Joe had stayed on for a couple of years he would have introduced more younger players at an earlier stage. After the stability of Diarmuid Healy, in three successive years we had three different managers and won three Leinster titles but lost the subsequent semi-final each time. With a bit more continuity maybe we might have kicked on.

Pádraig Horan took charge the following year and, operating in Division Two, we reached the National League final. I went back with the Offaly footballers that year and did a lot of hard training in the winter with them under Brendan Hackett, who more recently managed Westmeath. I liked Hackett and thought he was very much ahead of his time. I used to travel to training with him from Dublin so, when Offaly reached the League quarter-final in both codes on the same day, I felt a certain loyalty towards the footballers, having trained much more with them up to that point of the year.

I told Horan and he seemed to be ok about it.

As it turned out the footballers lost to Donegal after extra-time and the hurlers beat Waterford after extra-time. I was operating as a roving wing-forward for the footballers and missed two points from gilt-edged goal-scoring opportunities either of which, if converted, would have won us the game. I was back with the hurlers for the League semi-final and scored the match-clinching goal in a low-scoring 1-7 to 0-7 win over Tipperary. It didn't get much better in the final, in which we beat Wexford by 2-6 to 0-10. Still, it was a national title, the first time Offaly had won the League and we were optimistic that this young team was finally blossoming. Johnny and Billy Dooley were now on board. Hubert Rigney and Shane McGuckin, too. The likes of Roy Mannion and Brian Whelahan were maturing nicely. Horan was an iconic figure as manager and fiercely passionate. There was a great sense of excitement about where we were headed, but then the rug was abruptly pulled from under us.

We played Dublin in the Leinster semi-final and I hold my hand up and admit that I had a brutal game. As poor as I was, we were in control and, in the second half, I made a good catch to set Johnny Dooley up for a point. "Thank God, I might settle down now and play well," I thought. Next thing I was taken off. I can't really argue with the decision on one level, as I was playing quite badly but, at that stage, I felt I had earned enough kudos on the team to avoid the curly finger when I was out of sorts, especially when I had just made a contribution and looked like I might hurl my way into it.

Throughout the League I had finished most of the games around the middle of the field where I felt I could have made a difference in the closing stages against Dublin. I felt Horan was trying to teach me a lesson with the later rounds in mind as, at that stage, we didn't look like losing the game. Whatever about my substitution, the decision to bring Roy Mannion on for Aidan Fogarty at centre-back was disastrous. Mannion was imperious in the League final, winning the man-of-the-match award, but he couldn't start against Dublin because he had a dose of the 'flu. When he came on MJ Ryan scored a few points from centre-forward and generally went to town on him. Before we knew it the game was over and Dublin had beaten us by two points. It was the first time since 1979 that Offaly hadn't reached the Leinster hurling final.

I still had the football, but the Dublin-Meath saga that year held up the whole Championship. Training had been going very well and we genuinely felt that we could do something. We beat Wexford to qualify for the Leinster semi-final where Meath eventually came through after four games with Dublin and two with Wicklow. But, with every week that we were lying idle, the intensity of training dropped a notch and by the time we played Meath we were terribly flat. They beat us at their ease and it was my last game for the Offaly footballers.

The defeat to Dublin was the catalyst for a number of frustrating years not just for the team but myself, too. Prior to the 1992 Championship, I snapped the deltoid ligament in my ankle, an injury that would bother me intermittently for the next two years. I don't recall injuring it, just that it began to bother me. I went to see Dr Pat O'Neill, in Dublin, who was a bit miffed because the deltoid ligament is pretty much encased by the bone in your ankle so it's highly unusual to damage it without actually breaking your ankle. It tended to bleed into my foot, which was a rather ugly sight, and there was no hard and fast solution to it other than salt water and rest. Sometimes it would be fine but it came and went and I couldn't shake it off. It wasn't right for the Leinster semi-final against Kilkenny in 1992. I was a sub and was brought on but had to come off again at a time when only three substitutions were permitted. We looked to be in control of the game midway through the second half but ended up losing by six points and, with no second chance, another summer was gone.

It was a similar scenario in 1993. We were drawn to play Kilkenny in the first round but, again, I was only fit to come on as a sub. We were well on top for most of the game and were two points up at the death despite Mannion's sending off, when referee Pat Delaney made a scandalous decision to award Kilkenny a penalty. It wasn't that Shane McGuckin didn't foul John Power – he did – but Power was on his ninth step without soloing the ball when he was taken down just as he entered the penalty area. DJ Carey converted the penalty and they added another point immediately to beat us by two. They went on to retain the All-Ireland that year. Talk of a golden generation in Offaly went quiet.

By then Eamonn Cregan had replaced Horan as manager and we trained very well that year. He brought a physical trainer, Derry O'Donovan, with him and it was the first time we had done any really hard stamina training. The two lads couldn't believe how unfit we were. Derry made it enjoyable s though, and, while it was intense, he wouldn't have us on the field for any more than an hour. He was a brilliant foil to Cregan. If Eamonn was narky over something or other, the first chance Derry would get when he'd take us away for a run he'd say something like, "Don't mind Ned," as he used to call him, "he's a thick fucker!" We'd all be in stitches at him slagging Cregan off.

It took a while for Eamonn to get to know us and, over time, he learned to go with the flow more, though his patience was tested numerous times over the years when pitiful numbers turned out at training. A few times he headed back to Limerick insisting he wouldn't return. He always did, though. He had great faith in us as a group. I wasn't sure whether that faith extended to me initially, however. As well as the ankle, I was having a spot of hamstring trouble around that time too, and I began to doubt how much support I had amongst the management. I suppose I might have got a little bit paranoid but these things play on your mind when you find yourself on the periphery and, when it came to the first round of the Championship, with Kilkenny the opposition once again, I was on the bench.

· · · · ·

In his second year in charge, Cregan was getting to know the players better and some key changes in pivotal positions made a big difference. Unfortunately, Mannion became a casualty along the way. Him and Cregan had a difficult relationship and it came to a head one night when Mannion was marking me in training. I was trying to prove myself and here was Mannion cleaning me out so I asked him to let me win the next ball, which he did, and then Cregan came over offering a lecture to him about how he should contest a high ball, something Roy was an expert at. Sharp words were exchanged and that was pretty much the end of his Offaly career.

For the Kilkenny game Kevin Kinahan and Kevin Martin made their debut in defence, while Hubert Rigney was installed at centre-back. John Troy, with his goalkeeping days now long behind him, was given the platform to showcase his vast array of skills at centre-forward. The team had a much

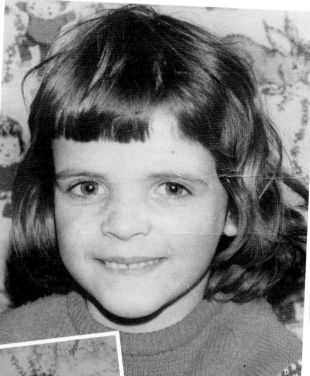

Edel, four years old, at home in Portlaoise.

My First Communion Day, with Roy Mannion for company.

Edel's First Communion Day, with her brother, Diarmuid.

The Garbally College senior team in 1986, with me fourth from left at the back.

The St Rynagh's minor team which also won the County title in 1986. A proud day for myself and my brother, Peadar. Our captain, Shane McGuckin, is out front!

The morning after the 1994 All-Ireland victory, outside Doheny and Nesbitt's in Dublin.

Myself and Edel enjoying ourselves the week after the 1998 All-Ireland victory, with friends Martin and Evelyn McKeogh, and David Malone.

The same week of celebration in 1998 and, left, I celebrate in Simon Lyons' in Banagher with my great friend Ciarán 'Sod' Daly.

Eugene Coughlan needs a lift home during our team holiday in the Canaries in 1991.

The Offaly team enjoying the good life (and lots of sun) on the beach in Florida in 1995.

John Troy is adjudged 'the winner' after some wine tasting on the Offaly team tour to South Africa in 1999.

Edel on our wedding day.

A happy couple on our wedding day.

The Offaly team holiday to South Africa in 1999 was so memorable for us.

Here we are having a magnificent dinner during the holiday with our friends, Deirdre and Ian Brophy.

Edel's 39th birthday party in the Bridge House in Tullamore, with Edel and Ollie Ryan.

Nine-month-old Seán in the Liam MacCarthy Cup.

At a party for Edel and myself, when we left Naas (for Durrow), we were presented with a drawing of our former 'local', Kavanagh's public house. Here we're with Ger and Norman Farragher.

Seán's First Communion Day in 2006.

Edel was so happy when we moved to 'the country' around Durrow in 2003.

Seán and myself grab a few winks.

Our family holiday in Marbella in 2006.

One of my best friends, Noel Farrelly, a garda based in Naas, was a huge loss to his family and, indeed, to all of us when he died suddenly at 47 years of age.

My sister Maura and David Doyle's Wedding Day in 1996 was a fantastic occasion for us – Peadar Jnr., Peadar Snr., David and Maura, my mother Jo, Sinéad, Brenda, Roísín and myself.

Edel's family celebrated their parents' 40th wedding anniversary in 2000. Back row - Niall, Ronan, Edel, Jerry and Diarmuid. Front - Anne, Jacinta, Chris and Linda.

Edel and her sisters on holiday in Italy.

Edel at her 40th birthday party with Evelyn McKeogh.

Edel on one of her many memorable trips to Medjugorje, with Betty Dooley, Joe Dooley, Marie Dooley and Niamh Dooley.

Edel was determined to run the Dublin women's mini-marathon which she did so bravely shortly before she died. Here she is with Ciara Leonard, Dolores Ravenhill, Marie Dooley and Breeda Fogarty. And also with our close friend, Tom Mangan.

On the night of the marathon Edel had every reason to celebrate with Dolores, Michelle Crilly, Ciara and Breeda.

Brian's First Communion Day, a day which Edel had vowed she would not miss, despite being informed three years earlier that her cancer had returned.

better shape and balance to it. There was a lot of pressure on us, though. To lose to Kilkenny for the third year in a row would have been disastrous and there might not have been a way back from there for that generation of players. Had we lost, things might well have panned out something like what we've seen in Laois football with their string of successful underage teams failing to kick on.

As it turned out we recovered from a bad start to play some fabulous hurling and beat them much more comfortably than the final four-point margin suggests. Joe Dooley's second goal could almost be described as total hurling, given the link-up play that led to it. I had to be satisfied with being introduced as a sub but, unlike the previous two summers, we were moving on in the Championship and I had a chance to stake a claim, which I did successfully by regaining my starting place for the Leinster final against Wexford. However, disaster struck about ten minutes into the game when the deltoid ligament snapped again. The pain was unmerciful but there was no way I was coming off. I played through the full seventy minutes with adrenalin driving me and we won by seven points. We scored another picture-book goal that day when Troy played a superb backward flick into Billy Dooley's path as he chased the ball in mid-air. Dooley's finish from a reasonably tight angle was lethal. The goal was listed at number eight on TG4's greatest ever hurling goals compilation. There's probably no other team that could score a goal like that and it showed the confidence we were now playing with.

The injury meant that I couldn't train ahead of the All-Ireland semi-final against Galway, so I was left on the bench again, which I couldn't have any complaints about. We were a very different proposition to the side that lost three successive semi-finals a few years before. The balance in terms of the age profile was just right and we weren't going to be overpowered as we had been before by Galway who, admittedly, were an inferior force to the one we had met four years earlier. I came on for the last twenty minutes, scored a point and did well as we secured a six-point victory to qualify for the final against Limerick. I aggravated the ankle, though, and missed a bit of training but felt I still had plenty of time to win back my place.

I think the expectation among the other players was that I would be starting the final, something I had been building towards my whole life. The trouble was that, although I scored a point against Galway, I also missed two opportunities that were probably easier than the one I had taken. If I had come on and scored three points my place would have been guaranteed. Instead, the night the team was being named Cregan called me over for a chat. He explained how, seeing as I had missed a quite an amount of training over the summer and had made an impact off the bench when I came on in the semi-final, he would be retaining me in that role for the final. I was devastated. "Impact sub" was not what I wanted to hear after all those years of striving to get to an All-Ireland final. Players can spout what they want about it being a team game and all that, but you think of yourself first and foremost, and it's amazing how some things go through your head, like the fact that you won't be in the team picture for the 1994 All-Ireland that is likely to adorn walls around the county for years to come.

I had a bit of a sulk in the car with Martin Hanamy after training and told him I was quitting. I calmed down after a few minutes and rejoined the lads. By the time the game came around I had accepted what my role would be and was prepared to throw my weight behind the team in whatever way I could. I certainly needed to be because, when I was introduced with about twenty minutes left, we were sinking fast.

Although we got an early goal after Joe Dooley scored on the rebound from Johnny's penalty, Limerick dominated much of the game and led by six points at half-time. We were out of sorts but scored the first four points of the second half, only for Limerick to pull clear again to lead by six with time running out. I scored what I felt was a fairly important point, to bring it back to five. We hadn't scored for a while at that stage. A few minutes later Billy Dooley won a free on the twenty-metre line, just to the right of the goal. Johnny Dooley was instructed to take his point but he shot for goal and it arrowed through a bunch of Limerick players and nestled in the corner. Suddenly we were energised. The gap was only two points. There were still five minutes left.

Joe Quaid, the Limerick goalkeeper, has taken plenty of flak since for taking the puck-out rather quickly but he landed it right in Ger Hegarty's hand. However, I was right up behind him and dispossessed him, flicking the ball to Johnny Pilkington who launched it goalwards again. It bounced nicely for another of our subs, Pat O'Connor, who rifled it past Quaid. Suddenly we were a point up. Would I have been as quick off the mark if Johnny Dooley had simply opted to tap over the free for a point? Hardly. Johnny Dooley and John Troy popped over a couple of points and then the ball worked its way out to Billy Dooley on the Cusack Stand sideline three times in quick succession for another three points. Incredibly, we scored 2-5 in four minutes and fourteen seconds to turn a five-point deficit into a six-point lead and, before we knew it, the game was over. We were All-Ireland champions.

"What's just after happening?" I thought as the crowd swept in around us and Martin Hanamy walked up the steps of the Hogan Stand to accept the Liam MacCarthy Cup. It was the most amazing finish to an All-Ireland final in history and I doubt if we'll ever see anything quite like it again. Having been poor for much of the game, we unleashed our full box of tricks on Limerick in the last five minutes.

It was difficult for Eamonn Cregan, probably Limerick's greatest hurler since Mick Mackey, having trained a team to defeat his own county. He gave an interview on television shortly after the game in which he was in a highly emotional state. It wasn't well received by some in Offaly but I felt sorry for him more than anything.

With the way the game ended his emotions must have been all over the place. On the one hand he had managed a team to win an All-Ireland, which is quite an achievement and must have given him huge personal satisfaction, but he had done it at the expense of his own county and could see the trauma that this had visited upon his own people and several players he had worked with previously.

Whatever about all that, there was no doubting his application in terms of preparing us for the final. He was a top-class manager and was ultra-professional. He certainly used his intimate knowledge of the Limerick players to our advantage, although the way the final materialised meant it never really came to bear. He was a really slick hurler himself and I think he saw our team, with the stylists we had, as a vehicle he could drive to play the game the way he believed it should be. He was preaching to the converted in that regard.

That aside, the elation was palpable back in the dressing room and then on to the function that night where Pat O'Connor and I were interviewed on the Sunday Game as we had both come on and made contributions. The disappointment of not being involved from the start wasn't to the forefront of my thoughts at that stage as we were carried along on a wave of excitement but, after a few days, it started to hit me. While I was delighted with what we had achieved, a sense of detachment kicked in, as I hadn't started the game. It almost felt as if, at twenty-six, my Offaly career was back where it started. Having been a key player on the Leinster three-in-a-row winning teams a few years earlier, I now had to establish myself all over again.

Before the year was out there was a tour of America and Canada lined up with the AIB hurling team. I was captain and took playing for the bank fairly seriously over the years. I was usually centre-back on both the hurling and football teams and turned out for the rugby team as well. I sometimes turned out for the bank team on the Friday before big games, such as county finals with Rynagh's. "I'm working for these people, they expect me to play," I'd tell the management. You'd never get away with that now.

I developed a firm friendship with Nicky English through playing alongside him on bank teams. He applied himself vigorously, too, and often picked up injuries that ruled him out of big Tipperary matches. We played in the inter-firms' and inter-bank competitions, winning the Leinster inter-firms' title once. The tour took in games in New York, Chicago, Toronto and San Francisco and I trained virtually every day, coming back in terrific shape. My ankle came good and, fuelled by the feeling of partial disconnection from our All-Ireland win, I vowed that I would never be a sub for Offaly again. As things turned out, I made good on that promise.

• • • • •

Before the idea of playing for Offaly ever came into my mind, making the St Rynagh's senior hurling team was my single biggest goal. Throughout my childhood the club was the standard-bearer in Offaly hurling and I wanted to be part of it. The group of players I grew up with enjoyed plenty of success at underage level and, initially, maintained those winning ways when we broke into the senior side. I was the first of our 1986 minor team to make it, earning my place on the side that reached that year's county final. We lost to Coolderry in a game laced with emotion for them, given the death of Pat Carroll only a few months earlier. It meant so much to them.

The occasion got to me that day. It was a huge thing to make the team, playing alongside Damien Martin and Pádraig Horan, and it's something that played on my mind rather than just going out and playing the game on its own merits. Very early in the game I took a sly dig into the ribs from one of their players. I dropped to the ground in a heap and he got booked. The net result of it, though, was that I was on the back foot. If that were later in my career I would have given it back to him. We both would have got booked but at least he would have known I was there. On reflection, I concluded that I had done the childish, rather than the manly, thing. That lesson would stand to me.

The following year we were back in the final against Seir Kieran of Clareen. They had never won the county title and were appearing in only their second final. This time I played the game and not the occasion. We beat them and I fulfilled the first ambition I ever set for myself in life. A year later that final pairing was repeated, but Clareen pulled off the victory this time, with a teenage Johnny Dooley scoring four points in a tight game. Of course it was very disappointing, but I did feel a certain satisfaction for them being such a small club winning their first title. Little did I know that they would go on to become the bane of our lives.

That win gave them the belief to achieve greater things in the '90s, particularly against us. We won further county titles in 1990, '92 and '93 and, by then, the club's ambitions were stretching beyond Offaly. Rynagh's contested the first ever All-Ireland club final in 1971, which they lost to Roscrea. Glen Rovers beat them in the 1973 final while Loughiel Shamrocks edged them out in a replay in 1983. No Offaly club had ever won the All-Ireland club title up to then. We lost to Portlaoise in 1987 in Leinster and, three years later, Glenmore beat us narrowly and went on to win the All-Ireland title. In 1992, we reached the Leinster final against Buffers Alley but their veteran goalkeeper, Henry Martin, had an inspired day between the posts and blocked shots with just about every part of his anatomy. While we probably weren't ready to win in 1987 and 1990, this was most certainly a chance missed, though we bounced back to finally take the provincial title the following year.

We had a tough encounter with Camross, in Birr, during that campaign, a game in which I pulled my hamstring, an injury that would haunt me later in my career. It was as if someone got a knife and stabbed me in the back of the leg. With various injuries I had over the years I always insisted on playing on, but this was different. I just couldn't run any distance whatsoever and had to come off. I played in the Leinster final against Dicksboro and, this time, we weren't to be denied. We beat them by a couple of points and I scored the game's only goal.

We took on the reigning All-Ireland champions, Sarsfields of Galway, in the All-Ireland semi-final the following February in Thurles. It was a damp and miserable day and, as anyone who has had hamstring trouble will vouch for, such conditions are a nightmare. I wasn't comfortable on my feet at all that day and didn't play well. While we had some brilliant defenders over the years, like Martin Hanamy, Roy Mannion, Aidan Fogarty and Hubert Rigney, we weren't blessed with natural scoring forwards. I did my fair share in terms of scoring and tended to create scores for others and win a few frees. That level of contribution wasn't available to the team from me that day. Hubie was stationed at midfield on the great Joe Cooney, however, and gave one of the finest individual displays that I have ever seen. He was just incredible. We were on top nearing the end of the game when our goalkeeper, David Hughes, fumbled a long ball over the line and we hadn't time to recover.

Sarsfields went on to beat Toomevara in the final and I often wonder if we had got there would that final ever have been finished. They had a few timber merchants, and there were no shortage of hotheads on our side either. I remember watching the final and being fiercely impressed by Sarsfields' discipline. They took every belt they got and retained their title. They also knocked the heart and soul out of us by beating us in that semi-final and we never recovered from it. We genuinely felt we had a team to win the All-Ireland, but it was a long way back to that stage. That defeat was one of several big games we lost from winning positions in the following years. Birr came out of Offaly later that year and became the first club from the county to win the All-Ireland.

We regrouped to reach the county final in both 1995 and 1996, but Clareen beat us both times. In '95 we beat Coolderry in the semi-final the day after Edel and I got married. The final was set for the following Sunday but we were flying out on our honeymoon for a fortnight the day after the Coolderry game. We tried to get the final put back a week but the county board wouldn't agree to it despite Clareen having no problem. I trooped off on honeymoon and missed the game, which ended in a draw. The club booked flights for me to come home a couple of days early and play the replay but it turned out to be a forgettable experience. I spent hours trying to find the American Embassy office to pick up the tickets and then our flights were delayed, meaning that I had a twenty-seven hour trip home with no sleep before the game.

Apart from losing, the biggest regret I have about that game is the fact that Aidan Fogarty was dropped to facilitate my return. He retired afterwards and it was a terrible way for one of the club's all-time greats to bow out. My contribution was limited in the 1996 final as well. We beat Birr in the semi-final and, during the game, I chased Declan Pilkington down and flicked the ball away from him. It bounced nicely for Hanamy who pulled on it first time – and straight into my unmentionables. He's arguably the best ground hurler we ever had in Offaly and I can certainly vouch for it after that experience.

The team doctor, Liam Dalton, came on and told me that I had to go off but I insisted on staying on. I also got a swipe across the hand and the back of my leg so, when I got to the dressingroom at half-time, I was a sorry sight. The pain started to kick in as the swelling increased but I somehow finished the game. By the time I got back to Naas that night I was in ribbons. While my illness in 1989 was the most distressing of my life, this was undoubtedly the most painful. I couldn't go to work the next day and eventually reported to the accident and emergency department in the old Meath Hospital. By then I was nearly passing out with the pain. It was unbearable.

I required an ultrasound and it turned out that I had a punctured scrotum and a fractured testicle. I'm told the testicles are particularly durable for obvious reasons, so it says a lot for the power of Hanamy's striking that he forced a fracture. I underwent major surgery, which was a success, and the doctor's parting words to me were, "Come back to me for a check-up in three months, but it's likely that it will be three to six months before you're able to play again". Yeah, right. I had already missed the intermediate football final and replay, which we lost, and the county hurling final was on a few days after I got out of hospital. "Are you going to tog out?" my father asked me, though his tone suggested it was more an instruction than a question. I wore my shorts and socks under a tracksuit and, when we were a few points down at half-time, I told Ger Fogarty, our manager, that I'd go on if he wanted me to. I was sent on and scored a few points, but we still lost by two.

By then thoughts of an All-Ireland were distant. We just wanted to put our stamp on the Offaly Championship again. Birr won the 1997 title and went on to win their second All-Ireland. We knocked them out in 1998 county semi-final and, yet again, Clareen broke our hearts by beating us in a replay. It seemed that every time we'd do their dirty work by beating Birr they'd pick us off. We'd often play Clareen in the early rounds of the Championship, which weren't knockout, and beat them, but, when it came to county final time at the latter end of the year in different conditions, they knew how to dog it out. We should have been able to adapt over time but we didn't. We returned to the final in 1999 against Birr but, by then, they were moving up through the gears while we were grinding to a halt with little talent coming through.

When Rynagh's got to the final again in 2001, I had transferred to Raheens, in Kildare. Birr are probably the only club in the county who continued to bring quality players through from 2000 onwards, and it was only then that they really began to dominate in Offaly year on year. From underage level all the way up there was very little between us and, in fact, we probably held the advantage over them up until the mid-'90s. For a few years after that it was still nip-and-tuck. They went and won their four All-Irelands, and you have to hand it to them. We wouldn't begrudge them but there'd be disappointment that we didn't get there first. We were close but, for a combination of reasons, didn't take the chances presented to us. When I think of what I won with Rynagh's, four county medals and a Leinster club title, the absence of an All-Ireland stands out more than anything, particularly as I had completed my haul by the time I was twenty-five. The remainder of my club career was nothing but a catalogue of sickening defeats.

Chapter 8

Croke Park, July, 1995

We rounded off the All-Ireland celebrations with a team holiday to Florida in January, 1995, before turning our attention to retaining the title. Having suffered first-round defeats in three successive years before 1994, we hadn't the opportunity to grow, develop and bond as a team. The 1994 campaign changed that and then the holiday in Florida was an extension of it. It also gave Cregan the opportunity to get to know us better and tap into what we were about that bit more. Having done that, I think he mellowed and learned to bend to our ways somewhat.

The image of our team as a bunch of boozing mavericks is blown wildly out of proportion. We were certainly different, yes, but we couldn't have enjoyed the success we had in the most competitive era in hurling history without applying ourselves rigorously to training and generally looking after ourselves off the field. I landed myself in hot water earlier this year as a result of a comment about the Offaly footballers and the application of some of the players, which is certainly questionable, and while we had our moments it was more the exception than the rule. I don't recall a player being thrown off the panel as a result of his social habits. The management had to roll with the punches or we would have got nowhere together.

The week before the 1994 Leinster final Johnny Dooley got married and a bunch of us drank the whole day long, even when Cregan and Derry arrived at the reception in the evening time. He couldn't afford to drop us all but we had to be taught a lesson. We were due to train the following morning and Joe and Billy Dooley, Kevin Kinahan, Martin Hanamy and myself were detained at the end and ran into the ground. That was very much the exception to the rule with Hanamy in particular though. A fanatical man to train, but he always said that, if a manager ever told him to give up the drink, he would have retired. He wasn't a big drinker anyway but he worked very hard all week, as well as training three or four times, and he reckoned if he wanted to have a few quiet pints at the weekend why should anyone tell him otherwise? And when you think about it, it's a very mature attitude to have.

In a good year you'd be lucky to have four or five big Championship games and Hanamy would be monk-like in his application during the build-up. He was a real leader in the team without being a mouthpiece and I felt he should have been retained in the role for several years after 1994, in a similar fashion to what Clare had with Anthony Daly. I think he found all the formalities that went with being captain a bit of a drag after we won the All-Ireland, but the management perhaps could have been more insistent on him remaining as captain.

Instead, Johnny Pilkington took over the role in 1995. He was very much the poster boy for the breezy perception of our team and I don't think that lent itself to being captain at that stage. He seemed to feed off it and was happy to be depicted as the joker in the pack but, in doing so, did himself a disservice. He wasn't even a big drinker behind it all and he was a savagely committed man. He may have given the impression that he could take it or leave it when it came to hurling, but don't believe a word of it. Hurling is Johnny's life. You can even see that since he's retired. He's taken charge of the Offaly minors and various club teams and is now throwing himself into the underage development, striving to get Offaly back on the map.

We reached the National League semi-final in 1995 despite being without the Birr contingent for much of the campaign as they won the All-Ireland club title. I had worked my way back into the team and stayed there all year, mostly at corner-forward. Kilkenny beat us in that League semi-final by six points, with DJ Carey scoring a hat-trick. We weren't too perturbed by it and they went on to beat Clare convincingly in the final. Having been All-Ireland champions in 1992 and '93, the vibe among the general hurling public seemed to be that we had caught them on the hop in 1994 and won a soft All-Ireland, mugging Limerick in the process. Kilkenny had stormed back and won the League and were clear favourites to win the All-Ireland. It was as if we were pseudo-champions. We were on a collision course to meet in the Leinster final that year and, after we laboured to a semi-final win over Wexford, that's what happened. It was the game of our lives.

We were a better side in 1995 than the year before. In the build-up to that Kilkenny game training was going well, everyone was fit. Confidence was high, particularly with Birr having won the All-Ireland on top of what we had done the previous year. We were absolutely flying it. The mood leading up to the game among the players was serious and Cregan tapped into it brilliantly. He stoked the fire in our bellies to ensure maximum heat was unleashed on Kilkenny. The team meeting we had in the Aisling Hotel a couple of hours before the game was epic. There was just a savage atmosphere in the room.

Cregan liked to have a meeting at that stage to get his points across clearly because you could have all sorts of roaring and shouting in a dressing room before you hit the field. Once he had the meeting, the idea was that you were in game mode. Now, that wouldn't be the case with all the players as everyone has their own routine to get them in the mood but, that day, we were all wired from the outset. Even Johnny P didn't raise a smile. Cregan spoke powerfully at the meeting, yet I can't clearly recall anything he said because I was so wound up. I can hum the tune though. He played on the perception that our All-Ireland win had been discredited and the charge that we had scraped a title in fortunate circumstances; that Kilkenny were overwhelming favourites despite the fact that we had beaten them comfortably the year before and been robbed of victory the year before that.

As the temperature spiralled during that meeting some of us were close to tears. If it went much further we would have stepped beyond the brink of sanity. It wasn't our style as a group generally, and there is a certain balance that has to be struck. Something like that won't always work. We brought the pitch back up to where it was in the hotel before we left the dressing room and nearly unhinged the door as we did so. As Leinster and All-Ireland champions we were to go out on the field second but, as if we weren't pumped up enough, there was no sign of Kilkenny when we got out there as the rain bucketed down. Hanamy took ownership of the situation and brought us back inside. He made a big deal of it.

"They sent us out in it and they wouldn't send Kilkenny out," he bellowed.

Unbeknownst to us, however, Kilkenny were out there and had taken shelter in the dugout amid the cracks of thunder and bolts of lightning as the skies opened. The match started a few minutes late but the weather didn't bother us. In fact I felt it was a positive because we had the more skilful hurlers and, in those conditions, your control comes under closer scrutiny. As it was, we walked on water.

My outlook when it came to playing Kilkenny was that they would have to be matched physically in the first twenty minutes and then let the hurling look after itself. We weren't too worried about the scoreboard early on. If you went out trying to simply out-hurl them from the off you were on a loser straightaway. They'd just walk all over you. You had to meet them head-on in the physical battle and then see who blinks first thereafter.

Some of the hurling in that first half was savage. The hits, the hooking, the blocking. I scored the first point after a couple of minutes, which was equalised by PJ Delaney. That was the only point they scored from play all day. Eddie O'Connor was marking me and started very well, bursting out with possession several times. Make no mistake about it, they were well up for it, too, and Eddie was their lightning rod. At one stage, as he launched a kicked clearance, Johnny Pilkington came in and buried him. No free was given and the ball worked its way back down to Billy Dooley. He picked me out and I whipped over another point. Eddie trotted back into the corner, effing and blinding at not having been awarded a free.

"That's it, Eddie," I said. "You keep soloing out with them and I'll keep tapping them over the bar, you fucking eejit."

And, with that, he went absolutely ballistic. Chances to goad Eddie should never be passed up. I was switched to full-forward in a swap with Pat O'Connor and him and Eddie took lumps out of each other, and both got booked. Elsewhere, another Kilkenny player pulled a dirty stroke on Johnny Dooley, jabbing the hurley into his face and breaking his nose. Johnny was a pure hurler and didn't get involved in that stuff usually, but when the next ball broke between them he lashed straight across him and shattered his hurley in the process. No quarter was asked or given. Every ball was contested furiously. Looking at the likes of Daithí Regan diving headlong to block players down, you couldn't but feed off it. It was low scoring at half-time, when we led by 0-5 to 0-3, but it was a breathtaking contest.

Early in the second half Daithí scored a fortuitous goal after Kilkenny goalkeeper Michael Walsh failed to deal with his delivery, allowing it to creep just over the line. That put daylight between us and we romped home from there with a collection of beautiful scores. The point that Brian Whelahan scored stood out for me and summed up him and our team perfectly: in terrible conditions he broke onto a loose ball, soloed up the field and pinged it over the bar from distance. Pat O'Connor scored our second goal with a brilliant overhead strike. All our skill, guile, teamwork and commitment came to the fore. Kilkenny had no answer bar two goals from DJ, one of them a penalty, in garbage time when the game was over. I popped over the last point of the game and our victory was emphatic: 2-16 to 2-5.

In so many ways it summed up what my contribution to the team was. Scoring a couple of points, setting up a couple more and going out to midfield for the last fifteen minutes and doing a job. It was a strength of mine that I recognised my role and didn't get ahead of myself. Others had their jobs. Whelahan would mop up and set the agenda for us; the Dooleys and John Troy would score the dandy points; Johnny Pilkington was the engine in midfield; Hanamy and Kinahan took no prisoners at the back.

Driving each other to different heights in training games isn't a phenomenon that only caught on in Kilkenny in recent years. I'm convinced that Billy Dooley became the gunslinging corner-forward he was in the mid-'90s as a result of marking Hanamy so often in training. Hanamy was no different in training to what he was in a game. Even in drills he'd put the ball out through you. It was all or nothing. No matter who Billy Dooley came up against after Hanamy marked him in training, he just couldn't have been as good. It was Championship hurling in training with him. I could be marking Brian Whelahan and he'd make a fool of you if you dithered for a split second. Kevin Martin wouldn't give you an inch. Shane McGuckin the same.

The four cornerstones of our team were Hanamy, Johnny Pilkington, Johnny Dooley and, of course, Whelahan. They were our four most special players, who would hurl in the best of company from any era in the history of the game. Pilky just had this incredible engine, up and down the field all day long. I can never remember him missing a match through injury, or even going down injured. He never let us down, regardless of the off-field reputation that preceded him. Johnny Dooley was the only player I saw in training that could take Whelahan to the cleaners. He could hit him for five or six points in the space of twenty minutes. He had great balance and power and was such a sweet striker off either side. Allied to that, he was a little bit greedy, which you need to be. There was no point in Johnny throwing out a pass to someone who was less likely to score than he was.

Whelahan was our most important player, though. I felt when Sid was playing at the top of his game we just couldn't be beaten. There were three strands to him as a player. Firstly, he just had huge self-belief without being arrogant. Throughout his career he basically ignored his man. He'd float around wherever he pleased and pick up so much ball because he read the game so well. The Franz Beckenbauer of hurling, as he was often called. You could say he left himself at risk of conceding a couple of points to whoever he was marking but that would be to take an extremely narrow-minded view of him as a player.

He could have played as an orthodox defender and marked his man out of every game if he wanted, but his net worth would have been reduced because we needed him sweeping across the back line and dictating the play for us. Secondly, he covered for everybody. He often drifted seventy yards from his right half-back position to prevent a goal or make a clearance. Finally, the quality of his deliveries was right out of the top drawer. When did you ever see him mis-hitting the ball? He could be under severe pressure in possession but would find the space to move out of trouble on the back foot and supply an inch-perfect pass up front.

I often marked him in club games and thought I'd have him nailed with a block, but every time I'd go on his right he'd clear off his left, and vice versa. He had an acute appreciation of everything that was happening around him, and that's something you can't coach. John Troy had that level of awareness, too, but he lacked the athleticism and movement to go with it. Despite his vast array of skills I wouldn't quite put him in the same category as the four lads because he wasn't quite as consistent as they were over a ten-year period or more. But, what a player!

The age profile of the team, fitness, ability and the confidence that ran through us meant that we were at our peak in 1995, and that Leinster final performance proved it. We had demolished what was a genuinely great Kilkenny team, a much stronger outfit than the one we hammered in 1990. The trouble was we put so much, physically and mentally, into that game that there would have to be a drop-off of some sort, particularly when we had the easier semi-final against Down. At that stage in our cycle we weren't going to suffer a mishap like Antrim in 1989, and we beat Down without any fuss to set up a final meeting with Clare, who had come from nowhere having won their first Munster title in sixty-three years.

After my personal disappointment of twelve months earlier, there was little doubt about my starting spot this time. I had played well all year and would finally get the chance to grace hurling's biggest day right from the off. We were well experienced from winning the year before, and most of us had featured in minor and Under-21 finals, but this All-Ireland was completely different and we weren't prepared for it.

We definitely underestimated Clare for a start. We felt that if we played any way well that we'd win. Another point was that we had no gripe with Clare and there was no history between the sides. We always felt that we needed that edge in big games but we just couldn't find it against Clare. There were other aspects of our mental preparation that were slack as well. We weren't ready for all the razzmatazz that went with that particular final, and it was only when Clare came out on the field that it hit me.

Throughout my career the crowd, regardless of the attendance, never bothered me in any way, shape or form but that day was different. We were out on the field first and when Clare came out a couple of minutes after us the roar that went up was extraordinary. It certainly stopped me in my tracks. If it were flagged in advance, it wouldn't have bothered us in the slightest what the decibel levels were when the Clare team emerged. I hadn't been well in the lead-up to the game and suffered with vomiting and diarrhoea the night before, something that I ascribed to nerves at the time, but now I realise that I simply just wasn't well.

We played very poorly but still looked the more likely winners throughout. I scored a soft goal in the first half after Clare goalkeeper Davy Fitzgerald failed to deal with an under-hit point effort and we led by two points at half-time. One of the things that stands out about my own experience that day was that Cregan never left me alone from start to finish. I was shifted around to various positions, and he seemed to be on my case the whole time. I always felt that the stylists on the team, like Sid, Troy and Johnny Dooley never had to put up with that. We couldn't shake Clare off and they were level with us when Johnny Pilkington scored our second goal. It looked to be enough to fend them off but then we missed a host of chances.

It was claimed afterwards that Brian Lohan pulled his hamstring yet played on, but I know from personal experience that he couldn't have. Maybe he twinged it because you just can't play with a torn hamstring. As it was, John Troy gave him a roasting, except for the fact that he spilled a few wides at a critical juncture that kept Clare in the game. They were two points down with a couple of minutes left when Anthony Daly took a free that dropped at crossbar height. Our goalkeeper, David Hughes, opted to bat the ball rather than catch and Clare substitute Eamon Taaffe was on hand to return it to the net. We quickly equalised through a Johnny Dooley free but Daly popped another long-range free over himself to restore their lead, and then Jamesie O'Connor scored from another placed ball in front of the posts. The final whistle sounded from the puck-out and, all of a sudden, we were beaten.

Clare fans were engulfing the field and Anthony Daly was lifting the MacCarthy Cup instead of Johnny Pilkington. It wasn't supposed to be like this. We were so close to retaining our All-Ireland title and cementing our status as the best team in the land at the time. Clare went on to become a great team, but they weren't at that point. Indeed, the team they had in 1998 and '99 was significantly stronger than the '95 team. If we had done ourselves justice we would have won the game reasonably comfortably but, then, I don't want to take too much from Clare either. Credit to them for restricting us, and they were a team that I have huge respect for in coming from where they did to win All-Irelands.

I'm a hurling enthusiast first and foremost and didn't begrudge them their win but it doesn't alter the feeling that we left it behind us and that was no one's fault but ours. I don't blame John Troy or David Hughes or Dickie Murphy, the smiling referee who never did us any favours down the years. It's a team game and we simply played shite. Ultimately, we have to take responsibility for that as a group, including the management for their oversights leading up to the game. It was a devastating blow. Johnny Pilkington took it very badly I felt. It would have been the ultimate for him to have captained Birr and Offaly to All-Irelands in the one year and he was only minutes away from doing it. He would have deserved it, too, for all he brought to that team. That defeat took a lot out of him particularly, but it took a lot out of us all.

• • • • •

It wasn't all doom and gloom after that defeat, at least not for me anyway. Edel and I got married the following month on October 14, 1995. Once we had been going out for a couple of years, we moved in together. We were living in Rathfarnham with a guy called Matt O'Brien, who was a smashing fella. He worked long hours so he wasn't there too much and charged us pitiful rent. He was just glad of the company. Edel was always supportive of me in my sporting pursuits, which was critical. I was already an inter-county player when I met her so she saw what she was buying into. I could nearly be shot for saying it, but when you're involved in a team at that level it simply has to be your number one priority, above work, family and everything else, otherwise you're wasting your time. It comes first for most of the year and then you unwind in the winter before getting back into it again. It's fundamentally a very selfish outlook that some people may struggle to understand, but it's the way it has to be if you want to succeed at the highest level. Any player would say the same if he's being honest.

It became obvious from an early stage that Edel and I were going to stay together so moving in together felt natural, even though it was awkward as we were still working together for much of that time. In 1994 we bought a house in Naas having spent a weekend down there with our friends, Ian and Deirdre Brophy. It was a bit of a punt because we had little or no money at the time but Dan Ryan, our boss in AIB, managed to wrangle a mortgage for us. We got engaged just before Christmas that year and picked out the ring together in Appleby's in Dublin.

I didn't quite get down on bended knee when it came to completing the formalities. Everyone was breaking up from work on the Friday before Christmas and we had a few drinks in the Glenside in Churchtown, one of the Mangans' pubs. I told Tom and Paul Mangan that we had just got engaged but that we hadn't told anyone yet. "Get the champagne ready," I said. Edel was sitting in the middle of a few colleagues when I called her and lobbed the pouch into her lap. "What's that?" everyone asked, as Edel fidgeted nervously before producing the ring. We had a great night afterwards and my family were delighted at the news. Edel got on well with all the Duignans and enjoyed a fantastic relationship with my parents.

We were married in Kilminchy church near Portlaoise the following year, with the reception in the Montague Hotel. We had a brilliant day though, typically, hurling was never too far away as the county semi-finals were in Birr the next day. I wouldn't quite say I had a dry wedding, but none of the other lads involved in those games did either, so it probably evened itself out. The sub-plot of the day was the Dooleys striving to get the Birr lads drunk ahead of their game the following afternoon! But this was a day when hurling most definitely took a back seat. It was the happiest day of both our lives. Edel looked fabulous and, when her father, Jerry, presented her to me in the church, I filled with pride. We were both just twenty-seven and our whole lives stretched out before us.

· · · · ·

Although losing to Clare was a massive setback, I felt we were hurling at a sufficiently high standard to regain the All-Ireland in 1996. We beat Meath and Laois to reach another Leinster final, playing particularly well against Laois when John Troy put on an exhibition. Wexford would be our opponents in the final this time after they had seen off Kilkenny and Dublin. There was no reason to expect that they would be any more formidable than they had been in previous years. They hadn't beaten us in the Championship since 1979, though, and I suppose they had to catch us some time. They did so by giving the performance of their lives in what turned out to be another epic Leinster final. We played well, unlike in the All-Ireland final the previous year. Not at our best, but we played better than we had on a number of the occasions when we had beaten Wexford before that. We weren't quite up to full tempo in training at the stage of the year, as we wanted to leave a bit in the tank. The warning signs were there for us to observe, however. Wexford beat us in both the Walsh Cup and the National League quarter-final that year.

We weren't too put out but, in hindsight, they must have taken confidence from that despite that we used to nearly always beat them, regardless of the competition.

Furthermore, we started to concede big tallies. Meath and Laois didn't exactly have heralded forward divisions but scored 2-12 and 2-10 against us, respectively. Then Wexford hit us with 2-23, though their win was embellished by a late surge, which didn't reflect how close it was. Approaching the game, I thought we were getting back to a good place and, if we had got over that game, the All-Ireland was there for us again. We didn't, though, and it took that Wexford team's greatest performance to beat us, so you can't take it away from them. They identified our half-back line as their point of attack and dismantled it on the day. Their half-forward line of Rory McCarthy, Martin Storey, and particularly Larry Murphy, went to town and scored twelve points between them. You simply can't win when your half-back line gives up that number of scores. Yet there wasn't a single change made to our defence despite the concession rate. It was crying out for something to be done from the line, though no action was taken.

I think Cregan showed a bit of blind faith in our half-back line that day by trusting them to get the grips with the situation, but they didn't. Out of all the teams I came up against over the years though, that Wexford side was probably my favourite and I was delighted for them when they went on and won the All-Ireland.

Cregan stepped down after that defeat. Four years was a long stint coming up and down from Limerick and we had given him his fair share of headaches at times. You could say that we were a difficult group to manage but, if you were clever about it, we could be managed very easily too. As time went on Cregan learned to strike that balance better. He's a man I have huge regard for and deeply appreciate what he did for us as a team.

He was replaced by John McIntyre, a former Tipperary hurler, who was a very eager young manager. He was inexperienced, though, and it was just a bit too much for him to come in and take over a seasoned bunch of players at that early stage in his managerial career. That's not to say that he was a bad manager, because he wasn't. He had a lot of good points and was ahead of his time in many respects. He introduced a psychologist but, as a bunch of players, we were very set in our ways. If we hadn't achieved success previously it would have been easier for him to get us to buy into his style.

He was very accommodating to me when I went back to play rugby with Buccaneers that year. We won the AIL Division Three title and McIntyre was happy enough for me to see out my rugby commitments when it overlapped with Offaly training. Once I resumed with Offaly full-time the training was tough and we made quite a good start to the National League. We might have expended more energy than we needed in some of those games and were a bit flat come the summer. We pretty much knew what the bones of the team was going to be year on year, so extending ourselves in the League wasn't a priority and our routine was perhaps upset somewhat that year.

Another area where McIntyre overdid it was in terms of his orations. He's a powerful speaker but his timing was a little off. He'd sometimes stop a training session in February to reassure us how exceptionally talented we were, when it would have been better practice just to get the session over and done with and save that for later in the year.

If we hadn't slipped dramatically from our peak in 1996, then we did in 1997. The fizz was gone. We hammered Meath in the first round of the Championship but then fell over Laois with a one-point win. We were very poor, and PJ Peacock came within inches of knocking us out of the Championship with a goal effort that just slipped past the post. We hit twenty wides and didn't improve much on that statistic against Wexford in the Leinster semi-final, when we struck a further seventeen wides. Such statistics were unheard of for a team of our economy. We were still unlucky to lose, though, and gave away some very soft goals, including one directly from a '65'. Only a wonder save by Damien Fitzhenry from Billy Dooley denied us a replay. McIntyre wasn't reappointed for a second year. Meanwhile, time was passing us by.

Chapter 9

Croke Park, September, 1998

1998 was the most remarkable year of my life for several reasons, not all of them hurling-related. Ask me to choose a highlight from those incredible twelve months and you may not get the answer you expect. It wasn't winning the All-Ireland title and scoring that point at the end of the final, which added the sheen for me personally. It wasn't the day in Thurles when we beat Clare in the most absorbing game of the year to confirm that we truly were back as a force in hurling. Neither was it when Johnny Dooley scored that last-ditch winning goal to beat Wexford, a strike that effectively extended the life expectancy of our team by three seasons. No, it was February 5, the day I became a father.

By then Edel and I were married more than two years but it had been eight years since we first met. Having children was something we always wanted, so we weren't going to hang around once we got married. We said we'd have a few fairly close together so that they could grow up as buddies. Living in Naas at the time, we had a worry that Edel might go into labour during peak traffic, which could leave us with a three-hour journey to the Coombe Hospital in Dublin. Luckily, it was early enough in the morning to avoid that complication. The two of us were reasonably cool about it, though Edel's patience began to wear thin as the labour stretched out for some twelve hours, and everything that goes with it. As I always say, it's not a spectator sport. Some of the abuse I shipped was worse than anything ever rained down upon me from the terraces or opponents! After Seán was born I went home to Naas and met a few friends in Kavanagh's.

"What was it like?" they asked.

"Jaysus, to be honest with you," I replied as I took a slug from the pint, "it wasn't as bad as I thought it would be."

This after Edel had endured a dozen hours of labour. The ignorance of that statement dawned on me just as the inevitable ribbing came.

When it comes to pregnancies I always simply wish a couple luck and nothing more because it's an experience you have to go through yourself to truly appreciate it. Thankfully, Seán (we chose that name as we liked short and snappy Irish names) emerged healthy with a shock of black hair and in perfect working order – two arms, two legs and a head and, of course, the wailing cry. I don't have the words to accurately describe exactly what it means at that moment when you become a parent. It's just unbelievable. The child is a manifestation of your relationship as a couple. Both Edel and I had good and bad points, and you're hoping that the better aspects from both of you might emerge in the child. That's something I see in the two lads all the time now.

Your thought process is immediately challenged on becoming a parent. I define myself as a father first and foremost and, as I'm sure all parents will relate to, am regularly consumed by a fear that something might happen to them, whether it be when crossing the road or cycling their bicycles. That mind-set is particularly exaggerated when it's your first child. Parenthood is peculiar in that, even though you have no real experience of it, you take to it rather quickly, simply because you have to.

Seán's birth didn't impact on my training with Offaly and I never missed a single session. I took a couple of weeks off work but, once I started back, a typical day might involve me getting home from training at around half-past eleven or so, in bed by midnight and up again a couple of hours later to feed Seán. I took on a lot of these duties as Edel recovered from the pregnancy and birth. Seán was a notoriously slow feeder and it could take up to two hours for him to finish his bottle. Later on, Brian was the opposite, and would sleep right through the night.

For all the changes that parenthood brought, we didn't become slaves to the role in the way some people do. Edel resumed work with AIB a few months later so we needed a minder, and how fortune smiled on us in that regard. We didn't like the idea of a creche and preferred something more personal for Seán, and a lady called Bríd O'Brien was recommended to us.

We visited her and, as soon as I walked through the door of her home, I knew that we had struck gold. Bríd is a truly amazing woman, as well as her husband, Michael, and their children, Lisa and Neil. We were incredibly lucky to come across them. There's an unbreakable bond to this day between Bríd and the lads. You could travel the world and not meet better people. Although we don't live in Naas any more, Seán and Brian still go up to stay with the O'Briens and they attend all the important occasions in their lives, such as First Communions and Confirmations. I firmly believe that Bríd played a huge part in shaping them into the pleasant kids that they are.

I often think back to those nights in the sitting room, willing Seán to take his bottle and trying to wind him. He'd be lying across my knees and used to look straight into my eyes, and you just had to love him. We're great friends, and I believe there was a deep bond created between us as a result of those long nights on the sofa. I didn't mind doing it one bit. At three or four in the morning I should have been in bed, but I was thinking, "I'm happy here with this little lad looking up at me," while wondering what direction his life would take. Nothing could come even remotely close to challenging the range of emotions brought on by becoming a father. Or so I thought.

• • • • •

By the time Seán was born John McIntyre had been replaced as Offaly senior hurling manager by one Michael "Babs" Keating. I must say that, initially, I was excited at the prospect because Babs had a larger-than-life personality. Through my friendship with Nicky English I had heard some hilarious stories from his time in charge of Tipperary. But he brought them from nowhere and achieved great success, though others would argue that he should have done better with the talent at his disposal. In the previous two seasons he had managed Laois when we played them in the Championship. In 1997, we were very fortunate to get over them, but that was probably down to our performance more than theirs.

He was appointed well before Christmas and I remember our first meeting with him in the County Arms in Birr. One of his strong points that Nicky would have impressed on me was that he was a players' man. He told us everything you'd expect him to at that meeting, how we were great hurlers that could win another All-Ireland, and all that jazz. He instructed us to go out and buy six new hurleys each, before turning to the County Board Chairman, Brendan Ward.

"That's ok, Brendan, isn't it?"

He obviously hadn't discussed it with him at all, and what else could Brendan do in that situation only give us the imprimatur to go ahead and get the hurleys. Next, Babs announced that our wives and girlfriends would be coming with us for post-match meals, be it Walsh Cup, Oireachtas, National League or Championship. Now, it would have been the norm for the girls to join us after Championship games but this new practice was a bit unheard of at the same time.

"That's ok, Brendan, isn't it?"

Offaly have a history of outside managers, both in hurling and football, and, given Babs's profile and achievements as a player and manager, there was a certain amount of excitement and anticipation attached to his appointment from our point of view. People might think that his relationship with us was fraught right from the start but I certainly didn't see it like that, possibly because I got to see a side to him that none of the others did. I would meet him at his daughter Orla's house in the Curragh, where she and her husband, Johnny Murtagh, the well-known jockey, lived. Orla and Johnny were hugely welcoming. I'd usually have a slice of their brown bread with a bit of cheese, while Babs might reduce an apple tart or a loaf to crumbs. Once or twice I arrived at the house to see that he was using the Curragh as a makeshift driving range, pinging golf balls over the busy main road. "Get in there beside me," he said as he got into the car. We then drove around until we had each ball collected. Being a jockey, Johnny had a sauna in the house, which Babs would often frequent before we'd depart. On the way down to training he could be backing a few horses. Massive craic. He'd make me feel ten foot tall, too.

"You're such a vital man on this team," he'd tell me. "We'll win the All-Ireland and you'll be a key player."

He certainly helped bolster my confidence. Early on in the year I recall a couple of lads being injured and Babs ensured that they were well looked after. Things like that were among his strong points as a manager.

Easily the best decision he made during his time with us was bringing Johnny Murray with him as physical trainer. Johnny was an army man, who was acutely aware of just how fit we needed to be and what buttons he'd have to press to get us to that level. The training we did in January, 1998, in Shinrone was animal. None of us will ever forget it. Circuit training, with Johnny barking out the orders army-style, but not in a condescending manner. He was well-spoken and had a real presence about himself. I got so sore from the training after a couple of weeks that I wasn't fit to do press-ups and had to devise a different routine. While Derry O'Donovan had improved our fitness substantially years before, this was raising it to another level again. Johnny was very much a student of physical preparation, and researched extensively to ensure he moved with the times. For example, he'd be able to impart to us what the All Blacks, or some other elite team, were doing. We were given various runs to do, up to 3000 metres, which had to be completed within time limits by a certain stage of the year. Although it came easier to some more than others, we all met those targets.

I remember the likes of John Troy and Hubert Rigney, who wouldn't have been the most natural of athletes, really struggled, but they never wavered and got there eventually. All this would stand to us later in the year and Johnny was a man that was held in high regard by each of us. He still is. However, there were early signs that Babs's heart wasn't in the job. For much of the early training he was nowhere to be seen, having decamped to Dubai where Johnny Murtagh was riding for a few weeks. It hardly sent out the right signals, even if the training was largely under Johnny Murray's control at that stage.

I had rugby commitments again that year, having been approached by Naas to play with them. It was a nice release and required less commitment than what I had given to Buccaneers the previous year and wouldn't impinge on my hurling too much. It was also an opportunity to play sport at a level that wasn't so intense and serious. As it transpired we had a great year and won the Provincial Towns Cup and Leinster Junior League. Babs, in fairness to him, was fairly accommodating. The day after we played Clare in a National League game I had the Towns Cup semi-final against Navan in which I scored a late try to win the game for us. We played Kilkenny in the final in Enniscorthy, which fell the day after Seán's christening.

We were coached by a New Zealander called Kevin West, who later took charge of Blackrock, and I must say I found the whole rugby culture of meeting up hours before a game, having drawn-out team talks and ridiculously extensive warm-ups rather grating. I was happy enough just to arrive half an hour or so before the game. It's something that Westy struggled with me on. I had a few pints at Seán's christening, nothing too hectic, but when the bus stopped in Tullow en route to the final the next day for a warm-up I certainly wasn't budging. In fact, I sent a young lad into the shop to pick me up a cone and bottle of Lucozade before Westy noticed I was missing.

"Duigs, what about the warm-up?"

"I'm not doing it, Kevin," I told him. "It's a load of shite. The match is not on for another two or three hours, what's it all for?"

I suppose you could say I was the diva on the team.

"Fucking hurlers," growled Westy as he rolled his eyes and went to rejoin the lads outside.

We won the final comfortably enough and, although I lined out with Naas the odd the time after that, that was pretty much the end of my rugby days. I was thirty and my body was finding it more difficult to recover from the physical exertions of playing various sports, and hurling was obviously going to be my priority. Nonetheless, while the Towns Cup wouldn't be near the top of my list of achievements, I got great enjoyment out of it and I retain strong links with the club. There were great characters involved, such as Ross Murphy, one of the players on the team and brother of Ireland international, Geordan, and club stalwarts, Gerry Prendergast and Anthony 'The Toe' Hayden who, sadly, has died since.

Although the National League was never a tournament we got too worked up about, the results and performances were generally poor. The only game we won was at home to Antrim, and the campaign ended with Dublin putting four goals past us at Parnell Park. A couple of weeks later we were due to play Tipperary in a challenge game in Clonmel. Babs was instrumental in organising it, with the proceeds going to Tipperary hurler John Leahy, who was under pressure at the time.

However, shortly before the throw-in there were only a handful of us in the dressing room. Our numbers peaked at thirteen and we borrowed a couple of players from Tipperary to play the match. Among the excuses put forward was the unusually large crowd that turned up at the League semi-finals in Thurles that day involving Cork and Clare, and Waterford and Limerick, with players caught in traffic. There may have been some substance to that though the fact of the matter is that a number of players, some of whom had been playing for their clubs that weekend, just didn't bother turning up.

It would be convenient to suggest that the apathy of the players was largely due to their disillusionment at Babs's management, but that couldn't wash as our group had plenty of previous when it came to incidents like this down the years. Clonmel was more or less Babs's home town and he got plenty of jibes from the crowd over it. It was embarrassing for him and for the players that were there. I had made the trip from Naas while others couldn't be bothered, which annoyed me. Babs actually resigned in the aftermath but was coaxed back later in the week.

If there was unrest in the panel at that stage I can't say that I was acutely aware of it. I just travelled to training with Babs, did the session and then travelled back with him. He was saying all the things that I wanted to hear about myself, I was in the team and playing reasonably well. But I was out of the county most of the time. I wasn't sharing a car and having discussions on the way back to Banagher, Birr or Lusmagh with other players after training. But the sessions certainly did lack the vibrancy that was needed to bring the best out in us.

While Johnny's fitness training was top-class, it spilled over into April, May and June, a time when stamina work would normally be parked in order to sharpen the touch as the ground hardened. Sessions would sometimes be halted abruptly as Babs gathered us around him for a talk, which usually carried a reference to his "thirty-four years involved in inter-county hurling". He was forever harking back to the '60s, which had no relevance to us. He'd lecture us about techniques in holding up the ball and arsing into fellas, which I tended to do anyway, but it was hardly something that you would try to coach to seasoned hurlers at that stage in their careers if it wasn't already one of their core competencies.

He once caused severe embarrassment to a player when he stopped proceedings to announce that "in my thirty-four years involved in inter-county hurling, I never saw a fella catching a ball with his eyes closed". More or less telling him in front of all his team-mates that he was afraid of his own shadow. Another night one of the lads needed a rub during a training session only to find that Babs was availing of one himself when he got to the dressing room. People sometimes wonder whether he tried to change our style of hurling and impose something alien on us. The truth is there was no real game plan or style of play that was mapped out. "If you don't want to listen to me, you won't listen to anyone," he might say to us, but listen to what exactly? Also, while he might like to give a different impression, it seemed that he couldn't see beyond Tipperary, Cork and Kilkenny in terms of the true hurling counties. Add all these things together, and throw in the fact that he went to Dubai in January, and you'd have to question how committed he was.

We beat Meath easily in the opening round of the Leinster Championship to set up a semi-final meeting with Wexford, who were rather depleted with injuries. They were comfortably the better side on the day but couldn't put us away. We managed to stay within two points of them late on when a break from a free lobbed in by Brian Whelahan fell to Johnny Dooley, who stroked the ball through a forest of legs and hurleys and past Damien Fitzhenry for the winning goal. We were steeped. The significance of that goal couldn't possibly be understated. In fact, it was one of the most crucial goals in Offaly hurling history when you think about it. If Johnny hadn't scored our year was over, the team would certainly have broken up with a legacy of underachievement and, in all likelihood, we wouldn't have contested any more All-Ireland finals in the near future. However, at that stage, given how we were playing, All-Ireland finals seemed a long way away as we prepared to face Kilkenny in the Leinster final.

It was the first Championship game Offaly had ever played for which losing didn't terminate your All-Ireland ambitions. The previous year was the first season of the "back door" system, as the beaten Leinster and Munster finalists paired off against Galway and the Ulster champions in two All-Ireland quarter-finals, with the Leinster and Munster champions going straight to the semi-finals.

Removing the knockout element from inter-county hurling was something that was met with no little opposition, particularly from Offaly, who voted against its introduction and, later, its retention. I felt it had a negative impact on the intensity of any Leinster final I played in thereafter though, and the 1998 final was a decidedly drab affair. Neither side covered themselves in glory, with Charlie Carter and John Troy trading scores at either end for much of the game. It was like the two teams were playing a different sport compared to the contest of three years previously. We hit some very bad wides and our touch and striking lacked the sharpness that defined us at our best. The contest was effectively decided by two 20-metre frees, from which DJ Carey went for goal and succeeded both times.

I think we would have been a much more determined and driven outfit if the outcome of the game was critical but then, maybe, the result wouldn't have been any different either. After all we had been poor against Wexford too. As a team we needed to have that edge to produce our best and it certainly wasn't there in that Leinster final in any number of ways. We were still in the Championship, of course, but only on life-support. We were petering out as a team and the win over Wexford was nothing but a stay of execution it seemed. We pondered this as Babs stepped out of the dressing room after the game to fulfil his media duties. And, boy, did the scribes get value for money that day.

"My job is to teach and show them what to do," he told them. "But it appears it's falling on deaf ears. The players just aren't listening to me. We're like sheep running around in a heap. I feel awful disappointed with the application of the stick and quality of the play. All of the negatives out there involve areas I've gone over and over again. I just wonder am I wasting my time in an Offaly dressing room. You'd like to think you have something to contribute but, equally, you'd like to think you'd be listened to. I'm not being listened to. It's a vein running through this Offaly team of individualism, of not thinking of their colleagues, not playing for their colleagues. The players just sail along. There's not a lot of disappointment in that dressing room. They just take every day as it comes."

It was effectively Babs absolving himself of all blame for the result and performance and heaping it on the players. That's not how a team works. Of course, we were the ones who took the field and few of us emerged with any credit after that display. We take responsibility for that, but not all of it.

Was the right environment created by the manager that would allow us to achieve our potential? Clearly it wasn't. Personally I didn't take any offence whatsoever at what Babs said and it didn't really cost me a second thought. To me it was just Babs shooting his mouth off, but he was wrong all the same. If he had something to say then he should have said it in-house rather than lambasting the players publicly.

With incidents like the Clonmel episode, Babs had reason to be frustrated with us at times over the course of the year, and Brian Whelahan went on a tirade in the dressing room after the game about players who had been drinking the night before. I never carried out my own in-depth investigation into who it might have been but I assumed Johnny Pilkington was guilty until proven innocent. We all had a few pints here and there and a few of us, say the Dooleys, Kevin Kinahan and myself, might go for three or four a couple of weeks before a match and have a chat about the upcoming game. Nothing major. But, as has been well documented, Johnny liked to have a few the night before. I didn't have a major problem with it because his performances were generally good, but the way in which he went about it framed the caricature that exists of him. If you feel that a couple of pints the night before a game will help you settle, then go and have them in some dark corner. I think Johnny liked to show people how he could have the few drinks and still perform well the next day. As I've said before, he did himself an injustice in that respect, as, when it came to the crunch, there was no one more serious about hurling than Johnny.

Ifs and buts. If Liam Horan of the *Irish Independent* hadn't picked up the phone to call Johnny the following day for a reaction to Babs's comments would we have ended the year as All-Ireland champions? Hardly. I can't be sure whether the players would have mounted a serious heave against Babs otherwise and we couldn't have picked things up sufficiently under him to mount a serious All-Ireland assault. But once Johnny took Liam Horan's call a sequence of remarkable events had been set in train. Babs had form in terms of criticising his players publicly, and did so rather cuttingly after we hammered his Laois side in 1996. Liam Horan called the one Offaly player that he certainly knew wouldn't take it lying down and the following day's paper saw Johnny cut loose.

"It is wrong for Babs to be talking like that," he hit back. "He's making it look like the Offaly players are idiots and indisciplined. It is stupid and unfair. Babs' track record is that we have won only three competitive games Antrim, Meath and Wexford, and we were very lucky to beat Wexford. Babs is washing his hands of all responsibility. I will stand up and say I didn't play well on Sunday. But other things happened. John Troy was taken out of centre-forward and Canice Brennan came really into the game. No one is sticking up their hand and saying that moving John Troy out of centre-forward was a bad move. You can't blame Babs for everything but you can't blame the players for everything either. We're all a team. We go down together and we win together. What he said will only cause trouble. Ground hurling has been one of our traits, but we haven't done any in training. I was asked recently to compare our former manager Eamonn Cregan to Babs Keating. At this stage of the year, Eamonn would have us doing nothing but hurling."

The mood in Offaly was one of anger at Babs, and the County Board underestimated that initially. The night after the Leinster final – before Johnny's comments had appeared in print – a meeting with Babs and the management team, along with Brendan Ward and County Secretary Christy Todd, was held in the Spa Hotel, in Lucan, as they plotted a way forward with an All-Ireland quarter-final coming up. Babs's comments were discussed but he didn't appear to be taken to task in a serious way, if at all. Instead Johnny's response essentially did that for them. Players were meeting and chatting in groups of threes and fours but there was no concerted move against Babs.

Living outside the county, I certainly wasn't party to anything at that stage, and I believe the discussions among the players centred more on restructuring training rather than trying to oust him. But the writing was on the wall once Johnny spoke out. Brendan Ward called Babs and outlined the situation to him and, though he was still keen to stay on and tackle the problems, Brendan eventually got what he sought when Babs told him he'd resign. It wasn't a case of the players collectively kicking up a fuss and forcing the manager's departure, something we see quite often nowadays. We didn't refuse to play for him. You must remember that, while managers coming and going in mid-season is common in most sports, and happens more regularly in the GAA now, it was unprecedented back then. We had to respond and we had to row in behind Johnny, too. Nobody said it, but we knew that's what had to be done.

My initial reaction to Babs's departure was, "Where do we go from here?" We were playing poorly, had been beaten in a dire Leinster final and now we had no manager. Conversely, as we chatted among ourselves, we knew we weren't too far off the mark. We were in excellent physical condition, thanks to Johnny Murray's training and, with the right ball work and drills, we could rediscover our brand of play. If the last thing a boxer loses is his punch then the last thing a hurler loses is his touch. But we needed a figurehead whose philosophy rhymed with ours. That's exactly what we got the Friday night after the Leinster final.

The name Michael Bond meant nothing to me. It meant nothing to any of us. We had never heard of him. Apart from Paudge Mulhare, of course, who knows everyone. Bond had played on a very highly regarded Ardrahan team that won three Galway Championships in the '70s and later managed a star-studded Galway Under-21 team to All-Ireland success in 1983, I was told. When I saw him in the dressing room I asked who he was and Joe Dooley, taking the piss, told me he was the famed Australian rugby coach, John Connolly. Worse, I believed him. "Oh, what's he doing here?" I wondered.

Bond gathered us out on the field with his usual, "Brostaigí, brostaigí" refrain. And for the next two months not a single negative word passed his lips. In fact, to this day that holds true any time I meet the man. He's incredibly enthusiastic in everything he does and exudes confidence in himself, though not in an overbearing manner. Crucially, he had just as much confidence in us, too.

"My name is Michael Bond," he announced. "I'm principal of Loughrea Vocational School, the best school in the country. You're the best bunch of hurlers in the country and you're going to win the All-Ireland," he told us sharply, with every syllable exhausted. "I can't tell ye anything about hurling. What can I tell ye about hurling? We'll just get back to basics, nothing but ball work – and mow the odd lad if you have to."

There is a fine line between talking crap to, and striking the right chord with, a bunch of players and, God knows our shower could spot a spoofer fairly quickly. Bond was just what we needed, though it would take time for the zip to return to our play. A week later we played Kilkenny in a challenge game in Nowlan Park and were absolutely destroyed after a bright start. Johnny Dooley broke his cheekbone and would miss the All-Ireland quarter-final. We were drawn to play Antrim, who were well short of where they were when they beat us nine years earlier. It bought us time we wouldn't have had if we had been paired with Galway, not that we would have feared them either.

Shortly after he took over, Bond held a team meeting just to get everything out in the open. He asked me beforehand to say a few words. He also approached Joe Dooley, Martin Hanamy and Brian Whelahan. Paudge Mulhare and Pat McLoughney had been retained as selectors from Babs's regime and Hanamy spoke first, criticising aspects of training and team selections over the course of the year. When Hanamy spoke, everyone listened. I glanced over at Paudge and could see the rage building in him as his face reddened. Sid and Joe followed up on Hanamy's comments and by the time it came to me virtually everything that needed to be said had been said. But I couldn't resist the opportunity to goad Paudge a bit more, so I re-emphasised all the points that Hanamy had made pretty strongly, just for the craic. By the time I was finished Paudge was nearly purple.

"That's terrific," Bond said. "We now have all the issues out in the open and we can work on improving them from here. Before we finish, Paudge, Pat, anything you'd like to add?"

"Fucking right I have," said Paudge as he ambled out to the middle of the floor. "I'm after listening to the greatest load of shite of all time. Oh, Jaysus, what I had to listen to," he continued as he made a point of eye-balling each one of us with the finger wagging. "I'll tell you one thing – there's only one thing wrong with ye, and that is that ye're a big-headed shower of fuckers!"

Well, to a man, we fell around the room laughing as Paudge slumped back into his seat; it was a major turning point. Although I was yanking his chain, what had been said in the meeting by the players was genuine and it allowed Bond to gauge the mood of the camp and act accordingly. And, in his own inimitable style, Paudge had a cut back at us, more or less saying that we had to have a good look at ourselves too, and he was right. This was all part of the cleansing process, but only Paudge could get away with it in the way he did it. It was a great finish to the meeting and we really gathered momentum after it.

If one positive came out of that challenge game with Kilkenny it was the introduction of Simon Whelahan at corner-back. He held his place against Antrim, at his brother Barry's expense, and won man-of-the-match in what was another uninspiring game, which fed the widespread belief that we were a busted flush as we laboured to a nine-point win. However, having lost so much ground in terms of our ball work, we continued to train hard right through the week of the Antrim game as we felt we'd get over them anyway. We couldn't afford to slacken off at that stage.

Everyone bought into it and we trained like professionals five times a week. On weekends we'd train on a Saturday evening, stay overnight in the Tullamore Court Hotel, up the next morning for another session, back to the hotel for a swim and home by midday. I basically did nothing else in that period only hurl for Offaly. I reported for work every day but was going through the motions. My mind was trained on nothing but hurling and seizing this opportunity to redeem ourselves. Our own people were still a bit iffy about us, even past players. Pat Delaney questioned "the blood in our veins", something which didn't go down well with a number of the players ahead of the All-Ireland semi-final meeting with champions, Clare. Meanwhile, Babs was sniping away in his *Sunday Times* column, claiming we weren't up to it from midfield up.

Clare had plenty of distractions themselves that summer. Essentially Ger Loughnane was a ringleader in an unnecessary circus that had been started with Colin Lynch's suspension following the Munster final replay against Waterford. Now, Clare had reason to feel hard done by, given that Lynch was the only player singled out for retrospective punishment, but the fact of the matter is he could have no complaint at a three-month ban for his wanton wielding of the hurley that day.

Loughnane was banned from the sideline for the first game against us while Brian Lohan was also suspended, having been sent off against Waterford. Loughnane waged war on the Munster Council, but it was one he couldn't hope to win and he needn't have got involved in. We paid no heed to it at the time and carried on with our preparations. The effect of matters like this can be skewed depending on the team's eventual fate. The infamous Keady Affair is said to have cost Galway an All-Ireland in 1989, but Keady's replacement,

Seán Treacy, actually played very well against Tipperary in that All-Ireland semi-final and won an All Star. What was much more damaging was the two players they had sent off that day, as they only lost narrowly. So, if Clare won by a point, the fallout would have united them, whereas if they lost by the minimum it would have been viewed as a distraction.

As it was they were clear favourites to win by much more than a single point, but unknown to the hurling world, we had turned a corner under Bond. We weren't quite back to our best, but we had definitely found a rhythm in our training that hadn't been apparent for a couple of years at least. We had been off the radar really since 1995 while Clare had developed into a much more rounded and forceful outfit in the meantime. Maybe they could intimidate the greenhorns from Cork and Waterford that they had blown away in Munster earlier that year, but they wouldn't do that to us. Not with the zone we were now entering. We hadn't been there for a few years and thought we'd left it behind for good. We were still hurt from '95, and the hangover from that defeat played a big part in our decline in the subsequent seasons. Avenging that defeat was certainly on the agenda. Other players felt that Clare's behaviour, when leaving us waiting on the field for a League game earlier that year, had been disrespectful. If we couldn't find an edge against them in '95, there were no such problems in that regard three years on.

Still, we couldn't be sure as to where we were at until we were pitched into battle. Straightaway, however, it felt different out there. We were on another level hurling-wise to what we had been all summer.

On a sweltering day, we were two points up at half-time and, as our confidence surged, I thought we were going to move away from them in the last ten minutes. Then Fergie Tuohy latched onto a breaking ball to score the game's first goal and he followed it up with a point to put them four clear. It was shit or get off the pot at that stage and it's at such times that the drive and determination to redeem ourselves came to the fore, and in pretty ironic circumstances, too.

Johnny Pilkington was spent by this stage of the game and had been sent into corner-forward as I completed his shift at midfield. He batted the ball to the net after Davy Fitzgerald failed to deal with an under-hit free from Johnny Dooley. With time almost up and the sides level he embarked on a run right through the Clare defence and, sensing he was going to be hooked, dropped the ball to the ground off his hurley and majestically arced it over the bar for what looked to be a sensational winning score. Not quite, however. Clare broke forward and referee Jimmy Cooney awarded what seemed a dubious free, from which Jamesie O'Connor equalised, though the referee later insisted it was for an infringement behind a ruck of players by Kevin Kinahan. Cooney blew the final whistle from the resultant puck-out. The replay would fall thirteen days later.

While we obviously would have preferred to win the first day, there was no sense of having blown it on our part. We were improving with every week and we felt another game against Clare was going to elevate us further towards where we wanted to be. For various reasons, though, we were on the back foot before we even got to Croke Park for the replay. Word came through on the morning of the game that Paudie Mulhare's father, Teddy, had passed away. He would also have been a relative of Paudge, our selector. Paudie was one of a bunch of new players, along with the likes of Stephen Byrne, John Ryan, Barry and Simon Whelahan, Gary and Darren Hanniffy, Ger Oakley and Colm Cassidy, who had come onto the panel in the previous couple of years. He was immensely popular within the squad and really came of age that year with a number of stellar displays. Oakley was drafted in to replace him at midfield. However, due to naïve planning on our part, we very nearly didn't even make it to Croke Park on time for the throw-in.

We had never played a Championship game on a Saturday before, yet we left for Croke Park at the time we normally would for a Sunday fixture, failing to take into consideration the traffic on a busy shopping day in Dublin. Having spent an hour crawling through traffic in Dublin, we arrived in the dressing room in a frenzy and just minutes before the game was due to start.

A ceremony was taking place out on the pitch following the Omagh bombing, which occurred the previous Saturday. The Clare players were present but we missed it. Bond had a ritual of running us through tactics and patterns of play he wanted us to observe on a flipboard in plenty of time before we went out, but that was out the window that day.

Although we actually scored the first two points, we were all over the place and Clare weren't long in swamping us throughout the field. The pace of the game seemed to have risen a notch from the drawn game and we were struggling to cope. I was moved out to midfield early on to try and stop the bleeding, but they zoomed clear. We even missed a penalty that would have helped to keep us in touch. Alan Markham got in behind Sid and Simon for a goal, which drove a real wedge between the teams. We just weren't tuned in. At one stage, as I went for the ball in the air, I accidentally pole-axed Ollie Baker with my two knees digging into his back. It's one of the hardest belts I ever hit anyone in a game and I was sure he was finished for the day. But he got back up. I couldn't believe it. He scored the point early in the second half, which put Clare ten points up and there looked to be no way back for us.

Our team had been drastically remodelled by then in an attempt to get us back into the game. For the start of the second half I moved to wing-back as Sid partnered Johnny Dooley at midfield. Neither of them had played there for Offaly in a big game before. Johnny P was up front and, soon after, Sid moved up there, too. I was on Jamesie O'Connor for the first few minutes of the second half. At one stage he pulled about a foot over the ball, what I considered to be a very sly stroke, and took a lump out of my shinbone. Now, that put me at boiling point.

Everything about the day had been crap. We were late getting to the ground, we were hurling poorly, had missed a penalty and were getting hammered. I had just made a routine hand-pass to Hubert Rigney, who fumbled the ball and then Kevin Martin did the same and Clare cleaned out the ruck and scored another point. It was so frustrating, and then I had this fella reddening my shins.

Whatever else happened, Jamesie was going to get it the next chance I got, but then he switched wings and David Forde came over on me. I was turning my back to lay off a hand-pass at one stage when he tried to close me down and his hurley accidentally clipped me across the top of the head. It was as sore as hell and I turned and struck him with the stick across the belly. Anyone who knows me as a player over the years will know that this was grossly out of character. I had taken far worse belts over the years and never reacted, but I was like an anti-Christ at that stage. It was all of my frustration coming to the boil. Having said that, and while it looked terrible, it's probably not the worst place that you can hit someone. When you're fit and strong a blow like that wouldn't take too much out of you, whereas across the knees, shins or head would be a different matter.

I know from watching games myself what the really dirty strokes are, like when a player pulls a second early or pulls over or below the ball. As it was, David got up and ran off straightaway, which was a great help to my cause as I awaited Jimmy Cooney's verdict. As well as David's reaction to the incident, it helped that someone like Jimmy was the referee, as he was a hardy, no-nonsense defender himself. That should have been beside the point, however, as there was no doubt I should have been sent off. It was inexcusable. I've met David Forde a couple of times since and he's a gentleman.

"He's after hitting me on the head!" I said to Jimmy in a desperate attempt for salvation, but that didn't seem to be getting me anywhere. "Jaysus, Jimmy, I was never sent off in my life," I told him, which was true. Still, I was sure he was going to send me off. To my disbelief I escaped with only a booking. I'm convinced Jimmy Cooney the hurler made that decision rather than Jimmy Cooney the referee. He admitted as much in an interview with Jim O'Sullivan in the book Men in Black some years later. The Cooneys are an exceptional hurling family and no doubt Jimmy gave and took worse flakes himself over the years. I didn't have a reputation as a dirty player and I'm sure that informed his decision. Given that we were so far behind, it didn't appear to be a call of major consequence to the outcome of the game on his part. That would come later.

Eventually, we managed to adjust to the pace of the game and gained some sort of foothold. Billy Dooley came off the bench and scored a goal, while Joe Errity converted a penalty. I hurled my way into it and made a run upfield that led to the penalty. As good as that Clare defence was, I always felt that, if you got them on the back foot and forced them to turn, their defensive skills weren't great in terms of hooking and blocking. If you could get in behind them and outwit them they tended to foul a lot. The numerous switches that we made around the field began to click and we now had real momentum entering the closing minutes, with Clare looking over their shoulders all of a sudden.

Over on the Cusack Stand side, Sid's hurley was broken as he contested possession. With the ball at his feet, he magically scooped it up with the bit of the stick he had left in his hand and was then fouled. Another hurley was immediately handed to him with which he converted the free to narrow the gap to three points. He then asked the linesman, Aodhán MacSuibhne, how much time was left and was assured there were a few minutes yet. Moments later, Clare's Barry Murphy had possession in the opposite corner of the field with Kevin Martin shepherding him when Cooney blew the full-time whistle. There weren't yet sixty-eight minutes on the clock.

I didn't realise this at the time but, straightaway, Martin Hanamy was on his case, gesturing at his wrist about the time. I wasn't too far away and I joined in, hoping that the game would be restarted before our momentum sagged. Security men quickly arrived at Cooney's side to usher him away. Kerry and Kildare were due to play in an Under-21 game as the curtain-raiser but it was put back until after our game due to the Omagh ceremony. Their players arrived on the field seconds after the final whistle was blown. Some of our players had already swapped jerseys. Barely a minute or two after his error there was already no chance of the game being restarted. The gates at the Hill 16 end were opened and Offaly supporters streamed out on the field.

I lambasted Cooney as he was escorted to his dressing room. Our All-Ireland chances disappeared down the tunnel with him, I presumed. Having wholeheartedly thrown myself into the argument over the lost time, I then quickly accepted our fate. "We're bet now," I thought as I headed back to the dressing room and had a shower.

· · · · ·

Pilky was usually one of the first to be togged in and I wasn't long after him this time. The two of us went up to the players' lounge for a drink. We were the first in there and he wandered over to the window overlooking the pitch. "Jesus, come here, look at this," he said. The pitch was thronged with Offaly people, who were sitting down in protest at the injustice. The Under-21 match had long been called off at this point. It was some spectacle.

Brendan Ward and Christy Todd eventually came out and were actually booed by our supporters, presumably in connection with how the Babs' situation was handled. Brendan assured the crowd that they were going to "fight this tooth and nail" and the jeers soon turned to cheers. Eventually the crowd dispersed, though many of them had missed their transport home at that point. It was all so spontaneous and very passionate on their part.

Offaly people are generally laid back in comparison to other counties. For example, every time Brian Lohan cleared a ball for Clare it was met with a huge roar from their support. When Kevin Kinahan did the equivalent the response would be much more muted, as if to say, "Well, he's the full-back, sure isn't that what he's there for?" But this was different.

A few drinks after a game like that can go to your head rather quickly and we later repaired to the Spa Hotel in Lucan for the post-match meal. The wives and girlfriends were present and it was decided to have a team meeting at the far end of the room. Talk of a replay was floating around but I wasn't getting too excited over it as I thought it was a pipe dream. We all had a few drinks on board at that stage, but I lost the plot when the idea of training the following day was mentioned. Pilky said he wouldn't be there, and himself and Billy Dooley had a frank exchange of views. Then I butted in and nobody was safe from the vitriol rolling off my tongue in what was a completely irrational outburst.

"Training? You want to go training at four o'clock tomorrow when we're out of the Championship? You wouldn't fucking train when we were in the Championship," I fumed. "Ye were out there today and half of ye didn't give a shit, swanning around and running over balls, and now ye want to train when we're out of the Championship?"

I turned to the county board officers, who I always got on well with, and unleashed my ire on them about gear and expenses and all sorts.

"Ye couldn't even arrange the day properly so that we'd get to Croke Park on time, we nearly missed the fucking match. And ye want us to train tomorrow as well? Ye're all great lads."

With that I leapt out over the table. I think I might have even declared that I'd never play for Offaly again.

"Edel, we're out of here," I said, and stormed out.

What a roller-coaster day it had been. Firstly there was the sad news of Ted Mulhare's death. Then we were nearly late for the match and had played rather poorly for the first fifty minutes or so, and I should have been sent off. We came back and had built up quite a head of steam when the match was ended prematurely. Our supporters launched a spectacular protest on the field as a result. We all went and had a few drinks and I ended up effing everybody out of it.

I woke up the next morning and went down to get the papers. I decided to drop into Kavanagh's for one and the bottle of Bulmers had only landed in front of me when my phone rang. It was Tony Murphy, the team secretary and outrageous sneer.

"How are you keeping? How's things? What sort of form are you in this morning?"

"Tony, what the hell do you want?" I snapped.

"Ah, but how are you getting on? How are you keeping? In better form this morning?"

"What's this all about, Tony?"

"We're going to do a bit of training at four o'clock. Would you come down for it?"

"Ah, Tony, I told you last night – what are we going training for and we out of the Championship?"

"Ah, but we're not out of the Championship. We're playing Clare next Saturday down in Thurles..."

"What?"

"Yeah, we've a replay."

The bottle of Bulmers went untouched as I raced home and got my gear together. Unlike the terrible injustice that Louth suffered in the 2010 Leinster football final, this scenario was provided for in the rule book in that, if a game was incomplete, it would have to be re-fixed for the full seventy minutes. It later emerged that Jimmy Cooney had played a thirty-minute half plus three minutes of injury time so, in total, he was five minutes short. However, when making my outburst the night before, it was fuelled by the fact that I presumed we wouldn't be together as a group for a number of months rather than a day later. I tiptoed into the dressing room anyway. "Howeya lads..." but it was quiet enough. John Ryan was never slow to seize an opportunity like this. He reached for a tracksuit and presented it to me.

"There you are," he says. "The way you're hurling you'll be needing it shortly!"

It broke the ice straightaway and we quickly knuckled down to preparing for the re-fixture.

Brian Whelahan later said that he was certain we'd win once he heard we were granted the replay but that wasn't in my thinking, though naturally I was confident. Clare had been gracious in agreeing to the re-fixture, and the word was that Colin Lynch would earn a reprieve as a result. I was sure they'd have him back but it didn't come to pass. I was enthused by the prospect of both teams going at it at full strength for seventy minutes in Thurles. Jimmy Cooney declined the opportunity to take charge of the game and, instead, it was passed to Dickie Murphy.

After three games Bond was getting closer to his strongest line-up and the team was well balanced for the third game of the series, with Clare with Billy Dooley and Joe Errity coming into the side from the start. We trained in Thurles once that week and Paudge pulled a stroke by asking the groundsman which dugout Clare preferred to use. When they emerged on the field the following Saturday all our spare hurleys and gear were laid out at that dugout. It's only a small thing but it shows how sharp Paudge was in his thinking.

A huge crowd turned out at the other night's training in Tullamore. We had a bit of a chat down the far end of the field when the session was finished and then turned to walk to the opposite corner, where the tunnel leading to the dressing rooms was. As we walked the crowd converged around the tunnel and began clapping and cheering for us as we approached. I felt very strongly about what our supporters had done the previous Saturday in Croke Park. It created what felt like an unbreakable bond.

My wrist was heavily strapped at the time having taken a belt, but I raised my fist defiantly to the crowd as we approached the tunnel and they went ballistic. Whatever about us, our supporters were definitely ready for action. There was a satisfaction that we were back in the zone as a team, where we hadn't really been for three years. It seemed as though time had passed us by and we'd blown our potential but now we were back and it felt terrific, with every man, woman and child in the county four-square behind us like never before.

With Ted Mulhare's wake and burial, as well as training, we spent most of that week together and all we thought about was hurling. For the 1984 All-

Ireland final, the Offaly lads felt they had erred by getting caught up in the hoopla around the town before the final, but now we embraced it. The square was packed with Offaly and Clare people and we had our pre-match meal in Hayes's Hotel, right in the thick of it. We were in a mood that was somewhat similar to the hours before the 1995 Leinster final, but not nearly as intense. We were more relaxed and comfortable in our skins.

At one stage Bond called me to one side for a word. "You could be in line for some heavy treatment from the Clare crowd today. Be ready for it," he warned me. My initial reaction to that was to think, "That doesn't happen in hurling," but after a few minutes it came around to, "Well, maybe it will happen. Sure, so what if it does."

Unbeknownst to me, Ger Loughnane posted a picture in the Clare dressing room of me striking David Forde the previous Saturday, saying, "Are we going to let that beat us?" before they went out on the field. The first ball that came my way coincided with a deafening chorus of boos. For me it encapsulated just how brilliant a manager Bond was. "Jaysus, he's sharp," I thought, "how did he know that?" It was excellent management because I was prepared for it and it didn't bother me in the slightest. In fact, I fed off it.

It can't have been easy for Clare going into the game because they must have been presuming they were in the All-Ireland final the previous Saturday night and, suddenly, they weren't. I don't fully accept though that it put them on the back foot approaching the game in Thurles, because they had a week to recharge the batteries and they still played very well for what turned out to be the game of the year.

Both sides were at, or near, their best in what was an enthralling contest. Once again we started well with four points without reply only for Clare to hit back with five on the trot. As opposed to '95, when we weren't prepared and rolled over, this time we matched them everywhere, including on the terraces.

We were two points ahead coming up to half-time when Ollie Baker committed a chop down on Brian Whelahan's hand as he completed yet another clearance in what was one of his most influential performances. Baker was booked, though fortunate not to be sent off, while Sid had treatment for a couple of minutes. Then he strode forward and belted the resultant free over the bar from where the ball landed, to give us a three-point lead at half-time.

Many people identify that as a key moment in the game, and it probably was. But it was a big moment when he got up off the floor in the first place. That incident also marked the end of the Clare crowd's booing of me. Like me, Baker wasn't a dirty player by nature and I think they realised that their man was lucky to get away with it, just as I was the previous week.

The game continued to ebb and flow in the second half but we held the whip hand for the most part. I remember one sequence, when Johnny Pilkington chased Alan Markham down in possession, and it summed up what Offaly hurling is all about. I always felt Johnny, along with DJ Carey, was one of the hardest men in the game to get away from. He wasn't going to jump up on Markham's back and foul him, he was just going to track him and hook him and not let him get his shot away. As it was the ball broke to allow Clare a shot on goal but Stephen Byrne pulled off one of several great saves he made that day.

Paudie Mulhare started the game but came off before half-time having, understandably, not been himself with the week he had endured. Gary Hanniffy came in and came of age, scoring three crucial points. Johnny Dooley scored a point that I'll never forget. His original effort was blocked but the ball came straight back to him and, with barely any space to swing, he lofted the ball over the bar from some seventy yards. Joe Dooley had his finest day in an Offaly jersey with five points from play from various angles and distances. A lot of lads played well and had to play well. It was serious stuff out there.

When the final whistle sounded we had won by three points and, not yet two months after we were managerless, were back in the All-Ireland final. It was such a special day and one of the standout moments in my career. After all we had been through that summer, to go down to Thurles and beat the Munster champions in such a great game to round off an epic trilogy was immense.

It didn't make up for losing to them three years earlier – nothing ever could – but it certainly helped. It can't have been easy for Clare but they handled themselves with good grace afterwards. Loughnane was gushing in his praise of Offaly hurling, saying that if they had to choose a team to lose to it would be us as our breakthrough in the early-'80s ploughed a furrow for them to follow.

For all that, we had won nothing yet and, with all the delirium that was engulfing the county, we had to be careful not to get carried away. We were experienced enough not to let that happen at that stage of our careers, though we still had to be mindful of the younger players in the group.

Given that the series with Clare stretched into late August we only had two weeks to prepare for the final against Kilkenny, who had beaten Waterford in the other semi-final. I'd say it's the only time in my career I wasn't in any way worried about playing them. We were on a roll and, as I said, virtually professional hurlers for those number of weeks, and were just able to keep it going for another couple of weeks to take us up to the final. I'm not sure we could have done it for much longer. With a carnival atmosphere at some of our training sessions, Bond took us down to Thurles again for a session ahead of the final. There was always a great sense of peace and quiet there.

Having started the 1994 final on the bench, a freak incident on the Thursday before the final almost ruled me out this time. I have had a bit of trouble with my back over the years and, as I got out of the car for our last session before the game, I twinged it and was barely able to move. Luckily the team doctor, Brendan Lee, was nearby and took me to his surgery immediately.

Brendan is well-known for treating back trouble and he set to work on me, with the vertabrae in my back crackling as he tried to realign everything. "You're going to be very sore tomorrow but you'll be perfect on Saturday," he told me. Mercifully, that's exactly how it turned out.

I went back up the field and passed myself but didn't take part in the session. I was named at midfield but would play at right half-forward in a swap with Johnny Dooley, who would see out the rest of his career there on the back of being shifted to that position as a crisis measure during the second game against Clare. It was actually the perfect position for him because he could influence the game more and still pick up his two or three points from play, such was the quality of his striking.

While we appeared to have much greater momentum going into the final than Kilkenny, it can work both ways. Had we lost, it would have been said that the Clare games took too much out of us and Kilkenny were coming in nicely under the radar. Many presumed that Clare would have too much power and fitness for us but we were well stocked in that regard from the work that Johnny Murray had done with us. The three games bolstered us further, and we were fortunate that we didn't pick up any serious injuries as we went along.

Kilkenny were managed by Kevin Fennelly, who tended to talk a lot and seemed from an early stage that year to be extremely confident that Kilkenny would win the All-Ireland, I've met him a couple of times since and he's a nice fella, but, back then, he struck me as being a little bit arrogant. Maybe that's to be expected, given all that the Fennellys won together with club and county.

While Kilkenny have since gone on to dominate hurling with the greatest side any of us has ever seen, this team was no pushover either, particularly when you consider some of the players they had, such as Pat O'Neill, Willie O'Connor, Michael Kavanagh and Liam Keoghan in defence, Peter Barry and Philly Larkin at midfield and DJ Carey, PJ Delaney, Charlie Carter and Andy Comerford up front. They had no shortage of flair. With all that happened in '98, between Clare's battles with the authorities and our fallout with Babs, followed by the three games between us, not to mention Waterford's breakthrough, the final that year has largely been forgotten despite the fact that, as All-Ireland finals go, it was a great game. It certainly bore no relation to the Leinster final a couple of months earlier.

That morning we arrived in the Spa Hotel as usual and Brian Whelahan was looking rather pale. He hadn't been well since the day before, having come down with a dose of 'flu. There was never any question that he wouldn't start the game, though. He was marking Brian McEvoy who, at that stage, was an unheralded member of the Kilkenny attack but he became a key player for them over the next few years, and I think his performance that day was the catalyst. He scored Kilkenny's first point from play after a DJ free and we were struggling to settle in the opening stages, had hit a couple of wides and were generally wasteful with possession. I swivelled away from Philly Larkin to score our opening point after a few minutes and I genuinely believe it was the most important score of my entire career. It helped to settle us and Joe Dooley quickly equalised, and then Joe Errity put us ahead. Charlie Carter responded with a goal for Kilkenny, but by then we were in the game and took it in our stride.

However, McEvoy was proving to be a real handful and added another point after a previous effort by him from out on the sideline had just drifted narrowly wide. Given that his switch up front had worked during the Clare games, and sensing that Sid was under pressure, the management decided to swap him with me once again and I was sent back to shackle McEvoy.

However, I wonder were the management overreacting somewhat to Sid's predicament, given that he hadn't been well that morning. With the form McEvoy was in that day, anyone would have had trouble keeping tabs on him. Although Sid was a brilliant defender, he wasn't a man-marker per se. Had he performed that role for us over the years, rather than sweeping and covering throughout the back line, his value to the team would have been diminished. His ability to read the game saved a certain goal while he was still in defence early on and summed up his worth to us.

Ken O'Shea played a cross-field pass, which broke nicely for PJ Delaney, who scooped it towards goal from a couple of yards out but Whelahan was there on the line to block it. Where did he come from? What was he doing there? I most certainly wouldn't have been in that position if I had been switched to wing-back by then. The ball was cleared only as far as McEvoy, who popped over his second point of the game. However, Whelahan's positioning meant that we had conceded just one point instead of a goal from that passage of play, even if it was his man that got the score.

When I went back on McEvoy my remit was simply to stick to him and curb his influence. The other five backs could look after their own patch. It took me a while, though. He added another point after I picked him up and won a free, which DJ converted. On another day, if he wasn't ill, the management might have concluded that Sid would sort it out for himself, as he often did, but the move up front took the pressure off him. He worked his way into the game coming up to half-time, setting up a point for John Troy, who typically caught the pass with his wrong hand but quickly acquired the technique to split the posts regardless. Sid added his first point from play shortly after and we were two down at the break.

He moved from the wing to full-forward for the start of the second half and Troy returned the compliment by delightfully stroking a sideline ball into his hand from which he pointed. We began to find a rhythm to our play, helped by some tenacious defending at the other end. At one stage there was a remarkable sequence of blocks by Kevin Martin twice on Comerford, followed immediately by Simon Whelahan on Carter. I was tight on McEvoy and, although he still had his moments, he wasn't as influential as he was in the first half. I was blocking and tipping balls away from him and eventually started beating him to the fifty-fifty breaks.

Joe Errity barrelled through and scored a brilliant goal from a drop-shot to put us three points ahead. We retained that lead when Kilkenny won a penalty entering the final ten minutes after Hanamy had pulled Delaney's helmet off. There was a peculiar swirling wind in Croke Park that day and, by that stage, it was in Kilkenny's favour. As DJ prepared to take the penalty I remember thinking, "If he hits this at all it's a goal". His shot whistled just over the bar. A DJ goal to bring them level at that stage in the game would have been a huge fillip for them. Pilky scored a point for us just as we thought we might be getting away from them but then Larkin popped one over for them from the puck-out. They weren't going away.

Typically, Sid made the critical contribution. He danced away from Pat O'Neill and Tom Hickey for a glorious point and then sealed victory for us when he stabbed the ball to the net after Errity skewed a shot for his second goal. With time almost up we could savour the prospect of beating our greatest rivals, Kilkenny, in an All-Ireland final, two months after they had beaten us in the Leinster final. From our lowest ebb, and after all the events that had formed such a tumultuous year, we were about to be crowned All-Ireland champions. All of this swept through my mind as Pat O'Neill launched a clearance down my wing.

• • • • •

The catch...

I remember the first ball that was ever sent careering in my direction. I first reported to the hurling field in Banagher, just at the bottom of our road, for training at about eight years of age. It was a wet evening and one lad, who was particularly big for his age, doubled on a ball perfectly and it hit me flush on the side of the head. My ear was throbbing and I ran out of the field in floods of tears. When I got to our front door, however, I reconsidered my

Heading for goal in Croke Park. There's no feeling like it!

Johnny Pilkington and Martin Storey of Wexford in the Leinster final in 1994.

Daithí Regan wins possession ahead of Galway's Liam Burke in the 1994 All-Ireland semi-final.

Johnny Dooley strikes a penalty early in the 1994 All-Ireland final. Joe Quaid saved his shot though another Dooley, Joe, was on hand to bury the rebound.

The Offaly team before the 1994 All-Ireland final with Limerick. Although I didn't make the starting line-up, it was a turning point in my career.

Martin Hanamy lifts the Liam MacCarthy Cup after our sensational victory over Limerick.

Tackling Jamesie O'Connor in the 1995 All-Ireland final.

Johnny Dooley comes under pressure from the Clare defence.

Things look good in the '95 All-Ireland final after Johnny Pilkington scores his goal.

Clare 'keeper, Davy Fitzgerald, shows his delight at finally landing the Liam MacCarthy Cup.

Our three great tussles with Clare in the 1998 All-Ireland semi-final started on August 9 and didn't end until our third meeting, a refixture, on August 29. In between, there was the extraordinary 'sit-down protest' by our supporters, which helped to form an unbreakable bond between them and all of the players. Here I am in the first game trying to halt the great Ollie Baker.

Ger Loughnane, Clare's irrepressible manager, gives instructions despite being confined to the stand.

An aerial dogfight between Kevin Kinahan and Ger O'Loughlin.

Offaly chairman, Brendan Ward, asks our supporters to leave the field after the premature ending of the replay against Clare. He also promised everyone: 'We're going to fight this tooth and nail!'

Referee Jimmy Cooney is escorted off the field at 'the end' of the replay against Clare in '98.

I read the riot act to referee Jimmy Cooney after he blew up our semi-final with Clare too early. I apologised to him years later!

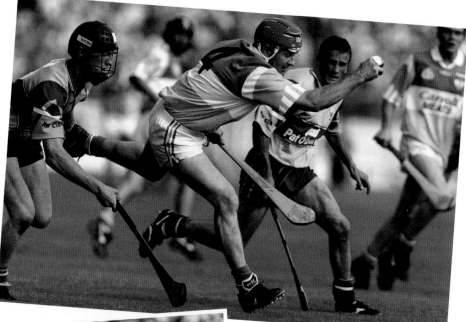

Martin Hanamy grabs the ball in the re-fixture against Clare.

Brian Whelahan and Alan Markham tussle in the same game.

At last, we have Clare behind us in 1998, and an All-Ireland final in front of us. Johnny Pilkington is carried shoulder-high from the field.

The Offaly team which started the 1998
All-Ireland final against Kilkenny.

Joe Dooley, at 34, enjoyed his finest season in 1998. Here, he
powers past the attentions of Tom Hickey in the final.

A DJ Carey penalty goes over the bar in the final.

Our manager, Michael Bond, came in and picked up the pieces after Babs Keating's resignation.

It sometimes felt that the Offaly players and Babs Keating were going in opposite directions.

We have Kilkenny on the run after our second goal in the '98 All-Ireland final.

Being challenged by Charlie Carter in the '98 final.

Hubert Rigney lifts the Liam MacCarthy Cup after a sensational summer.

I win the ball from Brian Corcoran of Cork in the 2000 All-Ireland semi-final.

The Offaly team which lined out against Kilkenny in the 2000 All-Ireland final.

The redoubtable Paudge Mulhare.

Johnny Dooley leads the team in the pre-match parade.

Kevin Martin chases down John Power in the 2000 final.

Willie O'Connor gets his hands on the MacCarthy Cup.

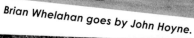

Brian Whelahan goes by John Hoyne.

DJ Carey scores Kilkenny's opening goal. We could see the relief coursing through the Kilkenny team after that.

I started my inter-county managerial career with Meath. Here I am watching the team against Dublin in 2002.

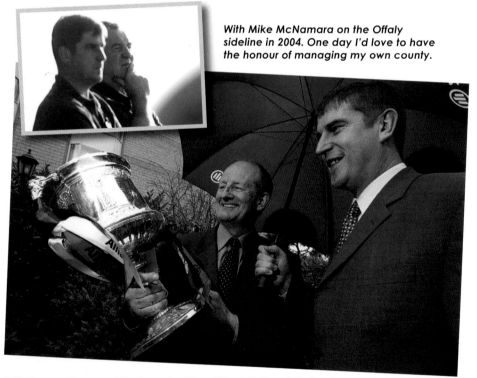

With Mike McNamara on the Offaly sideline in 2004. One day I'd love to have the honour of managing my own county.

With Eamon Cregan at the launch of the Allianz National Hurling League in 2002. We played our best hurling during his four-year spell in charge of Offaly.

options. If I went in whining about what had happened I certainly wouldn't have got any sympathy. "Sure, stay at home so," my father might say, "don't come around here crying about it." So I remounted my bicycle and returned to the field. I've always felt that I was tough and didn't want to give in that easily. It's a trait that served me well and, thankfully, I shared dressing rooms with lots of other players of similar ilk.

McEvoy had dropped deep to forage for possession by then. I caught the ball ahead of the inrushing PJ Delaney and moved forward.

The solo run...

Pat Joe Whelahan instilled great confidence in us as minors in 1986. He encouraged us to express ourselves and play without fear of any opponent. If the opportunity was there for us to take on a man and run with the ball to create space elsewhere, then go for it. We practised solo runs in training quite a lot under Pat Joe, something I don't recall doing to any great extent under any other manager. It's a fairly basic skill, but Pat Joe would incorporate it as much as he could to take the monotony off the physical training. His philosophy was that, when you're running in a match, you're generally running with the ball, so why not train like so? During a fifty-yard sprint, he'd throw a ball out in front of you. Much of that drive, in terms of showing no fear of your opponent, would have been instilled in me in Rynagh's from an early age by Tommy Fogarty and Jackie Ryland. You had to have that, along with guts and heart and determination, something our club was famed for, as a basic foundation before you could develop the confidence to be flamboyant.

McEvoy approached me as I accelerated with the ball on my hurley. I took the ball to hand and went past him as I continued my run.

The power...

Labouring in Boston in the summer of 1987 helped to bulk me up considerably. It was hard work, starting at five o'clock in the morning with Eamon Meehan. Temperatures could sometimes hit one hundred degrees and we'd have to finish by about three o'clock in the afternoon due to the heat, as the plaster wouldn't stick to the walls. On top of that we trained three or four times a week with a game most weekends. The hurling out there was tough and uncompromising and teenagers like Daithí and myself weren't spared. Some players out there had big reputations and were fond of mouthing and throwing their weight around, particularly when it came to young lads just out of minor, like we were. Let's just say they were dealt with according to the laws of the jungle. Working hard and playing hard in those conditions stood to me big time. A few weeks after I got home we played Seir Kieran in the county final. Towards the end of the game I gained possession in our half of the field and embarked on a lengthy solo run. As I progressed, I saw Eugene Coughlan emerging from full-back to meet me. I took the ball in my hand, flattened him and kept going. The year before he would have landed me on the embankment. I went to Boston that summer a boy and came home a man.

Philly Larkin advanced to try and make a challenge but couldn't get near me as I powered on straight down the middle.

The strike...

John Molloy was a key player in my development as a hurler in Garbally. He noticed how my striking technique was unconventional in that I would throw the ball up with my left hand and then place that hand at the top of the hurley as I struck it, rather than use my right hand as the pivot, as virtually every right-handed player would do. He forced me to change and often had me practising at the back of the class. I eventually mastered it and felt it was hugely significant. It only saved me a split second but, at the highest level, that's what makes the difference. Some players, like Gary Kirby and Kilkenny's Aidan Fogarty, have managed to get away with it. I don't know how my left-hand side would have developed otherwise but I probably would have been much more right-sided. I was never the most skilful player so I felt that all of the basics had to be in place for me to make it to the top. John Molloy's attention to detail facilitated that in a big way.

Having already caught the ball twice, I had to hit it or lay it off because Peter Barry was now moving in to cut off the channel of attack. Turning on my left-hand side, I struck the ball clean off the hurley from about fifty-five yards. It flew over the bar.

• • • • •

And that was my moment. I had been building towards something like this for my entire life and here it was now, at thirty years of age. The culmination. I had a determination from a young age to reach the very top level, which was winning All-Irelands with Offaly, and now it was all coming together for me. The frustration of failing to kick on from the three Leinster titles we won very early in my career. Early Championship exits and injuries in the years after that forcing me to prove myself all over again. Failing to make the team for the '94 All-Ireland final. Re-establishing myself in '95 only to lose the final to Clare. The team apparently on the wane following that traumatic setback. Babs coming and going. The three games with Clare and being fortunate to avoid dismissal by Jimmy Cooney. Losing to Kilkenny in the Leinster final and now turning the tables on them to become the first "back door" All-Ireland champions. Moving back and curbing their dangerman in the final. All those years of training since I first went to the field in Banagher, and the sacrifices that went with it. My whole career flashed in front of me as I scored that point. It was almost like an out-of-body experience. I spontaneously jumped in the air in a Riverdance-like celebration.

The lads slag me now, saying that they knew we had the All-Ireland won when they saw me scoring a point straight off the hurley on my left-hand side. Before the final whistle Kevin Martin actually embarked on a run himself, brilliantly flicking the ball over Barry's head before running around him and meeting it on the hurley. Thankfully, his shot tailed off, otherwise my score would never have been talked about! The final whistle soon sounded to bring an end to the most incredible year in the history of the hurling Championship.

Hubert Rigney, our captain, collected the cup from GAA President Joe McDonagh and declared, "We may have gone in the back door, but we're coming out the front!" For someone who was rather quiet and withdrawn, Hubie handled himself exceptionally well in his various duties once we won and probably surprised a lot of people. He was shy but a very capable man in whatever he did. He was very strong, mentally as well as physically, and had a great presence as captain.

I met Edel in the players' lounge after the game and we embraced. She knew more than anyone what this meant. The function that night was absolutely brilliant. Often, on occasions like that, you're too tired to take it all in but I savoured every moment. Brian Whelahan got man-of-the-match, having scored 1-6, though many people thought I should have got it, something I could never understand. Sid even told me as much as he went up to collect his award. But, no, this was a day when he franked his greatness ever more. Ger Canning conducted a live interview with Johnny Pilkington for the Sunday Game and finished by asking him what he thought Babs Keating might say if he was present.

"Ah, sure, he might say we're not a bad oul flock!" Johnny replied, quick as a flash.

Waking up the following morning after achieving something like that is always the sweetest feeling. We went to Doheny and Nesbitt's again and word came through that the Pat Kenny show on RTÉ Radio wanted one of us to come on air. Pilky was put forward and disappeared to a quieter part of the pub while we all listened attentively to the interview. He was more or less taking the piss as he went along.

"The question," Kenny addressed Johnny at the end of the interview, "on everybody's lips around the country this morning: is this man Michael Bond going to stay on next year?"

"I don't know," says Johnny, "I haven't decided yet!"

Well, we erupted with the laughter. Only Johnny could think of it.

The festivities didn't end there and we went on to have what could only be described as the greatest week of all time. The crowd in Tullamore that greeted us when we arrived back on the train was breathtaking. We eventually moved on to Birr, where we saw the night out, and the atmosphere was incredible. Hubie brought the cup back to Banagher the following night and I'd say it was the best night the town ever experienced. I certainly never had a night like it. We were in Corrigan's and ended up in Simon's where each player was cheered as the crowd sang their name. The place was heaving. "There's only one Johnny Pilkington, there's only..." The singing came to an abrupt halt when Pilky fell backwards off someone's shoulders and there was an awful crack as he hit the ground. Everyone went quiet. Next thing he jumped to his feet with a smile. "... one Johnny Pilkington," as the singing picked up seamlessly once again. It was priceless. You have to squeeze every last moment of enjoyment out of times like this.

We weren't yet home when we were signing autographs for kids going to school the next morning. Sleep could wait. The Wednesday night was spent in Killyon, near Clareen. All the Coughlans were there, as happy as when they won their own All-Irelands in the '80s. I thought that was brilliant because not all of the past greats like to see their legacies challenged. Paddy Connors, a giant of the club scene who played with Seir Kieran, was there too. As the night wore on I could see him looking over and I thought to myself, "God he's a thick man. He wouldn't even come over and say well done". Eventually we got talking and it was hilarious. He explained to me how his son had asked him to get my autograph. "I will in me hole," says Paddy back to him. "In a couple of weeks he'll be making a fool out of me in a county final." Sure enough, a few weeks later he was marking me in the county final and the first ball I went for, he nearly took the head off me. "Autograph that!" he growled.

By the Thursday morning I was in ribbons but Eunan Martin, son of Damien, who was also on the panel, ordered me out of bed to go to the schools with the cup. Afterwards we had a few quiet pints in Simon's, the first opportunity we had to relax without the back-slapping. We moved on to Cloghan to bring the cup to Sod's father, James, who wasn't well at the time. It gave him a great lift. There was a meal for us in the Bridge House that night but John Ryan announced that he was off to football training in Shannonbridge after God knows how many pints and that he'd meet us in Cloghan afterwards before moving on to Tullamore. They had a game that weekend in the latter stages of the County Championship.

Another epic night ensued in the Bridge House and, long after the bar was closed, Ryan managed to place an order for the two of us that involved "two Southern Comforts and red, two Tia Maria and milk, two Baileys on ice ... and two bottles of Bulmers just to wash it all down!" The following night came the GOAL Challenge in Birr against the Rest of Leinster. A few of the Kilkenny lads showed up, to their credit, and we somehow pulled a draw out of it. The week was rounded off in Shannonbridge that Sunday night and I stepped back into reality as I returned to work the next morning.

Before the year was out I won my first and only All Star award. Generally I'm not a big fan of these awards and, in fact, the man-of-the-match concept is not something that sits comfortably with me either. Some of the All Star selections are very strange from time to time and you'd have to question the credentials of some of the selectors. I was nominated a few times over the years, though not in 1995 when I thought I should have been very close to getting the award itself. Having said all that, I'm happy that I got one and it was nice that Joe Dooley and I received ours together having soldiered together for so long.

It would nearly have been too good to be true to add a county medal and so it proved as Seir Kieran got the better of us in a replay. It was hard to believe though that all of these things happened in the one calendar year, including winning the Towns Cup with Naas. I was aware that there might never be a time in my life like that again and, although we made a decent fist of it as a team in the following two seasons, that's how it turned out. At that stage I was thirty, flying fit and both Edel and I were in good jobs. We had just become parents and had settled really well in Naas. It doesn't get much better than that.

I've met Babs Keating a few times since at golf outings and there was no problem between us. To be fair, he's not that sort of person anyway. Maybe deep down he's regretful because, if things had worked out differently, he could have managed us to win an All-Ireland, though you'd have to doubt whether it would have come to pass with him in charge. I would acknowledge that he had his good points in terms of player welfare but, ultimately, I felt his heart wasn't in the job.

He later said that the comments he made about us wouldn't have offended people and players in the more traditional hurling counties, but that was proven incorrect by his most recent stint as Tipperary manager a few years back when he shot his mouth off far too often and really annoyed some of the players. Just like '98, he was left with egg on his face once again when Liam Sheedy guided them to the All-Ireland in 2010 following further scathing criticism by him after they lost to Cork in the Munster Championship.

I've got to know a number of the Clare lads over the years, particularly

Anthony Daly. They were a very special team that I have great respect for. Events of that year still come out in conversation every now and then between Dalo and myself. There's a bit of bite there and it's an easy way to get him going. They feel they were hard done by, but who's to say what would have happened if Jimmy Cooney had played the extra five minutes he should have that day? Obviously, with Clare three points in front, they looked more likely to win but we would have been in a similar position had he blown up early in the drawn game. The same in 1995 when we led in the last few minutes only for them to outscore us by 1-2 to 0-1 to win by two points. Look what happened in '94 when we beat Limerick. You just don't know.

Ger Loughnane put an uneven slant on things in his book when he claimed that Barry Murphy was bearing down on goal preparing to shoot when the final whistle sounded. Wildly inaccurate, as Murphy was over by the sideline with Kevin Martin shielding him from goal. While Ger took what happened at the time with good grace, and said that it was purely down to human error, he let himself down in 2005 when he revisited the Jimmy Cooney incident. It was an unnecessary and cruel dig at Cooney, heaping fresh misery on a man who had already suffered enough.

It coincided with my very first newspaper column and, while I defended Cooney, I still had an itch I needed to scratch in relation to the whole incident years earlier. I was quick to criticise him in the immediate aftermath of it as he left the field, and he said in the book, Men in Black, that I ought to have been the last person on his case after he had rather charitably decided against sending me off. I felt terribly guilty about that but, with the way things panned out, it never even occurred to me at the time that he should have sent me off twenty minutes earlier. I often thought of making contact with him. Initially I felt it was too raw and then I thought it might be patronising. After all, what was I going to say, "Thanks for not sending me off"?

In 2010, I was at the Galway Races, slipping out to the toilet, when I saw him. The easy thing to do would have been to duck away but I approached him. Well, we had a mighty chat. I told him how sorry I was at how things had turned out for him and apologised for having a go at him. His refereeing career had finished up shortly afterwards and he was on the receiving end of serious abuse in terms of crank phone calls and poisonous letters for several years afterwards. He was very gracious and his wife and children were ever so friendly, too. "You had nothing to do with it," he told me. I felt brilliant at having had that conversation with him. He was a thorough gentleman and was complimentary of me as both a player and a pundit. We parted on good terms and, as I walked away, a certain weight had been lifted from my shoulders. Twelve years on I had tied up the final loose end in what was the most the extraordinary year I have ever known.

Chapter 10

Ennis, May, 2000

Michael Bond hummed and hawed about staying on beyond the end of the 1998 campaign, for which he had only been appointed in a caretaker capacity. There was never any great doubt that he would, though. We had a phenomenal team holiday to South Africa in January, 1999. I was on five different trips over the years with the team, four for each of the All-Ireland finals we reached and then another for the Leinster three in a row from 1988-90, but this one topped the lot. There was little chance that any of us would go somewhere like that on an ordinary family holiday. It was so exotic, a perfect climate with little humidity and the food was amazing.

We visited Robben Island and Table Mountain, which I found fascinating. The guides are all ex-prisoners so we got an excellent insight. To observe the conditions in which Nelson Mandela served out a twenty-seven year sentence was humbling, not to mention the stories of how prisoners had notes smuggled in to allow them to further their education. Poverty and crime was rampant out there and the divide between the races was plain to see. We were playing golf one day and there were a few black men working on the green. We were waiting for them to move so that we could play our shots and one of the course officials, a white man of course, encouraged us to carry on regardless. If we hit them, we hit them.

One of the highlights of the trip was a visit to the Stellenbosch wine region. When tasting the wine some people swirled it in their mouths before releasing it, but none of our lads were spitting it out! We actually had a wine-drinking competition, with John Troy crowned the winner. That was the backdrop to what was probably his finest year in an Offaly jersey.

We were fortunate in 1998 that we didn't pick up many injuries, and none at all for the Clare and Kilkenny games. That wasn't the case in 1999. When the team was named for our opening Championship game against Wexford there were three vacancies, one of which related to myself. Throughout that year and the next I was constantly on and off the treatment table with hamstring problems, something that I ascribe to back trouble, playing too much too young, as well as the years of driving to and from training. I was deemed fit to line out against Wexford and played quite well, scoring one of three first-half goals that set us on the way to a comprehensive eleven-point victory.

Liam Dunne was just back from a cruciate ligament knee injury and claimed in his book that I had deliberately tested the strength of his knee early on. If I did that was certainly never my intention. I have huge respect for him as a hurler but I thought he and Martin Storey let themselves down in a Laochra Gael programme on TG4 a few years back when they virtually reconstructed the incident with John Troy that led to Dunne being red-carded against us in 2000. It was very disrespectful to Troy who, regardless of the history they had, didn't go out to get him sent off. Liam pulled the stroke of his own accord, and did it plenty of times before and after that in his career.

Kilkenny were waiting for us in the Leinster final, their first under the management of Brian Cody. They had everything to play for considering we had beaten them in the previous year's All-Ireland final whereas, again, I think we were affected by the fact that there wasn't a knockout element there. Under Cody you could see they were better organised, more focused and exploited our defence as a point of weakness. We still retained five of the six backs that won the 1994 All-Ireland and, while they were generally imperious over the years, Cody obviously reckoned that, collectively, we were losing that half yard of pace at the back. They ruthlessly went for goal with every chance they got and put five past us that day and ran out ten-point winners. It sent us into another All-Ireland quarter-final against Antrim, which we won easily to set up a semi-final meeting with a sprightly young Cork team. In atrocious conditions, it went down as one of the games of the decade.

We were excited about playing Cork because we hadn't come across them before. Kilkenny were the only one of the big three that we played regularly. Cork and Tipperary generally weren't reaching the latter end of the Championship when we were at our peak. Cork were back, though, with a team whose average age was twenty-two, so we were giving away a lot in that regard. It was probably the only time that we were beaten when Brian Whelahan was on the top of his game. We were a point up at half-time, though Cork powered ahead early in the second half. We recovered after a brilliant Johnny Pilkington score to lead by two points entering the last ten minutes.

I was left half-forward, alongside John Ryan and Paudie Mulhare in the half-forward line. The three of us had carried out our tasks reasonably well and scored a point each. I felt I had curbed Wayne Sherlock's influence on the game. Critically, having gone ahead, we made a substitution, Gary Hanniffy for John Ryan, which resulted in several positional switches that I felt upset the balance of the team. I was sent to the other wing on Seán Óg Ó hAilpín. At that stage I was thirty-one, had been troubled by hamstrings all year and here I was on an athlete like him in the last ten minutes of an All-Ireland semi-final. There was only going to be one winner to a breaking ball between us at that stage. Another critical aspect was that we tired. Bond had taken charge of the physical training that year and it wasn't near as tough as Johnny Murray's regime. After the final in 1998 I felt I could have gone and played another seventy minutes straightaway, but we were running on empty in those last few minutes against Cork. They picked us off with five unanswered points.

Our old friend Dickie Murphy was officiating that day and we were furious at how he handled the game. Several debatable decisions went in Cork's favour, the most obvious of which was John Troy's ingenious dispossession of Brian Corcoran, flicking the ball off his hurley and scoring a point only to find that Dickie had awarded a free out. In such a tight game, some of his calls were crucial to the flow of what was a magnificent contest. Our chairman Brendan Ward lashed out at him in the media that week, which wouldn't have been Brendan's form. As it turned out, he never refereed another All-Ireland final and only took charge of one semi-final, which was six years later. He didn't take charge of another Offaly Championship game until 2009, coincidentally against Cork in the qualifiers.

It was a heartbreaking defeat to take and I couldn't see a way back for us at that stage. We had often played worse in big games and won comfortably.

Cork went on to beat Kilkenny in the final, something we would definitely have fancied doing ourselves in the circumstances. While we weren't fully wound up for the Leinster final, we most certainly would have been for the All-Ireland. But that's all conjecture.

Bond stepped down and I was sorry to see him go. While his physical training contributed to our defeat, his sessions in the summer time were excellent and there was a great spirit among the group. I considered retirement at that stage myself but those thoughts were soon shelved when I heard that Pat Fleury was taking over. Pat was hugely respected by us as a group. He was like an embodiment of Offaly hurling.

He spoke to us the week of the third game against Clare in 1998 and we didn't take our game faces off until the final whistle sounded a few days later. He was so passionate about Offaly hurling and I was prepared to go through a housing estate's worth of brick walls for him. With all the managerial comings and goings over the years, I often wonder how things might have turned out if we had Fleury as manager four or five years earlier. By the time he took over we were going but weren't gone yet. He brought Pat Cleary and Ger Coughlan with him as selectors, two men I also had high admiration for, while Tom Donohue was an extremely efficient physical trainer and brought a bit of craic to the set-up as well. If we were growing old as hurlers at the time, we certainly weren't as party animals, however. A few weeks before the Championship a challenge game was arranged against Clare in Ennis and Fleury told us that we'd all have a few pints after it. I approached him afterwards.

"Pat, are you for real? It's bad enough going to Ennis for the weekend but to tell the lads we're going on the beer afterwards? If you said there was no drinking they'd still have a few." Having given us the imprimatur to let our hair down, there was likely to be carnage. And, even at that, we outdid ourselves this time. When we arrived at Cusack Park I could already see that Clare were training furiously. We played the game and they beat us up a stick. With that formality out of the way, we could look forward to the main event. I was friendly with Liam Doyle from my college days in Waterford and was chatting with him after the game.

"Are you around for a few pints?" I queried.

"Sure, we're playing in a few weeks," he said.

"Sure, so are we. We're going for a few pints anyway. Come on in for a few."

"No, I can't. I'd love to but we're off the beer."

The session went on until all hours. I was caught a couple of times in the hotel kitchen trying to prepare sandwiches for the lads at around five in the morning. I was rooming with Joe Dooley and the two of us felt like hell when we woke up. We trudged downstairs to assess the fallout only to find that, at about eleven o'clock, the session had already restarted. What could we do at that stage only join in. Might as well be hung for a sheep as a lamb.

The National League final between Galway and Tipperary was in Ennis that day and punters were arriving for lunch before the match only to be treated to Johnny Pilkington giving a rousing rendition of 'Sweet Caroline' with a bottle of Bud as a makeshift microphone. The bus stopped in Portumna on the way home and we had another few pints as we watched the League final. We went our different directions once we got back to Offaly and Joe and I carried on in Tullamore and got completely pie-eyed. Fleury had underestimated our penchant for excess and, realising the error of his ways, called an impromptu training session the following night when he ran the shite out of us. All's well that ends well, though. A few weeks later we dished out a thirteen-point drubbing to Wexford in the Leinster semi-final, while Clare were well beaten by Tipperary.

"What's the point?" Doyler later said to me. "I should have went with ye."

The Leinster final against Kilkenny was a ding-dong battle for about fifty minutes but, once Charlie Carter scored a goal to put them six points up, we clocked out and ended up being well beaten. It was the third year in succession we had given a limp display in a Leinster final, though that's not to suggest that we would have won but for the back-door element. We played Derry in the All-Ireland quarter-final and, after the display against Kilkenny, Fleury overhauled the team and gave a number of fringe players a run in the expectation that we'd still win comfortably.

We were in control without ever killing them off when Derry got a run on us in the second half and drew level. We recovered to win by six points but I was very angry at how I was treated that day and, for the only time in my career, felt like quitting the panel. I was selected at right half-back for a change and had done fine, but I was moved up to full-forward as Brian Whelahan was introduced in the second half to stem the Derry tide. Minutes later I was taken off. I felt scapegoated. An apology was conveyed to me from the management, which helped to cool my anger, though John Troy left the panel, having also been substituted, and didn't return until after the semi-final against Cork.

My hamstring trouble flared up again ahead of that game, for which we were rank outsiders. I was barely half-fit. Sid and I were in the Old Bawn Clinic the morning of the game receiving last- ditch treatment so that we could be wheeled out to play. The general feeling was that we had regressed from the year before while Cork had moved to a different level. They started strongly and we hung on through sheer know-how and experience in the first half and gradually hurled our way into the game.

In the second half we strangled the life out of them. Kevin Kinahan had been given the runaround by Joe Deane in the first half but dominated from the edge of the square in the second. While Cork were clipping in nice passes for him to run onto in the first half, we didn't give them that platform in the second. We got our shape and structure spot on in that second half. Our six backs were tightly packed, with the midfielders tucking in in front of them. Our half-forwards withdrew to the middle of the field and the space was there for our full-forward line instead.

The other aspect to it was that Cork were crowded out and, as a result, delivered bad ball into their forwards, who struck several wides under severe pressure from our defence. Simon Whelahan had his best game for Offaly that day, as did Gary Hanniffy, who dismantled Brian Corcoran to the extent that he was switched in to corner-back on me. Johnny Pilkington scored four beautiful points off Ó hAilpín. One of them was from such an acute angle that he was nearly sitting in the front row of the Canal End. He scored another from sixty yards while falling on his arse. Incredible stuff.

We finished with a flourish and, having restricted Cork to just two points in the second half, won by four to reach another All-Ireland final. The apologists for Cork claimed that they had taken us for granted, but there was no rush to make similar excuses for us the year before. I later spoke to

Jimmy Barry Murphy, who resigned as Cork manager after that defeat, and he assured me that they were ready and well prepared for us.

• • • • •

In hindsight, that win took a lot out of us. There was great excitement around the county at having beaten one of the game's superpowers even though there were far more All-Ireland medals in our dressingroom than in theirs. But we bought into the party atmosphere in the county following the win, rather than immediately setting our sights on the final, which would be against Kilkenny.

Hindsight can crystallise everything in your mind but, at the time, I was sure we'd win the final, even though our consistency was gone at that stage. The idea was that, if we could stay with Kilkenny and be within three or four points of them with twenty minutes to go, we'd beat them. Despite the fact that things worked out rather differently, that logic still holds true. Kilkenny were under severe pressure going into that game having lost the previous two finals and we felt that would become a major factor in the closing stages if we could swell the doubts in their mind.

Instead, we gifted them a dream start when our corner-back Niall Claffey dropped a ball into DJ Carey's hand after a couple of minutes and he buried it. You could feel the whole Kilkenny team relaxing straightaway and they followed it up with another goal, a rebound effort from DJ again, and a few points to boot. We actually settled down after that and played quite well for a period to reduce the deficit to a more manageable five points when the ball broke for me right in front of goal and I somehow managed to drag the shot just wide of James McGarry's post. I felt it was a hugely significant moment in the game. It was a sitter, and I still think about it quite often. We could have been going in at half-time just a couple of points down after a horrendous start, and what would Kilkenny have been thinking then? Shortly afterwards DJ broke through again and, although Stephen Byrne pulled off a great save, Charlie Carter was on hand to lash in the rebound. Kilkenny had weathered the storm and retired with a ten-point half-time lead.

The second half was a fairly even affair but there was no way back. We were too far behind to exert the kind of pressure that might have made them crack in the closing stages. While it's difficult to make assertions when you're beaten as soundly as we were that day, Cody's tenure in Kilkenny would probably have ended if we had upset them and the last ten years would most likely have turned out rather differently. Ifs, buts and maybes. They deserved it and we could have no complaints.

As a group we really loved our hurling and our pride in the jersey was immense. We were sore losers but that night was the exception. Nobody articulated it, but we knew that this was the end of the road for us. Although a few new players had come on board a couple of years earlier, the established players weren't being challenged and their powers were now starting to wane after years of service. The reception we got when we returned to the hotel that night was phenomenal. It was almost like a going-away party. Martin Hanamy and Billy Dooley had already retired the year before. More would follow in dribs and drabs in the next couple of years but that team, as we knew it, was gone.

That final turned out to be my last Championship game for Offaly. Fleury resigned as manager having had to deal with a lot of rancour during the year, which peaked when he left Hubert Rigney out of the panel for the final as well as his own clubmate Aidan Mannion. Hubie had been out all year through injury and there was a lot of fallout after the final. I think Pat didn't want to be at odds with his own people, while the job of replenishing the team probably wasn't all that appetising either. Michael Bond made a surprise return as manager and I gave a commitment to play on but my circumstances changed when I took on a job with Caterpillar, working in asset finance. I had moved into that field when I left AIB in 1995 to join Lombard & Ulster and later rejoined AIB, working in the same area but the step-up in workload with Caterpillar was immense.

Before that though, I had become a father again with Brian's birth on October 19, 2000. That day I had played in a golf classic with Noel Farrelly, Nicky English and John Hanley at Luttrellstown Castle as Edel wasn't due for another couple of weeks. Although Nicky wasn't having one of his better days, we were going great guns coming up the back nine when we decided to play a trick on Noely as he disappeared into the bushes to relieve himself. I would pretend that Edel had gone into labour when he arrived back.

"Noel, I have to go," I told him.

Now, if the world was coming to an end even that wouldn't be reason enough to desert the golf course in Noel's book, particularly when we were compiling such a good score.

"Why the fuck do you have to go?" he snarled.

"Edel has been on, she thinks she's going into labour. I have to go. Sorry about this lads but what can I do?" I added sincerely.

"Hey, Digger," Noely called to me as I walked away, "could you ever ring her back and see could Nicky bring her instead?" Classic stuff.

We managed to absorb Nicky's poor form sufficiently to win and, when I got home that night, Edel was sauntering around in her dressing gown without a care in the world.

"I think this baby's on the way," she announced, cool as a breeze.

I dropped Seán off at my sister Maura's place in Sallins and made for the Coombe with Edel, where Brian was born after a few hours – a much less harrowing ordeal for her than her previous labour. I was sitting on the edge of the bed with Edel holding Brian in her arms when a nurse poked her head in the door.

"Tea and toast?" she queried.

"Yes, please," I said quickly, not having eaten for hours, having been out on the golf course. Talk about putting my foot in it – as if the nurse was talking to me!

It had been more than two and a half years since Seán had been born so now we had a little buddy for him, we thought. We hoped we could have a little girl next. Brian was the complete opposite to Seán and slept right through the night, no feeding required.

I needed every wink of sleep I could get because, by the following spring, I was in every part of the country with work and driving like a demon in an effort to make training. I played a couple of League games and, in what turned out to be my last appearance against Limerick, I could see things were slowing down. I was in possession at one stage and was waiting to lob a handpass into John Troy's path, only he wasn't arriving quite as quickly as he used to so I had to delay the pass for a split second. In the meantime, TJ Ryan arrived and nailed me. At our peak, I would have had the pass made to Troy in plenty of time to meet TJ's hit head-on. I remember going off the field at the end of the game thinking, "I'm not going to get a chance to get him back for that". I knew I was finished. Only seeing out time.

Things came to a head shortly afterwards when I was on my way back from Killarney for training and got a blowout in Limerick that sent the car flying across the road, narrowly avoiding an oncoming truck. It was dark and pissing rain as I got out to change the tire only to find that the spare was a space saver, a miniature that's only designed to get you moving again at a vastly reduced speed. That really capped it. I went to a garage and they told me they couldn't source a replacement tire until the next morning. I booked into a hotel and called Edel.

"I can't do this any more," I told her. "It's crazy stuff."

I was finished. I was thirty-three, crocked with injuries and had nothing left to give. Work was incredibly busy and I now had two young children to think of. I called Bond later that week and told him I was retiring. He was hopeful that I might return in a month or two if the workload eased but it was never going to happen. It was the right decision, and I didn't even miss it initially. That would come later. As it happened, Joe Dooley decided to retire at the same time. I contacted Brian Carthy in RTÉ and we announced it jointly. It was a strange coincidence. We had done so much on and off the field together and now we were signing off together on something that defined us more than anything else.

It was an honour to have played with such an incredible bunch of players over the previous thirteen years, particularly from about 1991 onwards, when the core of the team that won the All-Ireland in 1994 and '98 began to take shape. Between 1992 and 2000, 1997 was the only year we didn't either win the All-Ireland or were beaten by the team that went on to win it. We had a knack of being involved in the game of the year on nearly an annual basis, win or lose; against Limerick in '94, Kilkenny in '95, Wexford in '96, the third Clare game in '98 and the Cork games in '99 and 2000. People say to me that we should have won more than we did given the abundance of raw talent we had. It's a fair comment, but in the most competitive era hurling has known, we won two All-Irelands, both of them in fairly different circumstances and with the bit of good fortune that you need along the way. Against that, we were unlucky in 1993, '95 and '99 but then you can't begrudge Clare their couple of All-Irelands, Wexford theirs in '96 or the two Kilkenny won in 1992 and '93.

Hurling has moved on now in terms of the power that the current Kilkenny and Tipperary teams have brought to the game. While we had some big men, and weren't short of natural power, we didn't build that into our armoury in the '90s because it wasn't as dominant a feature as it is now but I'd like to think we'd have adapted to it if we had to. We managed to do so when we upped our training considerably with the arrival of Eamonn Cregan and Derry O'Donovan and, later, we coped when Clare came along with their commando-style training.

Despite how we may have been depicted, we took our hurling very seriously and trained hard when we had to. We couldn't have survived, never mind flourished, at that time if it had been any different. Yet we still had our fair share of craic together. Moreover, we played the game in a sporting manner and went from 1993 to 1999 without having a player sent off in a Championship match.

There will always be debates about who the team of that era was and, of course, I have to plump for us. We had more special players than any of our rivals at that time. Flair players who could make something happen out of nothing. We were often labelled the Brazil or Harlem Globetrotters of hurling. In July 2011, *The Sunday Times* picked the top ten hurling teams in the history of the game and we came in at number nine, one place ahead of the Clare team from the same era. The passage summed us up neatly.

"Their character was reflected through the abandon and flair of their hurling. And they were probably the most beautiful team in history to watch in full flow. The pace of their hurling was like lightning, their technique an amalgam of unconscious first touch, beautiful crisp striking, ground hurling and an almost hypnotic ban on solo running. With fantastic skill levels, they were one of the purest hurling teams ever."

More than anything, I believe our legacy is defined by the thrilling brand of hurling we played. I wasn't one of those special players on our team but I felt I could do a job and I knew how to do it. Others bought into that as well. As a group we're not in constant contact these days but, when we meet, we pick up seamlessly from where we left off. That warmth and friendship is there. We know what we did together and I, for one, am immensely proud to have been a part if it. We could have won more. We could have won less. That's life.

PART THREE

Chapter 11

Tallaght Hospital, September, 2002

When I consider the direction our lives took as a result of that day, it's almost bizarre how breezy we were about it at the time. I had agreed to be a guest speaker at a lunch in Naas Rugby Club one Friday afternoon in September, 2002. It's an annual affair and usually the orators are rugby legends, the likes of Gareth Edwards, Martin Johnson, Willie John McBride or Fergus Slattery. They branch off occasionally though and people like racehorse trainer Ted Walsh and well-known businessman Feargal Quinn have also been asked to fulfil the role. Given my obvious connections with the club and profile through hurling and punditry, I was invited as one of the two speakers back then and, indeed, have fulfilled the role since.

Firstly, though, that morning there was the matter of taking Edel to the Adelaide and Meath Hospital in Tallaght for tests on a lump I had noticed on her right breast a couple of weeks before. It was just a couple of square centimetres but a reasonably solid mass all the same, and I suggested to Edel that we get it checked out. She went to her GP in Naas shortly afterwards and was referred to Tallaght fairly quickly. It's hard to believe now, but it wasn't something that either of us was particularly nervous about. Although we were aware there was a chance that it could be something serious, we approached it in a more blasé manner of just dropping by the hospital for an hour or so and then back down home in plenty of time for the lunch; Edel would pick the lads up and we'd kick on with whatever else we had planned for that weekend.

They carried out a fine-needle biopsy and mammogram and we waited for the results. Edel was one of, maybe, ten or so women having the same procedure that day and each one was being called for their results according to the order they had attended the hospital that morning. That was until they skipped Edel and went on to the next person. Something twigged with me immediately. Why would they do that?

They saw a few more people and those of us who were left were told to come back after lunch. I put a call through to the rugby club to inform them I wouldn't be able to make it. Edel told me to go ahead with it rather than cancel at such short notice but I said "no way", and Charlie McCreevy filled in for me instead in any event. We walked over to Eddie Rocket's in the nearby Square Shopping Centre for a bite to eat. We discussed the fact that she hadn't yet been called back in and we both found it strange. I wasn't scaremongering, but, privately, I had a very bad feeling about it.

Dr James Geraghty was head of the breast clinic in the hospital and very highly rated. He spoke to us when we returned from lunch and delivered the devastating news that Edel had a tumour in her breast. Hardened by the environment they work in, some doctors can be rather stiff when it comes to these matters but Dr Geraghty had a gentle way about him and a genuinely sympathetic demeanour. But there was no easy way of imparting this news to us. At that early stage he didn't know what exact course of action he would be taking but surgery was obviously in the offing. He tried to reassure us on the grounds that Edel was young and otherwise healthy, and it appeared to be in the early stages.

I know so much about it now, but words like chemotherapy and radiotherapy meant nothing to me at the time and ran right over my head. While neither of us were ones for bawling uncontrollably, even at times like this, we were still naturally very upset. Though Edel always had a tough exterior, she wasn't bullet-proof and this was terribly distressing and a massive shock. It just couldn't be happening, we felt. She was only thirty-four. That morning all was fine, but now everything had been turned upside down and our lives were headed on a completely uncharted route. We didn't know the destination, and we most certainly didn't know the way.

We stopped by the Poitín Stil on the way home for a couple of stiffeners, given the bombshell that had just been dropped. As a husband you want to be able to assure your wife that everything will be alright and that she'll be fine but pragmatism was always at the root of our relationship. It had, by and large, served us well so I wasn't going to start signing cheques that couldn't be cashed at that stage. That would have been pure nonsense to Edel anyway. The fastest route to dealing with any scenario, however difficult, is to recognise it for what it's worth initially and move on from there, rather than trying to cod yourself. So, instead of telling her we were going to live happily ever after, I would have said something along the lines of, "Look, it mightn't be too bad". We discussed the practicalities of what was stretching out before us. We didn't immediately start calling everyone and telling them, but those closest to us would have to be informed all the same, and soon.

Everything moved along pretty swiftly from there. Although he was optimistic as to how treatable it was, Dr Geraghty strongly advised that we didn't hang around and Edel was booked in for surgery ten days later. We went to Portlaoise to tell Jerry and Chris, Edel's parents, and, that Monday morning Edel went into work to talk to her boss in AIB and arrange the lengthy time off that would be needed.

All the while, further analysis was carried out ahead of the surgery to determine the nature of the cancer, thereby informing Dr Geraghty of the course of action he would need to take. The best case scenario at that point was a lumpectomy, a procedure which would just involve the lump itself being taken away followed by a period of radiotherapy, which is relatively straightforward. The nuclear option, as any woman will know, is a mastectomy, which results in the whole breast being removed, and the traumatic news came from Dr Geraghty, pre-surgery, that this was what was required.

Edel was admitted on a Sunday night for surgery the following afternoon. She came to later that evening and was obviously quite groggy given the amount of drugs she had on board, but also in a very distressed frame of mind after what she had just gone through. It's not within my gift, or that of any man, to relate to what a woman goes through at times like this so I'm not even going to try. But it was horrendous. Outside of the final week of her life, this period was the most traumatic out of all the time she was ill. Having been fit and healthy, she had quickly been faced with her own mortality and had undergone major surgery. Later, when we talked about it, Edel was apprehensive about how I would feel about her now given the nature of the surgery she had undergone, and worried that I might look on her differently. But it was a complete red herring to me. While of course there was a physical attraction there when we first met, in any loving relationship it largely becomes an irrelevance as things progress to a more serious level and you eventually get married and have children. I reassured Edel in the strongest possible terms that, in my eyes, she remained the same woman she was before entering that operating theatre.

She stayed in hospital for another week as part of the recovery process and then readied herself for chemotherapy. It was a giant leap into the unknown for us but, like most cancer sufferers, Edel bought into it straightaway, fiercely determined to come out the other side of it and continue with her life. It was like she entered a zone in her approach to the treatment. Rather than being a passive patient, she quizzed Dr Geraghty on the various courses of drugs she would be on, why this drug was better than that drug in these circumstances, and she was very quickly up to speed on all the various aspects of her treatment. The chemo would be in St James's Hospital, where we first met Dr John Kennedy, the oncologist who would become such a central figure in Edel's life over the next number of years. It would involve eight sessions, one every three weeks.

Edel received her chemotherapy through an intravenous drip over the course of eight sessions. There are various ways of administering the dose in that some may receive it in two separate sessions a week or so apart, but Edel was strong enough to take it all at once and she would then have her few weeks of recovery before having to return to St James's again.

Chemotherapy typically acts by killing cells which divide rapidly, a strong characteristic of cancer cells. The trouble is, it also kills cells which divide under normal circumstances and that we need to function properly, thereby bringing about the side effects of extreme tiredness and lack of energy, hair loss in certain circumstances, and so on. Curiously, she never once suffered from vomiting, as a lot of people do following chemotherapy. She would have been on various tablets to prepare her body for it in the immediate run-up to the chemo each time, but it was still a measure of her toughness that she withstood it reasonably well in that respect.

She wasn't immune to all the side-effects, however, and she lost her hair a number of times over the years. She'd wear bandanas and scarves to cover her head and, in later years, began to look into wearing wigs. Edel had always had a thick head of hair and for it to suddenly start falling out in clumps wasn't easy for her. She also became bloated at times from all the drugs, while nobody can avoid the sheer and utter exhaustion that chemotherapy brings. It's just a savage tiredness, with several other debilitating spin-offs as well. That week immediately after the chemo is the most difficult, and then you build yourself back up gradually until the next session.

The day is so long when undergoing chemo, particularly for Edel as she was having relatively large doses administered. You'd arrive in James's that morning and there would be so many people for the staff to get through that you'd swear that they couldn't possibly do it, but they always did. By six o'clock that evening everyone was gone. There were never any complaints from Edel about what she was going through; she just approached it as something that she had to get through, and that was very much the way among all the patients I came across. You could hardly start whining about your lot when there may be someone sitting beside you far worse off.

While Edel was only thirty-four at the time, there were others half her age getting treatment, which was quite a shock to see. Some people quite literally looked like death warmed up, possibly only six stone in weight or less. It was like we had been transported into a parallel universe that we never really knew existed up to then. One young girl that we used to see quite often in Tallaght stuck in my mind. She was only about eighteen, a beautiful blonde-haired girl, who also had breast cancer. "How could she be here?" I thought to myself. The fact that patients were generally on different rotas for their chemotherapy meant that forging lasting friendships wasn't really a runner, but Edel did speak to her a couple of times. I don't know how she fared out, but I remember her prognosis certainly wasn't good.

The health service has been a hot topic in Ireland for a number of years now but I have to say that my impression of it through Edel's experiences was that it was first-class. Within a month or so of having visited her GP, she had undergone surgery and started chemotherapy. But, then, if you talk to anybody who has had cancer they'll most likely say the same thing about the quality of the treatment, and that's probably largely down to the seriousness of the condition. It simply has to be treated quickly and efficiently and the staff are well-trained. Oncology nurses seem to have a special way about them, and they have to, really, given the amount of hardship they encounter on a day-to-day basis. Edel was treated in a compassionate and professional manner, with a bit of fun and craic along the way with the staff, too.

After the six months of chemo, she began radiotherapy in St Luke's Hospital under Professor John Armstrong. Compared to chemo, it's a walk in the park. It's basically a laser treatment to control the malignant cells and seal off the affected area to help prevent a further spread. A bit similar to putting a weld around it, if you like. She had an appointment every day, Monday to Friday, for around six weeks. Before she finished radiotherapy we had moved from Naas to Tullamore, and with all that was going on at the time I don't know how we managed to do it. We were both very happy in Naas and didn't particularly want to leave as we'd had some brilliant years there, but it was also a big ambition of Edel in particular that we would move out the country a bit at some stage, and houses in a rural setting certainly didn't come cheap in Naas. Back in 2003 we would have been looking at an outlay of possibly up to €800,000, a mortgage which would have crippled us.

We decided that we would sell our house in Naas and buy elsewhere. Up to that point I could never have seen myself leaving there. We both had a lot of friends there, were well settled and Seán had just started school. There was a real cosmopolitan feel about the place, given that it's essentially a suburb of Dublin. You could go for a few pints in Kavanagh's and see all sorts; judges, barristers, guards, nurses or dustbin men and everyone was taken at face value. There was a cross-section of people from every part of society from all over the country, a great mix of counties. There were mighty characters in Kavanagh's golf society and then there was the rugby club and the horse-racing side of things, which I also have an interest in.

Whether I would have retained the same love for all those things associated with Naas as I got older, I'm not so sure. While it was always our intention to relocate from the three-bed semi we had, Edel's illness certainly hastened the move. Had she not fallen ill it wouldn't have been so high on the agenda and, while I was working for myself and was more flexible in that regard, Edel most likely wouldn't have been able to secure a suitable transfer from the job she was in at that time that would have allowed us to move as far as Tullamore. But, once she had been diagnosed with cancer and the fright that went with it, it was very much a case of not allowing other factors to dictate what we did, and so we just went for it.

Before we left Naas, there was a leaving do for us in the golf club and the place was packed. There were hundreds there and all sorts of presentations to us, including a €1,600 voucher for golf equipment for me. Oddly, we were also presented with a painting of Kavanagh's from the owners, Ger and Norman Farragher. It says a lot for how much trade we gave the place! But, while leaving Naas was a wrench, setting up home in Tullamore would prove to be the best move we ever made.

In terms of deciding where to move to from Naas, we resolved not to go to either Banagher or Portlaoise, where the two of us come from. I'd always thought Tullamore was a good town, though I didn't know it particularly well. It was near enough to Dublin and Kildare and the other areas that I was dipping into for work, while it was central in terms of proximity to our families in Banagher and Portlaoise, as well as the fact that both of us had siblings in surrounding areas like Athlone, Oranmore, Sligo and Sallins. Our great friends, Joe and Marie Dooley lived there, and that was certainly a factor in our decision given our close relationship with them. I clicked with Joe pretty quickly once I joined the Offaly panel. It was at a transitional time where the team of the 1980s was starting to break up and we became good friends, despite the fact that he's a few years older than me. It was natural then that Edel and Marie would hit it off once we became a couple a few years later. In fact, Marie played a key role in the purchase of our house in Tullamore.

Edel and I had been down a few times, popping into the various auctioneers' offices but couldn't quite find anything to suit us. Marie had a friend who she thought was interested in selling though, and put us in contact with Stephen and Dolores Ravenhill, who would ultimately go on to become firm friends of ours and were immovable pillars of support during Edel's second illness. They were looking to sell their house in Durrow, just outside Tullamore, and build on a site just up the road. Marie brought Edel out there one day to meet Dolores. The house ticked all the boxes for Edel and I rambled down there myself one Saturday morning on my own and knocked on the front door. Stephen, whom I'd never met before, answered and brought me inside to the sitting room.

"Are you interested in selling the house?" I asked him.

Stephen played a bit of hardball, or at least that's how I saw it, saying that there were other people interested and that he was waiting on a valuation. I cut to the chase.

"Forget about the others and the valuation, how much do you want for the house?"

He mentioned a figure, probably thinking that I'd try and bargain for a lower amount, but I told him that's exactly what I'd give him for it. Done deal. It was similar money to what we were selling the house in Naas for so it worked out well that way. I like to slag Stephen now that I gave him too much for it, and that he built a big house beside me out of the proceeds with plenty to spare. He'd say that if he had waited a bit longer until the property boom hit its peak, he would have got far more for it, which he would have. But, overall, it was a win-win scenario for us both.

With the help of a courier friend John McGrath, I moved into the house in late July 2003, with Joe and Sod also lending a hand. Edel was on a pilgrimage to Lourdes at the time with my mother, which was when she first came in contact with Fr Simon. Although Banagher was hardly a sprawling metropolis, I had no prior experience of living out the country but I took to it surprisingly quickly and we settled well. Sod also happened to move to Tullamore around the same time and my circle of friends has swelled considerably in the intervening years. There were quite a number of people, more than I appreciated initially, living in the town that I was acquainted with over the years and who have since become good friends.

Edel finished radiotherapy that September and took a few months out to recuperate further before returning to work. Prior to falling ill she had been a human resources manager for AIB and was based in Finglas, with responsibility for the various branches in that area of Dublin. She applied for a transfer to Tullamore, or at least somewhere near there, during her illness and wasn't given any guarantees, but they told her they would do their best to accommodate her. Thankfully, she secured work in the Tullamore branch and started a few months after her treatment ended.

Within a few weeks of completing radiotherapy she had a scan and was given the all-clear. Thereafter, her appointments were three-monthly, six-monthly, annually and so on. Edel was looking into breast reconstruction at the time as well, which would have kept her in the system a bit longer. Now, I'm no medical guru but I'm of the opinion that these check-ups are generally worthless. Knowing what I know now, I'm always a bit perplexed when I hear people, somewhat elated, saying, "I had my six-monthly check and I got the all-clear". But it's only a physical examination, it's not as if they carry out a scan or blood tests every time you return for a check-up, so nothing is going to show up anyway. I think it's more for people to reassure themselves but I don't see any true value in it. If the cancer is to resurface it will most likely be as a result of a noticeable deterioration in your health in some respect or other, and you then act on it, which is incidental to a physical examination every few months.

It wasn't so much a case of us being relieved at Edel getting the all-clear when the treatment finished – at that stage that's what you would have been expecting after all she had gone through. It would be some kick in the teeth if that hadn't been the case given the intensity of what she had endured over the previous year. Five years is the ballpark timespan which is mentioned at that stage, as in, if the cancer doesn't return within that period, there's a good chance it won't come back at all.

The single biggest consequence of Edel's treatment, however, was that it eventually brought about an early menopause. She didn't have a menstrual cycle during the chemotherapy and though the hope was that this would only be temporary, it ultimately didn't prove to be the case. She had to stay on a drug called tamoxifen for five years and there was an outside possibility of having kids beyond that, but, even at that, it would have been precarious given that hormones can have an impact on the prevalence of cancer and another pregnancy would have heightened the risk of it returning. In any event, Edel had fallen ill once again within the five-year period so it was never a runner. While she was having her treatment the thought of not being able to have any more children wasn't to the forefront of our minds as just getting through the chemo and radiotherapy was the only objective. But, undoubtedly, having more children would have been high on the agenda for us in the normal course of things because we were both hugely into parenthood. Having had two, we wanted four at least and, possibly, five in total. Of course you'll take them any way they come as long as they're healthy, but a daughter would have been nice after the two lads arrived reasonably close together. In other respects, though, you don't miss what you never have and, rather than being crestfallen at not being able to have more children, we thanked our blessings for the two wonderful boys we had. Nonetheless, Seán and Brian would have liked more siblings and they still say it to me now. Seán had a preference for another brother while Brian, funnily enough, was more into having a little sister.

All in all, it had been a hugely difficult and traumatic time for Edel, as it would be for anyone struck by cancer, but it was particularly trying for a woman to go through having a breast removed, frequently losing her hair and then being resigned to the fact that she couldn't have any more children when, of all the things she did so well, motherhood came naturally to her. But, for all that, we had so much to be positive about once the treatment was behind her as we settled into our new life in what was an ideal setting for us in Durrow.

Chapter 12

Only a few months before Edel's diagnosis I had started my own financial services business and, as if that wasn't enough to keep me active, I was back on the inter-county hurling carousel too. Not quite at the level I had left it but, when I was contacted in relation to the Meath senior hurling manager's position in the autumn of 2001, I allowed myself to dream of the possibility of elevating them to a standard something near that of Offaly.

It all started when I took a call from Paddy Kelly, a former Meath hurler with whom I had played alongside for Leinster in the Railway Cup. Paddy was a mainstay of the Meath team when they beat us in the National League in 1995 at a time when we were reigning All-Ireland champions. The following year they ran us to six points in the Leinster Championship. I met Paddy with Martin Donnelly, the team sponsor, one day in Dublin and the one thing that came across more than anything was their passion for Meath hurling. I was offered the job and I took it. I thought that, just maybe, Meath were in a position similar to where Offaly had found themselves twenty years earlier and that with better application they might have the potential to move up the rankings. I was genuinely excited as to where this could possibly lead.

I immediately recruited Johnny Murray as the physical trainer as I had rated him highly when Babs Keating brought him to Offaly as part of his backroom team. Although he was Babs's man, I always got on well with Johnny. Paddy and Pat Potterton, another former Meath hurler of repute, came on board as selectors. We devised a winter training schedule to get the players in shape and they put in a decent effort. Early in 2002 we progressed to the Walsh Cup semi-final and welcomed Kilkenny to Navan. We gave them an awful scare and they were relieved to escape with a six-point victory. We had some talented hurlers like Nicky Horan, Mickey Cole, Ray Dorran and Kevin Dowd, brother of Tommy, while former county footballer Jimmy McGuinness, a brilliant character, came on board too.

Some long-serving players wielded too much influence in the dressing room but that didn't wash with me. Everyone was the same as far as I was concerned and management's orders were to be strictly followed, whether we were right or wrong. It's a code I always followed as a player. One of the first things I noticed about the players when I took over was that they weren't fit enough, but that was easily solved with Johnny's winter training. It wasn't so simple to correct the standard of their hurling, however. It was a huge drawback in Meath in that hurling is essentially a summer sport, yet these players were doing very little of it at the prime time of the year. The county team would be finished in the championship usually by May or earlier, and then the football kicked in. With the county footballers generally going well, the priority would be to get the county football championship finished, so the Meath hurlers had essentially been reared on winter hurling. With that backdrop, they couldn't improve significantly. I think that was recognised generally around this time and the Christy Ring, Nicky Rackard and Lory Meagher Cups were introduced a few years later.

Meath were operating in a twelve-team Division One in the National League at the time and, while we were able to make a nuisance of ourselves in the Walsh Cup when our fitness was probably more advanced than the top teams, we were found out in the league, shipped some heavy beatings and were relegated. Justin McCarthy had just taken charge of Waterford back then and I remember overhearing his team talk before they played us. He was roaring and bawling at them, and the general tenor of his address was to go out and hammer us, which I found bizarre. You'd swear it was an All-Ireland final. Perhaps that's partly why he could never guide Waterford to one in all the years he was down there. You have to choose your moments carefully when unleashing that kind of tirade.

While a few of the players we had could hurl comfortably in anyone's company, in general the speed at which we played the game was far too slow. Many of the players were lacking in the basic skills of the game. When a fella joins an inter-county panel he should be the finished article and then, as a coach, you work on improving him from there. Basics such as striking off both sides, picking the ball, holding the hurley correctly, catching, hooking and blocking should all be in place, but in many cases they weren't. It came as a surprise to me that I had to coach these skills and essentially try and manufacture inter-county hurlers, but I worked very hard on improving that ahead of the Championship and it was made easier by the fact that the players were so eager. I always felt they would get better when exposed to hurling in the right conditions, and that's how it turned out.

We beat Carlow in the preliminary section of the Leinster Championship to set up a meeting with Laois in Navan. While Laois were reasonably good and had always been operating at a higher level than Meath, they had slipped a bit from where they were in the '80s and '90s and I sensed an opportunity to cause a shock if we could stick with them into the closing stages. They were strong favourites, and that isn't something that would rest easily with them. Well into injury time we were trailing by two points and had a free around halfway. The ball was lobbed in and it broke to Mickey Cole. He whipped it to the net and the final whistle sounded from the puck-out. It was Meath's biggest victory in years and it was a brilliant feeling. The real satisfaction for me came with the fact that the lads had really put in a massive effort and improved so much from where we had started only a few months before.

We went on to play Dublin in the next round but, by then, our cover had been blown and they had too much for us. Our summer wasn't over, though, and, as fate would have it, we were paired with Offaly in the qualifiers. While training a team to beat my former team-mates barely a year after I had retired was hardly ideal, I wasn't found wanting in my commitment to Meath in the run-up to the game. In a way it was a good draw in that, while I didn't show it, I genuinely didn't expect us to beat Offaly but felt we could be competitive against them, and that's how it turned out. Offaly were in control at half-time but a Nicky Horan goal brought us within striking distance until Johnny Dooley came off the bench and struck three brilliant points to see them home on a 1-20 to 1-11 scoreline. Johnny's knee problems came to a head that summer and resulted in his retirement shortly afterwards so that was his last significant contribution as an inter-county hurler, and you can be sure he was determined that I wasn't going to get one over on him that night!

With the year over, I approached the county board and told them I wanted a team holiday. The lads had put in a huge effort, had trained like every other panel in the country and I felt they deserved to be rewarded for that. We had a race night in Athboy to raise funds and it went very well. I arranged for a letter to be sent out to prominent former Meath footballers like Bernard Flynn, Colm O'Rourke and Gerry McEntee seeking contributions. Although the letters were signed off with my name, I didn't actually see them before they went out and apparently they weren't presented very well, with no contact details provided. I was driving to Dublin one day when I took a call from a Dublin number.

"What sort of a letter is that to send out?" barked the person on the other line.

"Who's this?" I asked.

"I'll give you ten seconds to identify me or I'm hanging up," came the response.

"Is that you, Gerry?"

"Correct," he said.

"What's this about holidays for hurlers and promoting hurling in Meath? Meath is a football county."

We continued to exchange pleasantries and the upshot was that Gerry sent out a cheque towards the holiday fund and a comical note to accompany it. It read: "Dear Michael, further to our telephone conversation please find enclosed cheque as promised. In my opinion any improvement in Meath hurling is to the detriment of Meath football and should not be welcomed. Yours sincerely, Dr GP McEntee."

We raised enough for a holiday to Lanzarote the following January. By then Edel had fallen ill so I didn't travel, but I was looking forward to supplementing the work we had done the previous year once the players returned to training. That was a dangerous presumption to make, however, because not everyone came back. There was a feeling among seven or eight players that, after the commitment they had just given the year before, that they wouldn't be able to justify doing that again. Their reasoning was that they had improved as much as they were going to and they wouldn't be able to scale further heights in 2003.

Although I was bitterly disappointed at their narrow-minded outlook, I could see that they may have had a point but they were failing to see the bigger picture. While the biggest gains were always going to be made in the first year, if Meath could have kept the players together and trained to a high standard over a three- or four-year period it would have made a huge difference as more players would have come on board and bought into it. Players who might have been down the pecking order with the county footballers and were useful hurlers may have seen inter-county hurling with Meath as a more attractive proposition and a genuine alternative. But that couldn't happen overnight and too many players weren't prepared to put the work in over a period of years to raise the status of the team. It's a shame because we wouldn't have been too far off Dublin's standard back in 2002, and look what they have done since. I'm not suggesting that Meath could have made the same progress in that space of time but they do have the advantage of a genuine hurling heartland, something Dublin doesn't quite have.

Inevitably, the second year turned out to be a massive disappointment and more or less left us back where we had started. I made up my mind to quit at the end of the year once I became involved in a public spat with the county board after they scheduled a full round of club football games the night before we played a National League game, and it was no great wrench for me to depart by then. Although we had been very well looked after in terms of training facilities and food, there was often wrangling over ordering hurleys and sliotars and other essential gear, which is a given in the serious hurling counties.

It turned out that my initial hopes and dreams about establishing Meath as a hurling force were sadly misplaced and, with the small-town mindset that prevailed, I now wonder whether it's possible to really elevate the game in counties like Meath or whether the GAA should concentrate on consolidating the dozen or so counties that are serious about hurling. There was no real will at county board level to drive the game, but they can't take all the blame either when you look at what the players did. I suppose in one way my time in Meath had a happy ending – the lads got their holiday and Gerry got his wish!

· · · · ·

After finishing with Meath following the 2003 season, my involvement with inter-county hurling wasn't long being rekindled. Offaly started the 2004 National League campaign well in what was Mike McNamara's second year in charge. They beat Tipperary and looked set to reach the top six, which was a crossover between the top three teams in Division 1A and 1B, but a couple of defeats condemned them to the bottom six instead. Unlike the previous year, points from the first phase didn't carry over and they lost to Kilkenny before suffering a freakish twenty-two point defeat to an unheralded Dublin team. The final game against Laois saw them slip to another shock loss by a point in Birr, which meant that, incredibly, Offaly were relegated. This was far worse than being relegated under the 2011 National League structure, as there were twelve teams in the top flight at the time rather than eight. It was a disaster that had far-reaching consequences for Offaly hurling and which are probably still being felt to this day.

In the meantime, however, the knives were out and flak was directed at McNamara's set-up, with Pádraig Horan the most vocal critic at one County Board meeting. It was felt that the players' touch was blunt, with not enough concentration on sharpening their skills. While Offaly's successes in the 1980s and '90s were built on a foundation of doggedness and resilience, those qualities were supplemented with immaculate stickwork that made us so easy on the eye when at our best. It was felt that this was being lost and that a coach should be added to the management team ahead of the Championship to help restore these values. To that end, I took a call from the County Board, was offered the role and was only too happy to get involved with Offaly again. I was now living in Tullamore, where Offaly's summer training always took place down through the years.

I didn't know Mike McNamara well but was acutely aware of the fact that he had a very strong personality. Having said that, I'm not sure if, in his position, I would have accepted having someone foisted upon me as I was on him. I'd probably just leave and let them get someone else. The first night I arrived at training I wasn't exactly welcomed with a warm embrace. Mike rolled out his own session while I watched with my arms folded and had no involvement. Not even an introduction, as would normally be the case, to say, "Lads, Michael is coming on board with us to help out for the rest of the year, let's drive on together for the Championship..." or something like that.

I wasn't asked to contribute to the session in any way whatsoever but, given my passion for Offaly, I was prepared to look past that. Gradually things improved and I was integrated more as time went on. To be fair, I think Mike had a lot of the fundamentals in place for Offaly to maximise their potential. His physical preparation, others might call it torture, from what I could see was right in terms of where Offaly needed to be to compete on that level with the likes of Kilkenny, who were injecting more and more power into their game with every passing year. While his latest involvement with Clare a couple of years ago may have depicted him as being far too old-school, I thought he was a good trainer in lots of ways and, from talking to the Clare lads from the '90s, he was a massively influential member of that management team. There were two aspects to that, firstly how fit he had them, but and, secondly, that take-no-shit demeanour that he exudes, the manliness that underpinned the success that Clare had back then. He's the sort of person I'd like to have involved if I was heading up a management team, but how to utilise him properly within that would probably be the main conundrum.

There wasn't anything drastically wrong with his training sessions, but I could pick holes in them all the same and tried to tighten things up. For example, one of the drills would involve a player soloing the width of the pitch before giving a hand-pass to another player, who would then make the return journey. Another was three players pucking the ball to each other from one end of the pitch to the other, with the ball coming to you from seventy yards uncontested. These aren't scenarios that typically, if ever, arise in a match situation. My philosophy was to get everyone in tighter with more movement and balls buzzing about the place to help sharpen the skills which would be needed in a high-octane Championship match. While I didn't reinvent the wheel, I'd like to think that I brought a few things to the set-up in that regard, getting that first touch right and making us that bit snappier in how we went about our business. We had light forwards so the key was to let the ball do the work, keep it moving by playing nice diagonal deliveries inside, with the half-forward line offering support. Regardless of my input, or otherwise, we were blessed with a straightforward route to the Leinster final, which would most likely have been negotiated in any event. Although Laois and Dublin had surprisingly beaten us in the League, it was never going to happen in the Championship and we breezed past both of them, scoring a combined total of 4-48 and it was generally felt that we were playing a nice brand of hurling.

The whole thing was thrown wide open by Wexford's shock defeat of Kilkenny in the other semi-final. It just turned everything on its head. By now Kilkenny had been dishing out routine beatings to Offaly but there was no psychological barrier with Wexford. Make no mistake about it, this Leinster title was there for the taking. The Friday night before the final we had a team meeting in the County Arms in Birr, which was very positive. I drove over with Jim Troy, who was now a selector. Mike spoke and I said a few words, too. Wexford had devised a puck-out strategy in the semi-final which that played a huge role in their sensational victory and left Kilkenny and Brian Cody perplexed. Damien Fitzhenry didn't aim for a man as such from his puck-out, more a particular space where he knew a purple and gold jersey would be running into and it worked a treat. From analysing it, I didn't reckon there was any great rocket science to combating it, however, and I instructed our wing-backs not to follow the Wexford wing-forwards when, not if, they took off on a run to the opposite flank ahead of one of Fitzhenry's puck-outs.

"What you do," I told them, "is stay where you are and, when he comes across, bury him with a shoulder and then you're there with the ball. By following him you're only creating space for the other lad to run into."

At this stage it was nine years since Offaly had last won the Leinster title. I got a clip of the 1995 final when we beat Kilkenny in that monsoon. It was the same clip that had been played on The Sunday Game that particular night, with the Van Morrison number, Days Like This, providing the sound track to the key scores in the game.

"Lads," I said, "we were winning Leinster titles for sport for fifteen years and now it's nine years since we won one. That's going to change. That's the last time we won it and that's the type of passion we need today."

It seemed to hit the right note as we hurled up a storm in the first twenty minutes. However, for Fitzhenry's first puck-out, the Wexford wing-forwards sprinted across the field and switched positions as we anticipated and, for all I had said the previous Friday, our wing-backs duly played into their hands by following them. Despite our utter dominance of the game, we didn't make it count on the scoreboard. I rate Fitzhenry as one of the all-time great goalkeepers, but we made a hero out of him that day. His performance won him an All-Star, and is probably ranked by many as his greatest, but he shouldn't have had any business making the saves he did because he ought to have been given no chance. And, in fairness, he admitted himself afterwards that the saves were pretty comfortable blocks by his standards. He made four saves from clear-cut, goal-scoring chances, including a penalty, and from one of them the rebound was driven wide from a few yards out despite the an open goal. We missed easy frees as well. Mitch Jordan got a soft goal at the other end and, to our near disbelief, we were only a point in front at half-time.

I still felt we were in control of the game in the second half, though, and Brian Whelahan was dictating the play from centre-back until his hamstring snapped as he went for a breaking ball. I was patrolling the Cusack Stand sideline and was linked up to Mike on the far side through an earpiece.

"Move Rory Hanniffy to centre-back," I told him, as Brian hobbled off the field. Mike wanted to rejig the half-back line by moving Barry Whelahan back but I insisted, "Barry is fine at midfield but he doesn't have the pace to play back there."

Next thing I knew, the line went dead, Barry was switched and, soon after, his man, Paul Carley, got free and scored the goal that shifted the momentum of the game back in Wexford's favour. Eventually Rory was relocated to centre-back but we had lost our grip on the game and were beaten by four points. I firmly believe if my advice had been taken on board at the that time that we would have won that Leinster final, but then the game should have been well wrapped up by that stage in any event. It seemed that day that anything that could go wrong, did go wrong.

Wexford were well beaten by Cork in the subsequent All-Ireland semi-final and have slipped downhill ever since. I often wonder would we have taken much more value and sustenance than they did from that Leinster title had we won it. We had a lot of young players at the time who would have grown in confidence and possibly kicked on to become much more than just Kilkenny's whipping boys in the early stages of the Championship in subsequent years. It would also have bridged that gap between Leinster titles for Offaly, which would have been something in itself. Now it's sixteen years. And counting.

The year wasn't over yet as we had a qualifier game against Clare at the Gaelic Grounds in Limerick, but it was a disaster. Clare were still recovering from an awful beating from Waterford in the Munster Championship and were hardly riding high themselves. That was reflected in the opening twenty minutes when they hit a spate of wides that kept us in the game but, even when Damien Murray goaled from a twenty-metre free to put us in front completely against the run of play, there was still no interest from our lads, which was criminal. The game petered out to a heavy defeat and, despite having the option of another year, Mike subsequently quit, feeling there was no great appetite among delegates at a County Board meeting for him to stay on.

As well as the criticism he had shipped earlier on in the season, it was hardly too appetising for him to continue with Division Two hurling on the menu the following year, and he was unlikely to get a better chance to deliver silverware than the one which that had just been lost. I never really got to know him properly but have the feeling that, if I did, we'd get on very well. I ran into him at a game in Portlaoise a few years back and we ended up having a few pints together afterwards. I really enjoyed his company.

I was asked if I was interested in taking on the job at the time but I said no. There were a number of factors for this, chief among them my auctioneering business, which was getting off the ground at that stage and, given the property boom of the time, would prove to be hugely time-consuming. To actually manage the team I would also have to forego much, if not all, of my media work which, apart from being a decent earner, had a number of positive spin-offs that would help me in business. Another aspect to it was the attitude of some of the players, though not all of them, it must be said. The Clare game was a sickener in that so many of them simply didn't want to know about it and threw in the towel, which is unacceptable. If it was a case of having the opportunity to take over an ambitious bunch of lads who would die on their feet for you and the Offaly jersey then I may have thought differently about it, but that wasn't the case with a number of individuals. The thirty-one-point beating they took from Kilkenny the following year was one of the darkest days in Offaly hurling history. It had taken Offaly so long to become a serious force in hurling and, suddenly, within a matter of a few years, it had gone full circle. You'd almost be blaming yourself, thinking you may have stayed on too long but the most disheartening aspect to it was, once again, how the white flag was raised when not so long before we were renowned for having such heart and pride in the jersey.

For all that, since I retired it's been an ambition of mine to manage Offaly and I was sounded out once again when John McIntyre stepped down in 2007 but it wasn't a runner with Edel's condition. Given Seán and Brian's age, they're my priority for the next few years until they're able to stand on their own two feet. I just hope the chance to manage Offaly doesn't pass me by in the meantime.

I've had other offers down the years, too. Wexford sounded me out in 2006 before they appointed John Meyler, but driving all that distance down to the south-east a few times a week wasn't a runner given the situation at home. In late 2008, I took a call from Dublin County Board Secretary, John Costello, who was looking for a successor to Tommy Naughton. DJ Carey and Nicky English had already been courted and when Nicky couldn't commit to the role he mentioned my name to Costello, who I met in the Johnstown House Hotel in Enfield one afternoon. It was a brilliant meeting and I was hugely impressed by him and where he wanted Dublin hurling to go. His passion for, and knowledge of, the game surprised me somewhat as I had always marked him down as more of a football man. I have to admit I was seriously interested in taking it on and, although the job wasn't formally offered to me, I got the impression that it was mine if I wanted it. The appointment process had been dragging on for a while at this stage and I'd say they were hoping and expecting that Nicky would have taken the job. I thought about it and Edel didn't have a problem with me doing it, but it just wasn't workable. I could have been in the job for a month and then have to quit if Edel had deteriorated and required hospice care at home, for example, meaning I would have to take full responsibility for looking after the lads. My priorities simply had to be at home and nowhere else as I didn't know what was coming down the tracks, and it wouldn't have been fair to Dublin or my family if I had accepted the job under those circumstances. Another factor was that I had already turned down my own county when my interest was gauged twice before and I was thinking to myself, "How can you commit to another county now?" While it was hugely appealing, the timing was just all wrong. I phoned Costello and explained my predicament and he understood. I suggested Anthony Daly as somebody who would be worth talking to. Now, maybe Anthony was on their radar anyway, but I think it's worked out pretty well for both parties since.

· · · · ·

If managing Offaly is an ambition, then so, too, is taking charge of St Rynagh's, and I filled that role for a year back in 2006. A few of the players had been on to me over the years to get involved and, given my fanaticism for the club, I eventually took the reins at that time. Funnily enough, Birr contacted me the year before that as Pat Joe Whelahan was concentrating solely on managing Limerick, but I could never countenance training Birr to beat Rynagh's. Save for the year when I repeated my Leaving Cert back at the Vocational School, I had lived away from Banagher since I was twelve years of age and then, as inter-county commitments dominated my summers from the minor success of 1986 onwards, it would have been levelled at me at times that I didn't train with the club as much as I might have but I always tried to do as much as I could. No better man than myself to have the craic, but I was always a stickler for getting myself right and training properly. That attitude didn't prevail in Rynagh's any more by 2006, thirteen years after our last county title.

I installed Pádraig Horan and Seánie White as my selectors and set about changing the culture. It wasn't easy, however, in fact far from it. There were constant excuses from players week after week. There always seemed to be something – a stag, Christening, Confirmation, First Communion, wedding. The only excuse that wasn't exhausted was a Bar Mitzvah.

Anything came first bar training and there was quite a drinking culture at play. A number of the players would have been tradesmen who were doing well at that time, making good money and hurling seemed to be more of a hobby than anything else. When I was playing, my social life was accommodated around my hurling, whereas now it seemed more as if hurling was accommodated around the players' social lives. In fairness, it wasn't the case with all of them but it was sufficiently prevalent to erode the spirit within the camp. I can guarantee you Pat Joe didn't have to put up with it a few miles down the road in Birr during that era when they were collecting county, provincial and All-Ireland titles as a matter of routine.

We eventually got things moving reasonably well but ahead of the first round of the Championship against Ballyskenagh I felt I had to make a stand. A number of the players went to Cork for a stag the weekend before the game and I dropped them all from the starting fifteen. We lost by a couple of points but it wasn't a knockout game and I felt it was a stand well worth taking. Rynagh's had fallen so far behind in so many respects over the years that things weren't going to be transformed overnight. It was going to take a couple of years to change the whole mindset of what it meant to play for Rynagh's and the discipline that should go with it and, if there had to be pain in the short-term to achieve it, then I was prepared to swallow that.

However, I made a fatal mistake by allowing my better judgement to be swayed. Pádraig was also Chairman of the club and was anxious that the players I had dropped be brought back into the team. To be fair to them, they're sound lads that I got along fine with and there was no bitter animosity between us over the fact that I had left them out. But, rather than stick to my guns, I went along with Pádraig's suggestion and, once I did that, I had reneged on the promise I had made to myself about facing down this culture of laziness and apathy.

The year finished with a defeat to Kinnitty in the quarter-final, but in one of the earlier group games against Birr, although we were beaten by seven or eight points, I saw something that evening that led me to believe that we were going in the right direction. It was still going to take quite an amount of work, though, and it was a three-year project at least. We had very few players on the county panel, but some of the core issues that I had resolved to tackle had been dealt with to a certain extent. The training was good and the players were in reasonable shape. I could have had a blinkered approach and looked at the year as a means to an end and we might have slipped into a county semi-final, or possibly even a final, but in terms of long-term development it would have been worthless.

My affection for the club and desire to see them restored to the top of Offaly hurling very much informed my decision to take on the job initially, but it would take another couple of years for the reforms that I envisaged to really take hold and, once Edel was re-diagnosed with cancer that summer, there was no way I could carry the job through. Even for the year I was there, I was tearing down the road from Tullamore to Banagher at breakneck speed just to make training on time, devising drills as I went along. I wouldn't have had time to even think about how I would lay out a training session since the previous one given how busy I was at the time. A major overhaul had to be carried out and, if I was going to do it properly, the job needed to command more of my time, which I simply didn't have back then. I didn't go back with them in 2007, though I'd like to think the job will come around for me again at some point in the future when it's mutually suitable. There's only one team in Offaly that I'd want to train to win a county title and that's Rynagh's. If I'm honest, it's something I often dream about.

There is a lot of hope around the club that they can re-establish themselves as a real force at senior level in the near future. After our crop won the minor title in 1986, there wasn't another success at that level until 2005, and they've won three more since. But there was still just one Rynagh's player on the Offaly senior panel in 2011 and, while the standard of club hurling in the county has undoubtedly dipped over the last decade, if you're going out against the likes of Birr or Coolderry, who have a handful of county players and you have none, you're on the back foot straightaway.

There would be a school of thought that the correlation between the decline of Rynagh's and Offaly is more than a coincidence. "Offaly won't be back until Rynagh's are back," I often hear people say. Players from our club have always played a key role in successful Offaly teams. Indeed, three of the county's four All-Ireland winning captains were Rynagh's men, but it's more the type of player that we produced that I'm alluding to. People like Horan, Aidan Fogarty, Martin Hanamy, Damien Martin and Hubert Rigney were all tough men who were seriously committed and blessed with a big day temperament. Looking back over the years, there isn't any Rynagh's player that springs to mind as being particularly flashy; rather more efficient and uncompromising, and I'd put myself in that bracket, too. A team that wins All-Irelands requires various personalities and characters and Rynagh's players brought that bit of steel and backbone to Offaly in the 1980s and and '90s. Then you supplement that with your stylists and we were blessed to have the likes of Pat Carroll, Mark Corrigan, Ger Coughlan, Brian Whelahan,

Johnny Dooley, John Troy and several others in that regard.

I acted as a coach with Portumna in 2010 and although I am regularly approached by clubs and have managed Ballinamere-Durrow with Pat Cleary in recent years, I see myself being more involved in the underage section with them and possibly county-wide in the coming years. Pat has recently been appointed as Director of Underage Hurling in Offaly and a number of people like Johnny Pilkington, John Troy, Kevin Martin, Ronnie Byrne, Joe Errity, Stephen Byrne and myself are rowing in behind him and making our contribution. There have been numerous declarations from various officials in Offaly over the last number of years about us starting to seriously address the decline in our fortunes, beginning at underage level, but despite the establishment of academies and the insistence that we are going in the right direction, our minor teams are still being beaten by Carlow and Westmeath. However, with Pat in position I'm confident that we've finally started to address matters in a genuine way, and he's already made significant strides in the short period he's been in situ.

Although there is an input with the development squads from Under-14 level upwards, Pat is going right back to basics at Under-8, Under-10 and Under-12 level right around the county. The simple things, like instructing a young lad to hold a hurley properly from when he starts out to avoid bad habits festering to a point where they are unbreakable when he grows older. It's all about getting the basic technique instilled from a young age and then nourishing it from there. There's a template in place so that, at the end of each year, a player ought to have mastered a certain amount of skills and then build on that as he moves through the grades. At the appropriate age, speed and agility training will also be introduced, something which that is very much under-appreciated in Offaly. The lads that I mentioned are checking in on the various clubs every couple of weeks to mark their progress, take sessions and give the coaches in those clubs something to work on ahead of the next visit.

Kilkenny have been very much the standard-bearers in terms of developing underage talent and Pat has had some very useful meetings down there with Paul Kinsella and Pat Henderson, who are involved with their academies. We need to put our own slant on it, too, and maintain that Offaly style of hurling.

Ground hurling is something that has long been associated with Offaly and it's a facet of the game that some feel has become antiquated by now given that possession is king, but it's not as if we played it to such an extent that it was more like hockey. You should only really use it when it's a fifty-fifty ball and you want to keep it moving, but when the chance is there to gain possession you should take it.

Offaly's hurling style revolves around being clever in your use of the ball, switching the play and augmenting it with the nice touches and flicks, hooking and blocking; elements of play which wouldn't be as prevalent in Munster hurling as it is in Leinster. While, historically, there have tended to be more good inter-county teams in Munster at a given time, I've always felt that a good Leinster team is harder to beat than a good Munster team. It's very simple hurling but we seem to have gone away from it. We also need to focus on producing more physically powerful and athletic players, as we haven't been winning the type of aerial possession that we ought to be in recent years. It also has to be acknowledged too that there was a certain freakishness about how many quality players came through for Offaly, which itself is a small county, less than half of which is genuine hurling territory. From our 1986 All-Ireland winning minor team for example, twelve of the players came from Birr and St Rynagh's and neither club would have a particularly big catchment area to draw from. Look out to Clareen where Johnny Dooley and Kevin Kinahan were both born on the same day in a tiny village and who won six All Stars between them. While a number of really talented hurlers emerged around that time, the most important asset we had was that there were huge characters there whose determination and belief knew no limits. That, more than anything, is the single biggest thing we've been lacking in the last decade.

• • • • •

With the sparsity of success at underage level since 2000, it's unrealistic to expect the Offaly senior manager, whoever he may be, to produce a team capable of challenging for major honours any time soon. The remit is more or less to keep the senior team as competitive as possible so that when a talented crop finally emerges from underage level, they have a platform on which to maximise their potential rather than having to drag the team from hurling's backwaters, something which has happened in Clare over the past couple of years. If what is being rolling rolled out at the minute bears fruit, I would hope and expect that Offaly will be winning a Leinster minor title within the next five or six years and, as 1986 showed, that could spawn further success to reinvigorate hurling in the county for years to come.

Chapter 13

Bridge House Hotel, November, 2005

Having been living and working in or near Dublin for virtually all of my career with Offaly, I was more accessible to the national media and giving interviews to Gaelic games correspondents was never a problem for me. I can't understand why there is so much reluctance among players and managers to co-operate with the media nowadays. In fairness, it mostly comes from managers, who are far too over-protective of the players and simply don't trust them to give an interview to a journalist without saying something that will rile the opposition. But, in my opinion, if he can't be trusted to express himself appropriately in that setting, how can he be trusted to do so in front of tens of thousands of people at Croke Park? Refusing to co-operate with the media is not something that's relevant to winning games anyway. Have you ever heard a victorious player or manager say after a big game, "Well, the fact that we didn't take any calls from journalists this week was crucial when it came to the crunch in the last ten minutes out there today"? The GAA is up against it at the best of times in terms of competing with soccer and rugby for publicity without its own flagship teams making it ever more difficult through media bans that are counter-productive to the promotion of our games. If every team took that approach the print and broadcast media would be void of GAA coverage, which would lead to little public interest and sparsely populated terraces.

As well, too many players take umbrage nowadays about something that may be written about them. If a journalist was critical of me in an article when I was playing I can honestly say it didn't bother me. If I played rubbish and he or she wrote as much, then fine, they're right. It's no big deal. Plenty of them said I should have been sent off against Clare in 1998 but I hardly interpreted that as a vendetta against me the way players seem to now. And, anyway, of course I should have been sent off so I could hardly expect them to write or say otherwise.

Granted, giving interviews is not something that every player is comfortable with and if they are dead set against it then they shouldn't be forced into it, but it can have a positive effect on a player and give him confidence provided he doesn't make himself a hostage to fortune in what he is quoted on, and most lads are sufficiently bright not to do that. The vast majority of GAA reporters are genuine enough not to hang a player out to dry in a way that would be associated with other sections of the media, particularly across the water. There are all sorts of positive spin-offs from it as well in terms of product endorsements, which can be quite lucrative. That side of things hadn't quite taken off before I retired but my media dealings while I was playing have accrued benefits that continue to stand to me.

Having taken part in successive All-Ireland finals in 1994 and '95, the Offaly team had a high profile at the time. Before one of those finals I was interviewed by Michael Lyster for RTÉ Television and, afterwards, he asked me would I be interested in appearing on The Sunday Game at some point in the future and I thought, why not? I didn't think any more of it until I got a call ahead of the 1996 All-Ireland final between Wexford and Limerick and was asked to cover the game alongside Michael and Ger Loughnane in the old gantry by the scoreboard above the Nally Stand as it was then. It shows how the times have changed as I was still very much involved with Offaly while Loughnane was the Clare manager. Now, RTÉ work off a panel of pundits and very rarely stray outside of that in terms of their main match analysis. Nowadays, a manager probably wouldn't let you do it, but it didn't even occur to me to seek permission.

I remember the day well. I wasn't nervous in any way, but the noise from the crowd was deafening and I could only hear Michael through the cans I was wearing on my ears. Pat Horan, a clubmate of mine, was the referee that day and sent off Wexford's Eamon Scallan in the first half and I had no problem commenting on it at half-time, although it was difficult to see how Scallan could have too many complaints anyway, given what happened in that incident. Of course, I would have much preferred to be out on the field playing, as I had been the two previous years, but it was a brilliant occasion and I enjoyed it. Unfortunately we made an even earlier Championship exit the following year and I was called back again for the Munster final between Clare and Tipperary, which I covered from the studio in Dublin. In the last three Championship seasons I was involved in we enjoyed lengthy runs, reaching two finals and a semi-final so I wasn't called in at all, but, from 2001 on I became a regular fixture.

There is a certain prestige attached to doing it and, of course, it strokes the ego, something we all liked as players, whether we admit it or not, and this helps to fill the void somewhat. While I still enjoy it, the novelty soon wears off when you're on the evening highlights programme and you have to spend ten hours or so in Montrose. It takes a bit of getting used to but there is no formal training for it as such, which is a good thing, I believe. There's no one telling you that you have to come at something from a certain angle, whatever others may believe. One of the more difficult aspects to it is the heat in the studio. While it comes across as a nice and tidy set on your television, the camera is very much on top of you and the lights that beam down can be quite intense as the make-up melts on your face.

In the last few years I have worked more as the co-commentator during the live broadcasts alongside Ger Canning or Marty Morrissey and you need to get used to their individual style over time. I found it awkward at the start in terms of knowing when to interject with your own piece of analysis to supplement the main commentator, and I'd often look for a physical sign from them but, over time, it becomes more intuitive once you've developed a rapport. I've heard John Giles say how the best piece of advice he received in regard to doing co-commentary was not to speak just for the sake of it. If the match went on for five minutes and the nature of the play during that period didn't demand your input, then so be it. People sometimes say to me after a game that I didn't utter a word for ages but, if a straightforward point has been scored and Ger or Marty have described it in forensic detail and there has been a replay or two of it, there's not much point in me adding to it for no good reason. You also have to deal with the mutterings of the producer in your cans throughout the game. Most of the time, what he's saying doesn't relate to you but it can be distracting if you allow it to be. Something like, "Tell that lad to get out of the way of the camera!" would often be blurted out, or sometimes they can get wrapped up in the game and roar, "That wasn't a free!" But they could also ask you to comment on something that has happened, so you have to be conscious of what's being said in the background without being swayed by it either. I prefer the live commentary in that you do your seventy minutes and your day's work is done, but it's a far more difficult assignment than the analysis in the studio because, in that scenario, you have plenty of time to think about what you're going to say. It's all on-the-spot when the match is unfolding in front of you.

The more experienced I became, the less worried I was about what I might have said previously on a particular matter and trying to maintain a level of consistency on that topic. I've realised that you're allowed to change your mind if you want to. I don't prepare material to use on air before games per se, though naturally I think about it during the week in the run-up to a game. But, until that ball is thrown in, you don't know what's going to happen so there's no point tying yourself up in knots in terms of preparation beforehand. It's different if you're in the studio on the highlights show, when you'll pick out various clips for analysis.

It may be stating the obvious, but it's essential that you know the players and are familiar with their play, otherwise it will erode viewers' confidence in you. There is nothing quite so unprofessional as getting players' names wrong. It's also important to be conscious of the fact that the audience you are addressing aren't all knowledgeable GAA people and may only have a passing interest in hurling. In the modern game, players switch positions much more frequently on the field, and it's something that's difficult to pick up on from your armchair at home, so you need to point these things out, along with the more subtle aspects of the game where you bring your own playing experience to bear.

Of course you'll get calls wrong from time to time and that's when you really have the craic with it. If I'm honest, there is a perverse satisfaction to putting my foot in it because of the reaction it draws. One such incident fell during the Waterford-Clare Munster semi-final in 2010. The game was drawing to a close when I commented on Ken McGrath and how his career was all but over, his knee problems had caught up with him and he was barely able to puck around with his kids in the back garden. Next thing, Ger says, "Is that Ken McGrath warming up, Michael?" Straightaway the camera panned to him on the sideline. He came on and got a ball on the old stand side of the field in Thurles just under the commentary box and swung over a massive point to seal Waterford's win. Nice one, Michael!

Another time I was on the panel for a Saturday evening game with Paul Flynn and Ger Loughnane. I was just back from Medjugorje with Edel and only arrived shortly before the start of the programme. Just before half-time, Michael Lyster leaned in and said, "Ger and Paul, I'll get a quick comment off ye and then we'll go to a break and, when we come back, I'll start with you, Michael." That was grand, so I sat back in my chair and relaxed while Michael turned to Ger and Paul once we were on air in the studio. But, for once, I hadn't turned my phone off and it started ringing. I shoved my hand in my pocket and stopped it pretty swiftly though I wasn't able to turn it off and, sure enough, it started ringing again. I was fidgeting and rooting in my pocket when Lyster, being the messer he is, couldn't resist winding me up by drawing me into the analysis despite saying he would wait until after the break.

"And what did you make of that first half, Michael?" he asked.

For about a second I looked at him and was about to say, "Would you ever feck off you bollocks!" only out of the corner of my eye I could see myself on the screen so we were still on air. Words failed me.

"Well, I, eh, uh, ah, I suppose, yeah but, no, but..." making about as much sense as that character Vicky Pollard from Little Britain. I made a complete gobshite out of myself, but it was funny all the same.

Back in 2003, I got a lot of ribbing from Wexford supporters when I completely forgot that they were still in the Championship on air, unbelievable as that may sound. Offaly had just beaten Limerick in the qualifiers that year in a game that was, bizarrely, played on a Thursday night and Wexford were playing Waterford the following Saturday. After Offaly had beaten Limerick, the post-match analysis turned to the teams that were left in the Championship and I mentioned everybody bar Wexford in such a way that suggested that I was effectively putting Waterford through to the next round. It wasn't that I was snubbing Wexford and thought they had no chance of beating Waterford,

I genuinely just completely forgot about the upcoming game.

I was down in Nowlan Park that Saturday as Larry Murphy rolled back the years in spearheading a great win for them. The banter coming out of the ground was brilliant, with Wexford supporters banging on the windows in their buses and slagging me off about my slip. They were good-natured in their banter though and it was all in the spirit of a bit of harmless craic, which I knocked great fun out of. You'd wonder how you could be so stupid as to forget something like that, but I did it again in 2007 when, after Kilkenny had beaten Wexford in the semi-final and Waterford accounted for Cork in the quarter-final replay on the same day, I effectively placed Waterford in the All-Ireland final despite the fact that they had they still had to play Limerick the following Sunday. Sure enough, Limerick turned the tables on Waterford, just as Wexford had done four years previously. The Limerick fans didn't take it with the same good humour, though, and were a bit sore in their comments to me afterwards. Again, while you wouldn't be planning these things, it gets people talking about you and is good for your profile.

The Sunday Game has been criticised by players, managers and administrators in recent years for having what they feel is too big an influence on the GAA's main disciplinary body, the Central Competitions Control Committee. A controversial incident happens in a game, it is discussed at length on the show and then the player finds himself being proposed for a suspension. Does The Sunday Game wield an influence on the CCCC's collective thinking? I'd say yes, it probably does. It's only natural that it would, as those who sit on these committees watch the show like everyone else and are human. But, for me, that's not really the point. Whether an incident is highlighted or not, players should take responsibility for their actions rather than looking elsewhere for scapegoats. If you pull a stroke on someone during a game, nobody else is responsible for that only you. The player knows the risk he's running in doing it so, if it's caught on camera, he need have no complaints.

One of the high-profile suspensions of the 2010 Championship was that of Kerry footballer Tomás Ó Sé. His indiscretions against Limerick's Stephen Kelly were highlighted by various cameras and, while he naturally wouldn't have been happy about it, he took his punishment like a man. "It happened on the day and I wasn't going to go appealing it," he said afterwards, "it was there for everybody to see." Ó Sé is part of what seems to be a dying breed in that he doesn't get too perturbed what is said about him in the media and just gets on with it. A lot of the loopholes have been closed in recent years, meaning that the number of cases going all the way through the disciplinary process is falling as players are finally copping on to the fact that, while they may have got off on a technicality previously, that avenue realistically isn't open to them any more. It's about time it happened, too. I got away with it once in 1998, but if the referee had taken the appropriate action that day I wouldn't have gone exhausting the disciplinary process afterwards.

Bizarrely, sometimes people link the fact that I have commented on an incident during a live commentary, perhaps saying a player should have been sent off or yellow-carded, with the subsequent action taken by the referee – as if he has a live feed to my commentary as the match progresses! "You didn't do anything to help his cause anyway," someone might say, as though it made any difference to the referee's thinking. It isn't particularly pleasant having to highlight something that could land a player in difficulty. During the Kilkenny-Galway Leinster semi-final in 2009, I said that Tommy Walsh ought to have been red-carded having been involved in a number of flashpoints. It came up on the highlights show again the following night and I reiterated that view. Tommy is one of my favourite players, and I didn't take any satisfaction from saying it, but I had a duty to give my honest opinion, even though you know you could be landing the player in bother as well as annoying everybody in Kilkenny. The easiest thing would be to go and show the goals and key scores from the game another three times when viewers have already seen enough of that.

I sometimes get the feeling that some of the other pundits, particularly Pat Spillane, almost seem to revel in bringing these incidents to light knowing the impact it could have, which I find rather distasteful. Pat is no longer in the presenter's chair, which is no harm. He'd often try and set you up on air in terms of his questions. As I said, Michael Lyster would generally give you a steer as to what he will ask you about beforehand. Pat would do the same, only then he'd take a completely different slant once the cameras are rolling and throw you some sort of curve ball like, "There was racing on down in the Curragh today, Michael, with massive prize money and the players in

Croke Park are getting nothing. What do you think of that?" Quite honestly, introducing an argument like that is a complete red herring, which I couldn't care less about. He's a good GAA man but his knowledge of hurling was limited and you'd find yourself trying to educate him, which was awkward.

People might imagine that there is tension between Ger Loughnane and myself, given the events of 1998 when he pinned the picture of my wild pull on David Forde to the dressing room door before we beat Clare in the third game in Thurles. But, if you've learned anything about me from reading this book, you would know that it wouldn't bother me in the slightest. In fact, I thought it was a ridiculous thing for him to do and he could put up a picture of me every day for all I cared but I understand that he was using it purely as a motivational tool. It is my opinion that Loughnane is a very intelligent person and everything he says is carefully thought out, whereas others think he's trying to be controversial for the sake of it. Like, when he took over Galway, he said they had to win an All-Ireland within two years. I believe that was designed to put pressure on the players and, if they didn't deliver, then he was well able to take the flak anyway. Through the punditry I have got to know the likes of Anthony Daly and Tomás Mulcahy well and have struck up friendships with them through playing golf. I don't have that rapport with Ger but we always get on well when we meet. However, I think it's a shame how he pilloried Daly and a number of his former Clare players through his media work in later years, particularly in his newspaper columns.

While Loughnane's stern visage and outspokenness meant he was widely known long before he ventured into punditry, the same wasn't quite true for me and I am recognised much more now than I was in my playing days as a result of being on television regularly. It's bemusing at times how people think they know you and are entitled to approach you. I'd like to think I'm a reasonably approachable guy and I have no problem with it most of the time and usually the conversation will be about hurling but, occasionally, someone could come up to you and, without any formalities, say something like, "Jaysus... you're after getting shocking fat!"

Once, Edel and I were on holidays in Barcelona when a chap from Cork recognised me while we were having a meal one evening. He started chatting, which was fine for a couple of minutes, but when the conversation continued for the rest of our meal I began to wonder how someone could have such poor social awareness. Sometimes I could be in the process of having an important business meeting in a hotel when someone passing might think it's wholly appropriate to interject and start talking hurling. I often wonder would they be so prepared to do it if, say, Henry Shefflin was in the same scenario. Now, I'm sure Henry gets approached more often than he would ideally like, but I think people feel that once you are on television you're public property to a certain extent. That goes with the territory and, by and large, I have no problem with it, apart from a few awkward moments like I have just outlined. As I said, I often enjoy it, especially when I'm getting a bit of stick. One of my favourite comebacks in those situations is to stare the person down and ask, "Are you paying your TV licence?"

There are a number of positive spin-offs from punditry work and one of them was when I became a hurling columnist for *Irish Daily Star Sunday* in 2005. I was bemused to open the paper one Sunday to see a sub headline accompanying my byline that read, "Ireland's number one hurling columnist", though I thought the column went quite well. It was ghost-written by John Harrington, who very quickly grasped what I was about and wrote the column exactly as I wanted it to appear week after week. With The Sunday Game I was generally only commenting on games and incidents arising out of them but with the column, I had a platform to air my views on a wide range of GAA topics. Among them was a fall-out in Limerick with Justin McCarthy, which led to a shadow Limerick side taking part in the National League and Championship in 2010. While some of the Limerick hurlers may not have commanded huge respect for some apparent off-field misdemeanours over the years, they did seem to have some genuine difficulties with McCarthy. Limerick had level-headed fellas like Séamus Hickey, Brian Geary and Damien Reale, who are very serious about their hurling, withdrawing their services. McCarthy also had a relationship breakdown with a number of hurlers in the Waterford dressing room during his spell with them. I felt the whole thing would have come to a more satisfactory conclusion much sooner if the other players hadn't taken their place under McCarthy, whose position would have become untenable much earlier than when it finally did. I wrote as much in my column and Reale, whom I've never met before, sent me a text to thank me for the support, which was a nice touch.

The strikes in Cork weren't so straightforward, however. I was very supportive of their first stand in 2002 and was shocked at how bad things were down there. They stood firm together on it and managed to reach the next four All-Ireland finals in succession. I remember speaking warmly about them on The Sunday Game in 2003 on the night they won back the Munster title, a massive statement for them in terms of justifying the unprecedented stance they had taken. They took on Frank Murphy, a man who wielded such power in Cork GAA, and won. They also got their own way in the two subsequent strikes but, for me, they didn't retain the same level of public support, certainly outside Cork anyway. People just lost interest and yawned the more it kept coming up, and their cries started to sound a little hollow.

Overall I'd say that the Cork players took a brave stance and initially got where they wanted to go in terms of winning their two All-Irelands, but they haven't been so successful in the last number of years. They demand the very best in terms of preparation and, by and large, you'd have to say that they deserve it because of the time they're putting into it. On the other hand, though, there is a great inequality in terms of preparation across the board because resources aren't evenly spread. The likes of Cork, Tipperary, Dublin and Kerry will spend around €1million annually in preparing their teams, much more than a smaller county like Offaly can afford to so, if you extrapolate that, the strong will only get stronger and the weak will get weaker.

I'm not sure how widely read my column was by GAA people, but the paper clearly wasn't earning its keep and was pulled early in 2011. The column was something I really enjoyed doing, though, and I'd welcome the opportunity to put my name to one again in the future.

Another developing off-shoot from punditry has been a few appearances on the after-dinner speaking circuit and also performing master of ceremonies duties at various functions. The after-dinner speaking is something that is only relatively new to me and which I'd like to expand on in the future, but I've adapted reasonably well to it so far. You have to be wary of the crowd you are addressing and mix the anecdotes accordingly, but I also bring my working background to bear in these scenarios where appropriate. All of this has to be done in the right context and, generally, I don't plan what I'm going to speak about until I've had an opportunity to size up the audience and then adapt from there. Encouragingly, I've had a few gigs that have stemmed from previous appearances, so I must be doing something right. Leaving hurling aside, my career has been reasonably broad and far-reaching, and my public profile was no harm in that regard either.

· · · · ·

For a long time I had the idea that, while in my twenties, I would devote most of my energy towards excelling in sport, primarily hurling as it turned out, and then, in my thirties, I would redirect that level of application towards business, with the intention of being well set up by the time I reached the age of forty. I arrived at that milestone in February 2008, and things had gone pretty much to plan up to that point until the economic downturn took hold later that year. Having left AIB initially in 1995 to move to Lombard & Ulster to work in the area of asset finance, I returned to AIB in 1998, this time in the finance and leasing division, before leaving for the last time a couple of years later to take up a position as national sales manager with Caterpillar Finance.

I was working on a worldwide subsidiary, essentially leasing Caterpillar machinery to clients, usually over a number of years. During my second stint in AIB it had always been in my mind that I would go out on my own at some stage and, in April 2002, I took the plunge with the establishment of Michael Duignan Financial Services. By then Edel had earned a couple of promotions herself in AIB and was well-placed so it wasn't a huge risk by any means, especially given how the economy was gathering pace. I didn't have to process a huge amount of business to justify the decision, which was comforting. Working with Caterpillar was a good experience but very demanding. I had built up my own client base over the years and my thinking was that I would be able to attract a certain amount of business with a number of them that would be more than enough to keep me afloat.

While it was liberating to be your own master, for the first time in years I had to perform more regular tasks such as buying my own car and paying mobile phone bills, the like of which had been looked after for me in previous jobs, while there were overheads associated with running my own office, though it wasn't too bad in that respect initially as I worked from home. From a work point of view it was pretty straightforward: a client with an interest in buying a piece of plant equipment from a dealer would engage with me to organise finance for them, most often from Bank of Scotland or Lombard & Ulster at the best rate I could get, with commission on the side for me from the client. I was essentially the middleman. It was important to have an awareness of how your potential clients were operating and then to try and persuade them to share a certain amount of their dealings with you. I wasn't going to get all their business, and I didn't need it all. I had a good relationship with the banks, which helped, too. The period leading into the summer is usually quite busy so I was pretty much straight in at the deep end once I started and completed a number of nice deals to get me going. Things slow down towards the end of the summer and pick up once more in September and October before another lull and January to April then would be mayhem, particularly back then.

Edel fell sick a few months after I started, so I wouldn't say I was quite driving the business on as best I could at that stage, but, over the next three years I fared pretty well and then found myself gravitating towards the auctioneering trade. It all started when I took a call one day from someone wondering if there were any sites available within Tullamore for new housing developments. I looked into it and sourced two sites, which a developer later acquired through me. With the development set to be rolled out, someone was then required to sell the houses and it was suggested to me that it would be a good idea if I fulfilled the role and moved more towards auctioneering in general. Although I had no experience in auctioneering, it appealed to me in that I had been considering diversifying so that most of my work could be centred around Tullamore. As it was, I was travelling around the Dublin, Kildare and Wicklow areas quite a lot. The property boom was in full swing at that time and auctioneering licences were obtained as easily as dirt on your shoe. Finding a suitable office wasn't quite so straightforward at the time, given that there were few prime locations available and those that were came at exorbitant prices. It meant that, when the first big development that I was involved in as an auctioneer was going on the market, I didn't even have an office to sell from!

I rented a room in the Bridge House Hotel one Thursday evening in November, 2005, to launch the development, though a sod had yet to be turned. The way things turned out that night was a prime example of how extravagant people were with their money back then. I received deposits for about forty houses purely off the plans. Now, the development looked great on paper and the site was ideally situated, given its proximity to the town centre. The demand was just ferocious. It was bizarre to think that, with no background in auctioneering, no office and with not a single sod turned in the ground, that I was able to sell that many houses so quickly, not that I had to be in Arthur Daly mode to pull it off, so willing were people to part with their money. A few months later, three showhouses had been built and I had opened an office on Main Street in Tullamore. On the weekend we presented the showhouses for viewing there was mayhem. People were queuing around the block on the Saturday, some of them even getting narky at the fact that there were only a couple of houses available for viewing. We came back the next day and, such was the demand, prices had risen considerably from the day before.

Over the course of the weekend we took deposits on about another one hundred and twenty properties, making for up to one hundred and sixty in total, which was more than half of the development with only a couple of show houses on the site. Not all of those eventually went to sale but most of them did. A lot of it was speculation in that, while some of the buyers were planning to live in these houses, many of them were purchasing in the expectation that the prices would continue to rise and that they could make a healthy profit by selling them on again in another few years. From my point of view, it was a great start to the business. I had Mary Nestor and Jackie Moriarty working with me, both of whom, unlike me, had experience of working in auctioneering previously.

· · · · ·

While that start had me up and running nicely, I was also completing several other deals and was fortunate enough to start selling property for John Flanagan and Sons in Tullamore, one of the most reputable builders in the midlands. Because of my banking background I saw myself as being better suited to commercial property, while Jackie had a flair for the residential side of things and we dovetailed nicely. From the my time in the bank, I quickly learned to be strictly confidential in my dealings, unlike a lot of people who mouth off in pubs, and that's something you can apply to a lot of professions. I think people could see that in me once having dealt with me, and it stood me in good stead in auctioneering. There's no point in playing it down, we had a few very good years but, at the same time, and without meaning to sound wise after the event, there was a voice inside me wondering where all this would end.

The property market was at its peak when I became an auctioneer. I had come from nowhere and stepped right into the middle of it and it was surreal to see it in action, with ordinary people, not tycoons, climbing over each other to buy houses in Church Hill. It was like Black Friday in America. It was all so different from when Edel and I bought our first home in Naas in 1995, scarcely a decade earlier. From my own banking days, the changes were obvious. In '95, both of us had good pensionable jobs and could only borrow two and a half times our combined salary. When we bought the house it was a shell and we'd save bit by bit to kit it out. One month we might have put tiles on the kitchen floor, the next it might have been carpet for some other room. Dribs and drabs. A decade later, €300,000 had, rather dramatically, become a small sum but it was still a lot of money. People were buying houses that were fully furnished, with two new cars sitting in the driveway. Granted, wages had increased across the board and people were generally doing better for themselves, but the interest rates were driving this whole thing.

One hundred per cent and interest-only mortgages were being thrown at anyone, with finance made available to people for virtually anything. It wasn't like people were wondering, "Will I get the money?" more a case of "Who will I get it from and what's the rate going to be?" I found it hard to credit how access to finance had loosened so considerably from my time in the bank a decade earlier. The foreign banks that are now suffering couldn't wait to get a slice of the action and the whole thing was gone mad. A landowner only had to look at the fact that houses, which were once selling for €80,000, were now going for three times that so, naturally, they pushed up the price of their land. Where developers would once have worked off a model of, say, buy the land, build the houses, pay everyone what they're owed and finish with a fifteen per cent profit, instead they wanted a fifty per cent profit. The pace of it all was staggering and, of course, speed dictates the casualty levels when a crash occurs.

While on the one hand I was telling myself that it couldn't continue at this rate, like everyone else, it was hard not to get caught up in it and there were no clear indications that everything would grind to a halt so abruptly. I invested a lot of the money I had made in property and bank shares and planned to sell them on for a tidy profit at some stage in the future only for the arse to fall out of the market, which has left me with little option but to retain them for now. They could well turn out to be sound investments eventually but, if I were to sell now, I'd be looking at substantial losses.

Among my ventures was to row in with Joe Connolly and Michael Lynskey, from Galway, in establishing Connolly Duignan Lynskey, a separate auctioneering business in Portugal. It was a painstaking couple of years going through the lengthy application process to be granted a licence over there and we weren't long on our feet when people in Ireland suddenly became very reluctant about investing in foreign properties as the Celtic Tiger wheezed its last, leaving us with a number of rather significant properties still on our hands. I thought I had insulated myself reasonably well in terms of how I spread my money around with these other investments, safe in the knowledge, or so I thought, that money owed to me from other deals would come good. It didn't. I was certainly stung in that regard and paid a price for looking too far ahead. I was investing with a view to reducing some of my borrowings out of future earnings, which looked safe at the time, but then everything came to a standstill so quickly when I thought there were still another couple of good years to be had. If the slowdown had been more discernible from an earlier stage, and I had even got another twelve months out of the boom, I could have recouped the money from the deals I was involved in and escaped relatively unscathed.

But that's wishful thinking, and there are certainly others who have been scalded far worse than I have been. I wouldn't say that my standard of life has dipped noticeably as I wasn't brought up to be extravagant and, thankfully, having money at my disposal didn't change me in that regard. All I ever wanted was the simple day-to-day stuff like food on the table, providing for my wife and children, going for a few pints here and there. It doesn't take a huge amount of money to sustain that. We would have taken more holidays, especially with the Portugal connection business-wise, but nothing over the top.

As the auctioneering business went from strength to strength initially, I maintained the finance brokering on the side, but it, too has fallen flat in tandem with the property market. At this stage I'm wondering whether it would be a better idea to just cut my losses and move in a different direction altogether professionally, as overheads alone are nearly enough to drag you under at the moment. A lot of people don't quite realise how draining they can be on your resources when starting a business. To that end, I have withdrawn from the premises in Main St to a unit I own just outside Tullamore.

People in Ireland changed so much during the Celtic Tiger but now it's back to basics for many and a new-found modesty is taking hold, which is no harm either given how we had collectively lost the run of ourselves. A friend of mine from Galway explained to me how he once had flown back into Dublin from exotic climes and, rather than jump on a bus, train or even grab a taxi back home, he hired a helicopter for something like four grand in cash to get back to Galway. "What sort of a fecking eejit was I?" he said to me. You'd see it at race meetings in Galway and Punchestown, champagne tents densely populated by the nouveau riche when, a few years previously, people would be happy with their few pints. I was drinking modest champagne in Punchestown one day in the company of friends when one of them, who would only have been known to me among the group I was with beforehand, told the waitress to "take away that shit" and ordered two bottles of Dom Perignon for all of us – €250 each. Those who were used to that standard of living generally handled the Celtic Tiger lifestyle fine but a lot of the new entrants completely lost the plot.

Comparisons will be made to the 1980s recession, but I feel the current predicament is far worse. When I was growing up in the '70s and '80s people had very little. Even if you came from a middle-class background, it was still decidedly modest. Wages were meagre and families were bigger. There were some people who could be considered the elite, but very few, and there was much less diversity in society back then. One of the crucial differences between then and now is that, although they wouldn't have been well-off, people generally didn't owe money because they couldn't get it in the first place. It was simply a matter of getting them back to work. Some might have owed a few bob to the Credit Union but there was no second or third mortgage; they were lucky enough to get one. People saved for things they wanted and cut their cloth accordingly, whereas, now, the level of debt out there is massive. I know of regular people out there in ordinary jobs who could own up to twenty properties and are millions of euro in debt and you'd never think it of them. It's rife. Even if the debt is only a few hundred grand, it's still a lot of money, but it has been made to look small by the excesses of the Celtic Tiger.

There is now more of an appreciation in that, if someone has €50,000 in the bank, they know it's a lot of money when, not too long ago, such a sum was being tossed around like loose change. And for all the money that was in the country for more than a decade, a lot of issues didn't go away, such as the apathy towards the health service, although there were a number of advances, too. But, in the '80s, people never knew any different because it had never been radically different. Now it's a case of re-evaluating everything and asking ourselves what is important. That's something I feel is good for society and for the next generation, provided the economy recovers sufficiently to prevent them from leaving the country. I think it could be up to a decade before we see that, though.

I'm not bitter about the predicament I've been landed in. While I don't think I underwent a personality transplant in the way that some did during the boom, I'm willing to take my share of the responsibility, but I believe that everyone should have to do that and the banks, in particular, are getting away very lightly. I'm mystified as to how they forked out a lot of the money they did. A voice of reason was required but no one shouted stop. I'd like to think that, if I were still in the bank, at whatever level, I would have called for more strenuous financial checks as to people's ability to repay a loan before handing out such vast amounts of money to them. Now the pain is all one-way with the banks being bailed out, but there's nobody bailing out the client who is crippled by repayments. I think a deal will have to struck, some sort of write-down perhaps, that gives people a chance to survive for now because there is a risk that the private sector and entrepreneurial people will go to the wall, and who will lead the recovery then?

"Burn the bondholders," has become a catchphrase of late, but I don't think it's that straightforward, either. As I see it, there is roughly a €15billion deficit between what the country is spending and what we're taking in on a yearly basis and, if we burn these guys, how are we going to make up the shortfall in the meantime? There certainly wouldn't be too many prepared to invest in the country. But, while the banks are being given money hand over fist now, my gripe is that none of that money is filtering down into the business community. There are ordinary decent business people who have been in operation for years, say in terms of seasonal sales, and they would have always relied on an overdraft facility before paying it off once their money comes in at a certain time of year. Now these people are being refused that facility and smaller businesses are going to the wall, which only twists the knife in the back of the economy. Whatever money the banks are giving out it comes with crippling interest rates so, if you were to leave the bad debts to one side and look at their operating profits on a day-to-day basis for the last three years, I guarantee you that they'd be substantial because of those interest rates. When I started working in the bank all those years ago, it was very much a case of looking at the person, but that approach seems to be long gone now.

Nobody can be certain as to how things will unfold in the coming years, but I'd be confident that I can get my lads educated. If I lose my properties and end up owing some money, I wouldn't see it as a catastrophe. A lot of other people are worse off. I hope to be able to repaying everything that I owe, but I can't guarantee it.

Changing tack in terms of my career once again is something that I have been considering. You need to be flexible and I think that I am. I've been dabbling in property management but now that I've established myself reasonably well in terms of the media since I retired, I think there is a niche there in terms of how the GAA is covered in a whole realm of areas, social networking being one of them. I also think there is a demand out there for more GAA-related documentaries and feature-length shows. It's something TG4 have done well in recent years and I think it could be expanded on, possibly through setting up my own production company at some point down the line. I think it's doable, but obviously there's more to it than that and I need to tease out how financially viable it may be. I have built up a wide range of contacts from all walks of life through my diverse sporting and professional careers, and I suppose it's a case of working out how best to use that to my advantage.

In any decision I make about my future, it has to be taken with Seán and Brian in mind. They are my sole priorities over the next number of years and inform my thinking in virtually everything I do. I was presented with the prospect of a pretty radical career change recently when a leading political party asked me to run in the general election. There was a freakish element to the 2011 election, given that a number of quirky candidates came out of nowhere and won a seat amid the prevailing mood for change. With that in mind, I have to admit that I was tempted and it's something I considered, but only briefly. People may have been offering me encouragement to stand, but, of course, they weren't looking at the bigger picture. As a single parent, I have to be there for Seán and Brian every morning and evening and leading the life of a TD, where I could be away a couple of nights a week or certainly arriving home late at night, simply wasn't a runner.

Like a lot of people, I'd be angry at how things have turned out over the last few years. I train a number of youngsters at underage level in Ballinamere-Durrow and I'd like to be sitting up in the stand watching them win All-Irelands, see them getting married and having children in fifteen or twenty years' time rather than receiving their postcards from Australia. I'd hate for my own sons to attend college in years to come, knowing that they'll have to leave the country as soon as they graduate. It's just as well they're at the age they are in that regard as I would be more optimistic that the country will be on a sounder footing when that time comes around.

When I see people leaving the country in droves I find myself getting angry about the cronyism that has prevailed for so long in Ireland. I can understand why a stroke might be pulled here and there in politics and business, but only within reason. Some of the salaries, expenses, pensions and pay-offs that are being drawn down are absolutely crazy and we need serious reform on that front. Fianna Fáil took a lot of stick for overseeing this sort of behaviour, but some of the appointments since the new administration took over wouldn't engender confidence that radical change is on the way either. I'd see myself as being straight and honest and I expect the same from others, certainly from our public representatives.

Chapter 14

St James's Hospital, June, 2006

The withdrawal symptoms from playing inter-county hurling at a high level for so long can be difficult to withstand, though I suppose the couple of years I had with Meath, and my brief spell with Offaly in 2004, was methadone in that respect. Initially I was relieved at having cut ties, given how busy I was with work. One day I could be up north, the next day it could be Killarney. Trying to go training in Offaly in the middle of all that when injuries were continually catching up on me became less appealing and I know that I made the right decision. Having processed all that, it didn't stop me missing it terribly once the Championship came around, and it's something that took me a number of years to get a handle on.

Offaly were drawn to play Kilkenny in the Leinster semi-final in 2001, a straight knockout game at the time. The team's consistency was long gone by then but it was still felt that they could summon a big performance from nowhere, as had been the case against Cork the previous year. Ger Loughnane even predicted an Offaly victory. It wasn't to be, however, as Kilkenny cruised to a twelve-point win that signalled the break-up of the team, even though a few of us had already departed by then. There were a lot of miles on the clock for our key players. The likes of Johnny Dooley and Brian Whelahan, although not yet thirty at the time, had been playing minor hurling for Offaly when they were still only fifteen, had played another four years at Under-21 level and then had lengthy senior careers. The Birr lads had endured a number of draining club campaigns, too. I felt a bit of guilt at the time, as though I had left the lads in the lurch to take a hiding from Kilkenny but there's a fine line between staying on and helping to bring new players through or staying on and stunting their development. If I had been involved in 2001 I probably would have earned a starting spot, but my ability to contribute would have been very limited compared to when I was at my best. A lad of nineteen or twenty would surely have been a better option at that stage. Despite that, I couldn't help wondering at the time whether I should have given another year to help the transitional process after that Kilkenny beating. It hurt me then, and it hurts me now, that we had spent so long as a county trying to reach Kilkenny's standards and then surpass them, but now they had pulled so far clear of us.

What I missed most was the training. Not the drive to or from training, but the sessions themselves. Over the years our training sessions were brilliant and thoroughly enjoyable. With the stickmen we had, the quality of the hurling we played, even within training, was outstanding and I would look forward to it with relish. Added to that was the spirit we had as a group and the characters involved – the slagging and the craic, as I took my customary spot beside John Troy in to the left of the dressing room. Pilkington loosening the tops on the salt and pepper and continually catching lads out with it. Robbing a towel out of someone else's bag after training and then replacing it, soaked, before the unknowing victim arrived back to the dressing room. John Ryan might stack a few sods of turf in another gear bag. I had spent a vast portion of my life alongside a lot of these players and, while I was going to see them again in the future, it would never be with the same regularity, so retirement brought an abrupt finality to something that was an absolutely massive part of my life. At the time we were happy living in Naas and had no intention of moving so there was the factor of leaving Offaly behind as well. The couple of years after my retirement, rather than becoming easier, were even more difficult.

By then the buzz had gone out of playing for St Rynagh's for me. It wasn't helped by a fall-out in the club in 2000 with Hubert and Michael Rigney, who didn't play. We reached the county semi-final against Birr and I was centre-back. I played one of my best ever games for the club, but Birr still stuffed us and it hurt me deeply. It was frustrating for me personally that internal wrangling had led to two of our best players not lining out. I'm not suggesting we would have won if they were playing, but we wouldn't have taken a beating like that. For so long we were the one team in Offaly that Birr feared in knockout games but that was obliterated with that result. Having quit the county team, continuing to trek back to Offaly to train with the club wasn't very appetising, even if it was a wrench for me to leave Rynagh's.

I transferred to Raheens in Kildare at the behest of a great friend of mine, David Malone. He was an excellent footballer with Kildare that I had played against years earlier and who won a Leinster club title as a teenager, but Raheens had slid down the pecking order since. Now he was in his late thirties and this was as good a time as any to fulfil a promise I had made to him that we would play one year together before he retired. David and his wife, Mary, came to national attention in horrific circumstances in 1995 when a man called Jerome Kavanagh broke into their home and attacked the family with a knife, killing their son Ciarán, before David arrived home and disturbed him.

They were advised to stay in the house for a period afterwards on the basis that they'd never be able to confront what had happened to them if they moved straightaway. Having got that period under their belts they decided to build a new house out in Carragh but, in the meantime, they moved to Jigginstown Park, straight across the road from where Edel and I were living. I saw David pull up in the car one evening, recognised him and went over for a chat. We became very good friends, as did Edel with Mary. Out of our friendship he asked me to play with him for a year and 2001 seemed as good a time as any to do it while I was still in reasonable shape. Raheens had been down for a long time but, with the two of us in midfield, we had a brilliant year and reached the county semi-final where we were eventually beaten by reigning champions, Moorefield.

Back home, Rynagh's roused themselves to reach the county final against Birr and out of nowhere produced a stirring performance only to lose by a single point. Birr went on to win the next two All-Irelands, and no team got closer to them over that period than Rynagh's. It was very much an emotional decision that I had made to transfer to Raheens to play with David and I didn't regret it, but it was torture watching that county final. I love the club and felt terribly guilty. While there's no guarantee that my presence would have made any difference, I'd like to think that I would have been worth an extra point to the team anyway. I transferred back the following year and, in the county semi-final, when once more Birr provided the opposition, scored what looked to be a match-winning goal to put us a point up in injury time, though they snatched an equaliser and won the replay at their ease.

· · · · ·

Playing a bit at club level alone wasn't enough to fill the void that my retirement in 2001 had left. Initially I thought that it would be a good opportunity for me to do other things, such as playing golf and chipping away at my handicap. I did that but it didn't give me the same hit, though it didn't stop me playing either and, over time, I developed a very active social life around the game. Too active, Edel would have eventually argued, and she was right. After retiring she recognised the fact that I needed to let my hair down a bit and unwind, but it was a different story when it was still going on a couple of years later. Naturally, I had been around the house more than I was when I was playing with Offaly but not as much as I ought to have been. I might head out for a few on a Thursday night and there could be a golf classic on the Friday, which I would sometimes allow to swallow up the whole weekend. When Edel was ill I was thoroughly supportive but, soon after she got the all-clear, I resumed the selfish habits. Edel was easygoing but would take me to task in her own way. I cringe now when I think of how selfish and immature I was about it.

"I'm after having it so hard for fifteen years," I'd tell her. "You married the wrong person if you think I'm going to sit at home and watch Coronation Street with the slippers on. That's not me."

For a while I would have been a bit underhand about my movements.

"I'm just after getting a phone call to go and play in this golf tournament," I'd say.

Of course, she could see through it.

"Look, why don't you just tell me what you're doing?" she eventually snapped one day.

"Right so, where's your diary?" I replied, before filling in about three months' worth of outings. My good friend Noel Farrelly played off five and he was regularly asked to play in golf classics. He'd usually bring me along, as I was useful off my handicap at the time. A group of us played together quite often and I was captain of the golf society in Kavanagh's at one stage.

Edel didn't have a problem with me playing golf, or going for a few pints, all she was looking for was a balance. She was a very sociable person herself but she often said that when Seán was born her life changed dramatically, whereas I ploughed on as always. We weren't at each other's throats the whole time, or anything like that, and generally we were getting on grand, it's just that, at times, I was prone to looking at things from a personal, rather than a family, perspective when the opportunity for a social gathering presented itself. Edel's point was that, say, instead of being down in Kavanagh's three nights on a particular week, couldn't I just make it two? If I got a call from a friend on a Monday evening wondering would I come for a few pints, I immediately answered in the affirmative without any consultation with, or consideration for, Edel at home.

What really drove her round the twist was when I could go to Mullingar, for example, to play golf on a Thursday and then end up getting on a roll with the lads and not coming home until Saturday. I'd ring her and say, "I'm after having a few pints..." as if I had only been informed that a drink-driving law existed and obviously she wasn't going to encourage me to drive home then.

It was only in later years that I appreciated how I was bang out of order and wondered how I could have done that to her and not realised that being at home with your family is more important than the sideshows I was getting caught up in. Now, I'm sure a lot of men are squirming in their seats analysing their own habits as they read this, but I wouldn't say I was a bad husband in an overall sense. It's just that these things build up over time and can be quite damaging if allowed to fester. But, after my trip to the Galway Races in 2005, Edel had enough.

The two of us went down together, having been invited to the infamous Fianna Fáil tent by a friend of mine for the Wednesday meeting. We had a very enjoyable day and I got a hankering to stay on for the Thursday, which Edel was fine with and she went home. But when one day turned into four it was the plank, never mind the straw, that broke the camel's back. We went through a rocky period when I finally surfaced again and the upshot was that Edel insisted that I go and talk to a psychologist. She felt it wasn't normal that someone would go off like that for a number of days and wondered were there deeper-lying issues that resulted in my actions. At that stage, I wasn't sure myself.

I agreed to talk to someone and got in touch with a man called John O'Donoghue, in Athlone. All the while, I never feared our marriage was in mortal danger. We were far too much into each other and the lads to go our separate ways. We had our moments, but we generally got on really well when we were together, and Edel still readily acknowledged that I was brilliant with the kids at home. The critical factor was that there were times when I wasn't at home when I should have been, given these random sessions that popped up now and again, and this time I had gone way too far. When I first went to see John it was more a case of getting it out of the way. With regard to the drinking, I explained how I had always been very disciplined throughout my playing career and would have no problem abstaining for months at times.

"My initial reaction is that you're certainly not an alcoholic," he told me, "but a good barometer is to give up the drink for forty days and see how you get on."

I did that, no problem, and continued to see him throughout that six-week period. He told me that he had a staggering number of clients who were former inter-county players struggling to cope with retirement and had encountered all sorts of problems. It could be anything, drink, depression, women, various problems.

I explained to Edel that whatever my issues were, drink wasn't one of them. John reckoned it was a combination of things, ranging from going to boarding school at a young age, given that I was a bit of a home bird at the time, right up to the death of my good friend Seán Conway in 2000, my retirement the year after, Edel's illness and then moving from Naas to Tullamore. With the obvious exception of Seán's death and Edel's illness, not all those things would be filed under traumatic, but it's the little bits and pieces over the course of our lives that make us what we are as much as anything else.

Seán's death bothered me greatly. A Clonmel man, we became the firmest of friends during my time in Naas but he contracted Barrett's Oesophagus and it turned out that he had quite a sizeable tumour. He required a huge operation if he was going to pull through and a group of us raised money to allow him to undergo surgery at the Dana-Farber Cancer Institute in Boston. I travelled out with him and, while he got through the surgery and was in reasonably good spirits after he came home, he suffered from an infection and went downhill. He passed away in May, 2000, aged forty, leaving his wife, Trish, and son, Jack, behind. He was a shadow of the man he had been and it was painful to watch. John surmised with certainty that I suffered from reactive depression for a couple of years after Seán died, particularly when you throw in all the other things that were going on in my life at the time, like switching jobs and finding myself under pressure in that respect, not getting on with some of the people I had to deal with professionally. Back then, I had lost interest in work for the first time in my life and would often sneak home in the middle of the day to catch a couple of hours' sleep. All these were factors that fed into my sometimes-erratic behaviour.

The sessions with John also threw a spotlight on our relationship as a couple. At times we could be rather volatile. Some say that opposites attract but Edel and I could have polarised views on something and neither of us would budge. Both of us were strong and independent people and we were both equally determined to have the final word, which resulted in some late nights. When I explained all this to John, he suggested that Edel go to see him as well, feeling that it wasn't all one-way traffic. For all she had gone through with her treatment, Edel hadn't spoken to anyone and hadn't really dealt with all the issues surrounding what she experienced. While the Galway Races fallout was a serious incident, plenty of good came out of it for both of us. I was never going to pull a stunt like that again and I had got so much off my chest, talking to John about things I had never spoken to anyone about before. I benefited from that, and so did Edel.

Years later, another of my dear Tipp friends from Naas, Noel Farrelly, died suddenly of a heart attack in February 2008. He was just forty-seven, and his passing shocked us all to the core, not least his wife, Catherine, and daughters, Emma and Sarah. But my experience from seeing John, and his dissection of my reaction to Seán's death, helped me to deal with Noel's passing in a more controlled manner. Not that it wasn't traumatic, because it certainly was. He was a truly great friend. I was in Portugal, on the golf course appropriately enough, when the news reached me of what had happened and

I dashed home to be a pallbearer at his funeral – the only non-Tipp native who carried his coffin. It was quite a compliment given Noely's comical disdain for anything or anyone without a blue and gold tint. I still go to Naas quite regularly and it's certainly not the same without him.

While my relationship with Edel hadn't exactly been on the rocks prior to this episode and going to speak to John, we got a new lease of life all the same. In fact, if our marriage had been continually turbulent then it probably wouldn't have withstood that incident. That we had spoken to a professional about whatever issues we had, individually provided a platform for us to discuss things ourselves, which wouldn't have been one of the stronger points in our relationship over the years. Like, if I had just come home from Galway and said something like, "Well, that happened because I'm still struggling to deal with retirement", it wouldn't have been met with a favourable response, but that didn't mean it wasn't valid either.

I certainly became more considerate and thought about things and the consequences related to them before I went through with them or not. I obviously hadn't left that former mindset fully behind me either because it resurfaced in that period after Edel died, but while she was alive it didn't manifest itself again. I still maintained an active social life and Edel was keen that I would, just without the excesses. It dawned on me that it wasn't necessary to turn up at every golf classic or function that I was invited to, but there was nothing wrong with going to a few of them either. It was just about striking the right balance. At thirty-seven it was about time that I matured in that way, even if it was short of the level I've since acquired. Thankfully, I reached that platform when I did because we needed absolute stability to absorb the news that awaited us within a year.

· · · · ·

Once you stave off cancer, as Edel did in 2003, you're told that if it doesn't return within five years there's a good chance it won't come back at all. We didn't live our lives willing those five years to pass quickly so that we could box it off, but we were always conscious of it. Then, around May 2006, Edel complained of back pain. We weren't too perturbed by it initially, but then it wasn't going away and got worse. She was taking a few painkillers but later decided to get in touch with Dr John Kennedy in St James's Hospital again. He booked her in for a scan on the first week of June. We went to Dublin with an open mind, but we were nervous about it. The five-year threshold hadn't yet been breached and, suddenly, we were back in this zone that we hoped we had left long behind us three years earlier. The scan was carried out and we waited for the results.

Dr Kennedy spoke to us and explained that Edel had secondary breast cancer, which had manifested itself in both her liver and spine. The full consequences of what he said were lost on us initially. When Edel was battling the primary cancer, secondary cancer wasn't discussed, as there was no reason to do so at that stage. It just wasn't part of the equation and the hospital staff weren't going to start scaremongering by bringing it up when it wasn't an issue that affected us at that time. Having completed the treatment successfully, the five-year rule of thumb and negotiating that period was all we were concerned about, not the characteristics of what the cancer may be if it happened to resurface. My first thoughts on hearing the news was that Edel would have to go through the painstaking process of a year or so of chemotherapy and radiotherapy, just as she had before and then, hopefully, get the all-clear once again. I didn't appreciate the connotations that went with the term "secondary cancer". Edel asked questions to that end, though, and very quickly the conversation was dominated by some straight talking.

"This can't be cured," we were told, "it's terminal."

If it was primary cancer that had occurred once again it would have been different, but it was secondary breast cancer, which, by definition, is incurable. Immediately, Edel wanted to know what lay in store for her.

"How long have I left?" she asked Dr Kennedy.

"I can't say," he replied awkwardly. "I'm not God."

"You've seen people with symptoms like mine before," she persisted, "and I want to know."

He threw a look at me, hoping that I might interject and dissuade Edel from her line of questioning but I wasn't going to do that. She wanted an indication of how much time she might have left and eventually he relented.

"If you really want to know I'm obliged to give you my opinion but it's very difficult to say. It's in the very early stages and we'll treat it as best we can. Spinal cancer is the lesser worry of the two but, with the liver, you could be looking at twelve months, maybe eighteen."

The enormity of the situation hits you fairly hard at that point. It was obviously a very different bombshell to the one that was dropped on us a few years earlier. By now we knew the disease much better and what went with it. But it wasn't so much that the cancer was back, it was more that it was terminal. The first time was a life-changing experience but this, sadly, would be a life-ending one. While there was hope after the first diagnosis, now there was none. That was the stark and brutal reality. I held Edel's hands and looked into her bleary eyes as the realisation of her fate filtered through her body. I just felt so incredibly sorry for her. She had fought cancer so valiantly before and got on with her life, and now this. I thought to myself that, if I were in the same position, I wouldn't be able to accept it but I knew that, in time, she would. Even before we left the room that's how she was bracing herself. But she was angry, too, given that she had done everything stringently by the book and led a very healthy lifestyle.

"I've done everything that I could do," she said, "everything I was supposed to do. Why me?"

And there can be no logical answer to that.

Edel's sister, Anne, was in Dublin the same day and we had arranged to meet her. She was originally going to travel down to her home in Glasson, near Athlone, but came to Tullamore with us after hearing the news. I remember we stopped at Furey's, that well known pub in Moyvalley, on the way down for some food. It was a fine summer's evening and Edel and Anne sat out the back of our house and indulged in more than a few glasses of wine and became quite emotional. Seán and Brian were a bit perplexed about it to say the least. There were obviously going to be far-reaching consequences to the news that we received that day, but they genuinely hadn't even pierced my thoughts at that point. I didn't think of what the future held for the lads and myself, or anything of that nature. I only thought of Edel. I recall vividly looking out from the kitchen at her and Anne, both in tears, and thinking that here was one of the finest people you could ever hope to meet in your entire life, and she's been told today, at thirty-eight years of age, that soon it will be all over for her. Dealing with the consequences would come later, but the overriding feeling I had then was purely one of profound sadness for Edel only.

In the midst of all the devastation that prevailed that day, however, there was a beacon of light that would sustain us over the coming years. That same week Pattern Day, June 9 every year, fell in Durrow, the day on which First Holy Communion is always held in the parish. In shocked silence, we slumped down to the underground car park in St James's Hospital having received the chilling results of the scan from Dr Kennedy and sat into the car.

"Brian's Communion is in three years' time," Edel announced out of nowhere. "I'll be at Brian's Communion."

Chapter 15

St Colmcille's Church, June, 2009

Processing the fact that Edel's illness was terminal was a very slow burner. We only dealt with the unavoidable essentials initially, seeing as she was going to have to start a very aggressive form of chemotherapy straightaway. That was going to be extremely trying, as chemo is only meant to be administered over a set number of sessions lasting a couple of months. In that scenario, it's reassuring for the cancer patient in that after each session is completed, however exhausting it may have been, at least they can mark it off on the calendar and it's one less appointment to be fulfilled. That wasn't the case with Edel, who would be receiving chemo for the rest of her life. The option was there for her to have her treatment in Tullamore but she insisted on staying with Dr Kennedy in St James's given the rapport she had already struck up with him.

I don't think I could have lasted for three years if I found myself in similar circumstances to Edel. I'd be thinking, "What's the point, I'm gone anyway?" I think that's a mindset that would take hold with a lot of men in that situation. At first she was afraid of dying and leaving me, and particularly the lads, behind, but over time that subsided and she did everything she possibly could to elongate her life and thus allow her to shape Seán and Brian as best she could. She drank juices and multiple pints of water a day, kept physically active by walking, exhausted every manual she could, scoured the internet, and various types of alternative medicine were tried.

Maybe I would have undertaken such things if I found myself in her position, but I doubt if I could match her level of commitment to it. I have no doubt that all these undertakings allowed her to live longer. She effectively trebled her life expectancy. There was more to it than that though. Her positive outlook was a major factor, as proven by the fact that she confidently predicted that she would live to see Brian make his Communion.

This came half an hour after she was told that she had a terminal illness that would most likely claim her life within a year, and yet she was declaring she would be present for an event that was still another three years away. My immediate thought when she said that was one of disbelief and perhaps wishful thinking on her part. But then when I considered that this was Edel, and how disciplined and fiercely determined she was, I thought, "You know, she'll make it". That statement had a big bearing on the next three years. While it gave her a target, that extra time also allowed us, and her particularly, to deal with what was coming. There were different stages to her reaching a level of acceptance and, by the time she passed away, she was completely ready for it; she wouldn't have been in that space if Dr Kennedy's prediction had proved to be correct.

Her faith became a central part of her life over those three years, and the level of spirituality that she developed was the single biggest factor in her coming to terms with her fate. We were always regular churchgoers and, during Edel's first illness, she and my mother travelled on a pilgrimage to Lourdes with a group from Banagher. Her parents have a strong faith and Edel went to Knock with them on a regular basis during her childhood. I would have had good faith myself but, at the same time, Edel and I wouldn't have dropped to our knees for the rosary every evening. However, once Edel was diagnosed as being terminally ill her faith mushroomed, when a lot of people would probably go the other way.

Clonfert, just over the Galway border from where I come from in Banagher, was somewhere she visited quite frequently. Folklore has it that the statue of Our Lady of Clonfert was found in the trunk of a tree by a man who was chopping it down in the nineteenth century, and blood flowed from it when he unwittingly severed the arm. The statue was presumably placed there during a time of religious suppression. The other aspect to Clonfert is the presence of a man called Eddie Stones, originally a butcher from Clara who uprooted his family to move there and establish a centre for prayer and evangelisation, Emmanuel House, upon a calling from God. When he started down there it was viewed with scepticism but, with miracles having been attributed to his practice, the Church has come on board and backed it with a full-time priest now devoted to it. It's quite a sizeable operation down there now.

Edel went down most often with Marie Dooley. Eddie prays among those who come to see him and then there is an option of approaching him for a blessing, upon which several people faint on receiving it. I've seen it myself and it happened to Edel quite often. She'd be gently laid out on the ground for a few moments then until she came around. Aodh Horan, who played alongside me for St Rynagh's, and his wife, Carmel, are also very active in Emmanuel House and it was through them that Edel developed an interest in travelling to Medjugorje, a small town in the former Yugoslavia where Our Lady appeared to six locals in 1981.

The devotion to prayer wasn't a desperate attempt to bring about a miraculous recovery on Edel's part. Miracles are known to have happened and, of course, there would have been an outside hope that something like that could occur, but Edel was a realist. The longer her illness lasted, every day became a bonus, but her increasing spirituality allowed her to ready herself for death to the extent that eventually she had no fear of it and knew she was going to a better place, whereas when I held her hands after she received the news from Dr Kennedy more than three years earlier she was terrified at the prospect.

Her faith helped her through the hard times. It was impossible, even for someone of Edel's positive nature, to be upbeat all the time in those circumstances. She lost her hair a few times and I shaved it off for her once, something which was quite difficult, though the lads got a great laugh out of it. Her belief and spirituality helped her through times like that and then it linked nicely with the idea of her attending Brian's Communion. Over time we would have drip-fed Seán and Brian various different pieces of information about Edel's condition. The advice we were given was that, at particular ages, they would only have been able to absorb certain things. Being a couple of years older, Seán was more appreciative of what Edel was going through and would often help out around the house, loading the dishwasher and other such chores, while she lay on the couch. Brian had a rather different take on it and would hilariously admonish her at times. "Mam's very lazy, she was lying down there in the middle of the day!" The innocence of it.

While there were pressures and worries throughout that ultimately had negative spin-offs for me personally, those final three years we had together were certainly our happiest as a couple. The important things in life were accentuated and everything else paled into insignificance. The trips we had to Medjugorje played a big part in that. They gave Edel something to look forward to and she effectively recharged her batteries when she was out there. In all, I travelled there three times with her, while she went with a group on another occasion. I took a lot of out those trips as well as Edel. I remember in 2007, I reckon I hadn't been to confession since I was maybe twelve and I decided to break that duck.

"It's been ... a while since my last confession," I told the priest.

"How long?" he asked.

"Well, I was about twelve and I'm thirty-nine now, so twenty-seven years. I hope you have a while!"

Medjugorje is a very peaceful and serene place to visit, and hasn't been overrun by the cheap commercialism you see in some religious locations. The church is particularly sacred out there and silence is observed all around it. There wouldn't be anything like the mutterings you hear down the back of a church in Ireland on a Sunday morning. On our first trip we stayed in small dwellings with fairly basic meals and tough mattresses. There are processions at six o'clock some mornings, though Mass at ten is usually the starting point for the day and you find yourself slotting into a routine. The day would be filled out by climbing the mountains where our Lady appeared, Stations of the Cross perhaps and maybe a prayer meeting with Eddie, who travels there regularly. Edel did what she could with regard to the climbs; some of them were particularly difficult hikes.

There are various phenomena associated with Medjugorje, the most common of which is probably the sight of the sun spinning in the sky. I saw it once myself though Edel, who was standing beside me, couldn't so it must be down to the individual's mind. It was just like a ball of fire rotating in the sky. Another time I was waiting for Edel to come out of a public toilet when a man approached me and pushed a miraculous medal into my hand just as she returned. I showed it to Edel and, when I turned around, he was nowhere to be seen. I'm not suggesting he just vanished, but there was something strange about it. The medal joined Edel's pouch of religious paraphernalia. On one of the trips Edel got a private audience with Vicka Ivankovic, the most high-profile of the visionaries, and received a blessing from her. Even though she didn't speak English, Edel took a lot from that experience. Each time when I came back I assured myself that I would make an effort to devote a little more time on a daily basis to religious matters but, unlike Edel, that enthusiasm would wear off. I still manage my three Our Fathers, three Hail Marys and three Glory Bes most days though.

In our later trips we stayed in an apartment, which Aodh and Carmel owned, for a bit of extra comfort and made a holiday out of it as well. Some of the scenery beyond Medjugorje and along the coast is breathtaking, and then you drive through some towns that are still decrepit from the war. The relaxed setting in Medjugorje allowed us to have the sort of chats together that wouldn't be possible while sitting in the living room at home. It was a progressive thing with each passing trip and helped to bring us even closer together. We were able to discuss thorny issues like funeral arrangements, whether we would avail of hospice care or not and other such matters that were going to have to be dealt with as a result of Edel's condition, and, having boxed off all those things, it was a relief as we could then look forward without any of that hanging over us. It wasn't something that could be pushed though and the timing had to be right. We weren't at a stage where we could have those conversations a couple of years earlier. If Edel had only lasted the twelve months or so after her first diagnosis then we wouldn't have covered that ground. By the end, she had reached a point where she accepted she was dying, though still fought to postpone that inevitability for as long as she possibly could.

She once penned an article for a booklet called Thump the Lump, which was a compilation of personal reflections from cancer sufferers. She wrote: "I have been lucky enough to meet the most inspiring people on my journey and find no matter how ill we feel there are always others who are fighting a more difficult battle. There is no doubt when we are faced with any major issues in our lives it makes us sit up and evaluate what we have in our lives and what we need to do to ensure we hold on to a good quality of life. Over the last few years I have developed my mind spiritually and while I always had a strong faith I now find prayer relaxing and enjoyable and have strengthened my relationship with God. I made a promise to myself to try and get at least one good thought out of every day."

In 2008, she attempted to keep a diary but only managed to make entries in it sporadically. I found it some time after she died and the first entry in it read: "I thank God that I am here with Mick and the boys for the start of '08. It seems a long time since my news eighteen months ago – I pray to continue to receive the strength that I have and keep my hope alive."

The Dóchas Cancer Support Group in Tullamore was another great outlet for her in terms of keeping her spirits up and her mind occupied. She took up reflexology and photography while also taking art lessons from a well-known local artist and friends of ours, Siobhán Ryan. She also explored acupuncture, reflexology and Reiki.

I rekindled my appointments with John O'Donoghue in Athlone during Edel's second illness and he gave me some great advice. For example, with the pattern of chemotherapy, a patient should be reasonably well recharged in the week leading up to the next treatment. That was a time when I could pencil in something nice for Edel and I to do, such as a long weekend away in Spain or Portugal, or just a simple overnight stay in Dublin and go to a concert. The low-key holidays that we had in Ireland in 2008 and '09 would have been an extension of that. But the key, John said, was to afford her as much notice as possible for any of these events as it would then give her something to look forward to rather than surprising her at the last minute. His logic was that surprises are no good to anyone apart from the person that's springing them, and he was right.

In late-2007 I decided to throw a fortieth birthday party for her in the Tullamore Court Hotel. There were well in excess of three hundred people present with a full buffet, band and comedian booked. It was nearly more like a wedding and it may have been lavish, even for a landmark birthday, but there was more to it than that. Although it wouldn't have been articulated as such, in ways it was like a farewell because there wouldn't be another chance for Edel to meet and chat with many of the people who were there. Edel liked the idea of uniting people from various strands of her life and it was a wonderful night. There were no presents, only donations to charity were asked for.

While occasions like that were all well and good, it was the day-to-day matters in the household such as cooking, spending time together with the lads, throwing on the barbecue, going to matches and just being a family that counted most. We were definitely more appreciative of the simple things and grew exceptionally close the more time moved on. We always had a good relationship but I would have undermined it from time to time by going on those famous escapades. By this stage, doing things like that were of absolutely no interest to me, though Edel may have found that hard to believe and felt that I would prefer to be elsewhere. I still enjoyed a social life during her illness, and she did too, but the difference then was that the balance was right. As I said previously, because we were both strong personalities we would have had some serious bust-ups down the years over, with the benefit of hindsight, rather petty issues. That was all gone in those last few years because we knew what was important. Despite Edel's condition, we had a lot to be appreciative of. We lived in a perfect setting with great neighbours, a large circle of friends and two wonderful and healthy sons. I derive great comfort from the fact that we had those three particularly great years together before she died, even if it took her being diagnosed with a terminal illness for us to achieve that level of unity.

While I didn't notice it until some time later when she said it to me, Edel skilfully fostered a bond between the lads and myself that was independent of her. She'd encourage them to sit closer to me on the sofa as we watched television, or the three of us travelling to matches together, or simply going for a walk in the woods. It was very subtle on her part and it certainly wasn't a case of her detaching herself from Seán and Brian in any way. She had an ability to take a dispassionate view of what was required in order to minimise the impact her passing would have on them. Then, when she felt that bond between Seán, Brian and myself was sufficiently strong, she was happy to row back in with them and squeeze every last moment of pleasure out of being with them that she could. That probably reached its pinnacle when Brian's First Communion Day finally came around on June 9, 2009, and Edel was present, three years after she had boldly held the occasion up as a beacon that would guide her through all the dark days that lay ahead.

• • • • •

Having been so assiduous in dealing with her illness, and trying to maximise her life expectancy over the previous three years, Edel pushed the limits to such an extent in the lead-in to Brian's Communion that I genuinely feared she wouldn't be able to attend the ceremony. The week before, she took part in the annual Dublin Mini-Marathon on the June bank holiday Monday along with a bunch of friends to raise money for Dóchas in Tullamore. This was around the same time that we had received the scan results that hadn't painted a particularly cheerful picture and she was certainly experiencing more difficulty than she had previously. Edel always had a thing about pain relief, feeling she shouldn't take the full dose because it would only negate the drug's effect when she needed it most. What's more, she had only just fulfilled a chemotherapy appointment the previous Friday. "Are you sure about doing this?" I asked her beforehand, but she insisted, saying she would walk it or she wouldn't do it all. I never did quite get to the bottom of it in terms of how much she exerted herself that day, but even if she only walked it, ten kilometres in her condition was a big ask.

The lot of them took off on a bus that morning and Tom Mangan looked after them in Doheny and Nesbitt's pub on Baggot Street with food and refreshments as well as changing facilities. When she arrived home later that evening a few of the others came into the house but Edel asked them to leave as she wasn't feeling well, which was most unlike her. Soon she was in horrific pain with her back and neck. She took painkillers but she might as well have been popping wine gums for all the relief she was getting. It was the most helpless I ever felt for her, and the longest and most difficult night of all the time she was ill. The pain was relentless but even then she insisted that I wait until morning before calling a doctor. Eventually I got stronger painkillers coupled with steroids and it passed, though not without taking a lot out of her. On top of all that she would have a gruelling week ahead of her anyway as the side effects of the chemo kicked in, so it was very much a case of her summoning every last bit of willpower she had to get through the Communion day, which fell eight days after the mini-marathon. It didn't stop her enjoying the day though.

Pattern Day in Durrow, on which the First Communion is held on June 9 every year, is a big event in the locality. It's almost like a bank holiday and many Durrow natives who live elsewhere come back for it. Communion Mass is at ten o'clock in the morning followed by a procession to the abbey, one of the early Christian monasteries established by St Colmcille in the sixth century. There's another mass later in the day and then people gather by the well. Proceedings are rounded off by a sports day in the GAA field in the evening with activities such as three-legged races for the children.

In the previous couple of years, Edel would only go out socially if she really felt up to it. In truth, she wouldn't have been in flying form coming into the Communion day given the ordeal she had been through over the course of the previous week in particular, but her adrenaline was flowing given the significance of the day. Our neighbour Breeda Fogarty, a hairdresser by profession, arrived that morning to do her hair. Edel then set about dressing Brian in his suit. He loves dressing up by nature and I don't think there's a better picture of him than the one we have of him standing in front of the altar after the Communion Mass as proud as punch. We pushed the boat out that little bit and invited more people along than would normally attend for an occasion such as this. After the Mass and the traditional tea and sandwiches at Durrow Hall we went for lunch in the Clonmore House Hotel in Tullamore. The weather was beautiful and I brought the lads up to the field later that day for the sports and then we all went back to our place and had the neighbours over for a barbecue.

We didn't discuss the fact that Edel had made good on her promise to be around for the Communion on the day itself given that it was so busy, but it would have been mentioned beforehand. We even had a laugh about it when I told her I thought she was mad when she first said it. In the first couple of years after the second diagnosis it wouldn't have been discussed but then, once we reached the phase when we were more comfortable in talking to each other about the nature of Edel's illness, it would have come up more often. Even before that we were always conscious of it; Edel's remark in the car that day wasn't just something that was said and quickly forgotten about. I felt she took great resolve from having that day to aim for though, having reached that milestone, I partly feared that she would lose some of her drive to keep going without having a target like that. Although she died only three months later, I needn't have worried on that front at all as she was still as effervescent as ever following the Communion.

As the Communion day wound down there was a real glow of satisfaction. I was so proud of her. Her toughness had shone through yet again by not allowing the harrowing week she had just endured to spoil the day for her or any of the family. Despite that, she was wrecked by the end of the day; we all were in fact, though Brian insisted on counting his money yet again before he went to bed.

"How much did you get for your Communion, Seán?" he'd ask, only too delighted to hear that he had collected more.

Days like this are significant in any household, but this was huge for us, the apex of what was our happiest time together as a family. As I've said, most of that joy was derived from the more bland aspects of life around the family home. We had what we felt was an ideal location for us where we lived in Durrow, and that move had only been hastened by the onset of her illness originally in 2002. I believe that everything happens for a reason; things fell into place and the meaning of life was accentuated over those final three years we had together. We could be just sitting down together, comfortable in each other's company, and not a word had to be said. We may have had awkward silences at times earlier in our relationship, but it's a lovely silence when you don't feel there's need to fill it. This had largely been made possible by the fact that Edel had turned a most terrifying scenario on its head in reaching a point where she was able to enjoy life while remaining fearless about her fate, thanks to her faith. She had made life all about living rather than dying. That, for me, was a monumental achievement.

EPILOGUE

A few months before Edel died, she told me she intended to write a letter each to Seán and Brian for them to read after she passed on.

I queried what exactly she had in mind as, in these situations, some people write a series of letters to be opened in sequence at various landmarks along their children's lives, but no, Edel just wanted to write a single letter to each of them.

However, as she passed away relatively quickly, she hadn't alerted me to where she had left them. There was the possibility that she hadn't got around to writing the letters at all, but I considered that unlikely given how organised she was in everything she did. So, I went looking for them throughout the house.

I looked through her laptop to see had she saved them there. She hadn't. During Christmas, 2010, the three of us were down in Banagher when I had to go back home to Tullamore to get something from the house. The letters were on my mind on the way and, when I got there, I turned the place upside down looking for them. Still couldn't find them.

· · · · ·

Time is a great healer. How often do we hear that? It's a tired cliché but nevertheless true. What the lads and I have gone through will never go away, and nothing will ever change it, but life moves on relentlessly and, blunt as it may sound, you can't hang around moping for too long. Certainly not in this day and age with all the strife that has engulfed the country in the last few years, myself included. Edel wouldn't have wanted us to anyway. She frequently stressed to me that I should endeavour to move on once she'd gone, in every way. I always say to the lads that we'll never forget their mother. She'll always be there, in our thoughts and in our conversations.

Of course we miss her. I found her a great calming influence on me in terms of my work and business. I'd often tense up about things but she'd have the ability to stand back, take a wider view, compartmentalise each dilemma and present them to me in a way that was much easier to tackle. At times, I've felt completely overrun with the number of things flung at me and acutely missed that soothing effect she had. Of course, these matters pale into insignificance when set alongside what I've had to deal with in terms of her passing, but they don't go away either.

I sometimes wonder if I'm too easy-going with Seán and Brian when I encounter other parents who push their children a lot harder. I prefer to think that they'll be self-motivated and will go their own way and do what they want themselves. That's one of the perils of being a single parent; you make these kind of decisions on your own and, ultimately, you have to trust your judgement. Talking to my own family in Banagher of late, they detailed the trauma I have had to endure over the past decade or so for a young man and reassured me that, despite the odd hiccup, I had coped admirably and am setting the lads on the right course. It was strange, yet comforting, to hear it because I always looked on each of the travails as challenges that simply had to be addressed.

Overall, taking a look at myself at forty-three years of age, I know my qualities as a person far outweigh the negatives. Right now, I'm as happy as I could hope to be, and Seán and Brian are doing fine. I could write a Hollywood ending to this book, that we all live happily ever after, but life has taught me otherwise. So has death. Maybe we will live happily ever after. Maybe we won't. You don't know what life's going to throw at you and all you can do is limit the variables as much as you can. I'd like to think I'm doing that. Most of the time.

· · · · ·

In February, 2011, Edel's sisters, Anne and Linda, came over to the house to go through her clothes and belongings. I hadn't touched any of her stuff; a year and half on, her bag from St James's Hospital still sat at the foot of the bed. Her clothes remained untouched in the wardrobe. So, when Anne and Linda arrived that evening, there was a large degree of finality about it.

They went at it and were very organised, labelling different bags for recycling, others for charity. Edel's sisters, nieces, and some of her best friends, would have taken a piece of her jewellery as a memento, which was nice. I popped down to the room at one stage to see how Anne and Linda were getting on and they were reminiscing. "Do you remember the night she wore this?" one of them might say. I went to Edel's bedside locker with the intention of clearing it out and, as I walked away, I noticed a plastic bag behind it. It looked like it was full of rubbish but then I rustled through it and found that her letters to Seán and Brian were there.

I waited until they were going to bed later that night and read the letters to them, tears streaming down my cheeks. The letters were simple and thoughtful, but laced with love and emotion and gentle pointers as to how they should approach life.

"Life is for living," she wrote to Seán, "always remember that – enjoy every bit of it and get something good out of every day."

They can read those letters at any stage in their lives and still take something from them. Several times she wrote how she loved them – "with all my heart and soul".

Heart and soul.

It's something that sums up several strands of my life. Maybe I've exposed my heart and soul in writing this book. They are traits that all successful St Rynagh's and Offaly teams have been associated with. I'd like to think I left a bit of heart and soul on those jerseys when I wore them.

And Edel left more of it on us.

ABOUT THE CO-AUTHOR

Pat Nolan is a native of Tullamore in Co Offaly and has worked as Gaelic Games Correspondent for the *Irish Daily Mirror* since January 2007. He graduated as a Bachelor of Engineering in Computer-Aided Mechanical and Manufacturing Engineering from Dublin City University in 2004 and a Master of Arts in Journalism from Dublin Institute of Technology in 2005. Aged 29, this is his first book.